Collective Bargaining and Increased Competition for Resources in Local Government

Collective Bargaining and Increased Competition for Resources in Local Government

Arthur W. Spengler

QUORUM BOOKS
Westport, Connecticut • London

Library of Congress Cataloging-in-Publication Data

Spengler, Arthur W., 1942–
    Collective bargaining and increased competition for resources in
    local government / Arthur W. Spengler.
        p.   cm.
    Includes bibliographical references and index.
    ISBN 1–56720–290–X (alk. paper)
    1. Collective bargaining—Government employees—United States.
    2. Employee–management relations in government—United States.
    I. Title.
HD8005.6.U5S68   1999
331.89'04135173—dc21   99–10406

British Library Cataloguing in Publication Data is available.

Library of Congress Catalog Card Number: 99–10406
ISBN: 1–56720–290–X

First published in 1999

Quorum Books, 88 Post Road West, Westport, CT 06881
An imprint of Greenwood Publishing Group, Inc.
www.quorumbooks.com

Printed in the United States of America

The paper used in this book complies with the
Permanent Paper Standard issued by the National
Information Standards Organization (Z39.48–1984).

10 9 8 7 6 5 4 3 2 1

Copyright Acknowledgments

The author and publisher are grateful for permission to reproduce portions of the following
copyrighted material:

"TRIM-ing Property Taxes," *Washington Post* (editorial), October 30, 1978. © The Washington
Post.

". . . and Montgomery Issues," *Washington Post* (editorial), November 3, 1980. © The
Washington Post.

To Margaret

For your love, encouragement, and support.

To My Mother, Mary Quinn Spengler

For your love and for instilling in me the value of education
and providing me the opportunity to pursue it.

To My Sister, Mary

For your love and for teaching me to meet life's challenges
with courage and good spirit.

Contents

Illustrations

TABLES

FIGURE

Acknowledgments

I would like to thank those who read and critiqued the manuscript in its early stages: Roger R. Stough, Seymour Martin Lipset, and Timothy J. Conlan. I also wish to express my thanks to those present and former officials in Montgomery County, Maryland, whom I interviewed and who gave so generously of their time and insights.

I wish to acknowledge the 25 members of the Montgomery County Council for whom I had the pleasure to work during my 19-year tenure as a member of the council staff. They helped to make it both a challenging and rewarding experience. Thank you as well to my colleagues on the council staff and in the various public agencies in the county with whom I had the privilege to work over the years. They are highly professional men and women who do an outstanding job serving the citizens of the county every day.

I also wish to thank Alan Sturmer, my editor at Greenwood Publishing Group. His suggestions improved the work significantly.

1

Introduction

Approving the operating budget, levying the taxes to balance it, and establishing the compensation policies for employees are among the most important policy decisions made by many local governments in the United States. The goal of the research reported in this book is to contribute to a better understanding of the nexus between these policy processes in the last decade of the twentieth century.

This book explores the use of collective bargaining by full-time local government employees in the context of a local budgeting model. It is designed to ascertain if the wave of taxpayer revolts that occurred during the 1970s and early 1980s influenced these employees to use a *collective voice* strategy as they sought to achieve their goals.

UNION MEMBERSHIP IN AMERICA

Although it has declined slightly in recent years, union membership in the United States has been relatively stable since 1987. For non-farm wage and salary employees, there were an estimated 16.2 million union members in 1996, about 25 percent below the 1976 peak of 22.2 million (Table 1.1). Union membership as a percentage of non-farm employment (density) has been steadily declining since it peaked in 1953 at 32.5 percent. In 1996, density was 15.2 percent, less than one-half that peak level.

This decline in overall union membership and density, however, masks very different trends in the private and public sectors. Over the last three decades, the American labor movement has experienced the most momentous change since its founding in the nineteenth century. Its central features have been the

Collective Bargaining

Table 1.1

Employee Organization Membership and Density, All Employees, Private Sector and Public Sector, Selected Years, 1933–1996

Year	Membership (000)			Density (Percent of Non-Farm Employment)		
	Total	Private Sector	Public Sector	Total	Private Sector	Public Sector
1933	3,491	3,194	297	14.7	15.5	9.4
1945	12,254	11,674	580	30.4	33.9	9.8
1953	16,310	15,540	770	32.5*	35.7*	11.6
1960	15,516	14,613	903	28.6	31.9	10.8
1970	20,990	16,978*	4,012	29.6	29.1	32.0
1972	21,206	16,485	4,721	28.8	27.3	35.4
1976	22,153*	16,173	5,980	27.9	25.1	40.2*
1977	21,632	15,876	5,756	26.2	23.6	38.1
1982	19,571	14,007	5,565	21.9	19.0	35.1
1987	16,881	10,826	6,055	17.7	13.4	36.0
1992	16,390	9,737	6,653	15.8	11.4	36.6
1994	16,714	9,620	7,094*	15.7	10.9	38.7
1996	16,237	9,385	6,852	15.2	10.2	37.7

*historic peak.

Sources: 1933–1982: Troy and Sheflin (1985), Table 3.91; 1987–1996: U.S. Department of Labor, Bureau of Labor Statistics, *Current Wage Developments*, February edition, annually.

rise of unionism in the public labor market and its decline in the private market (Troy, 1994: 1).

Private sector union membership has declined rapidly since its peak of 17 million in 1970. Density peaked in 1953 at 35.7 percent; in 1987, density was 13.4 percent. By 1996 there were 9.4 million union members and density was 10.2 percent, less than one-third the 1953 peak. This decline occurred in all industrial sectors.[1]

In contrast, public sector membership in employee organizations has continued to grow, reaching an all-time high of 7.1 million in 1994. Density in that year was 38.7 percent, slightly below the 1976 peak of 40.2 percent.

Membership in public sector employee organizations increased about 6 million between 1960 and 1996. The era of rapid growth was between 1960 and 1976, when membership grew to almost 6 million and density peaked at a level higher than the private sector's 1953 level. While there was a brief period of decline between 1976 and 1982, since that time both membership and density have been increasing.

Table 1.2
Public Sector Employees: Membership in Employee Organizations, Selected Years, 1933–1987

Year	Local Number (000)	Local Density (%)	State Number (000)	State Density (%)	State & Local Number (000)	State & Local Density (%)	Federal Number (000)	Federal Density (%)
1933	na	na	na	na	19	7.0	271	48.0
1945	na	na	na	na	159	5.1	390	13.9
1953	na	na	na	na	210	4.8	512	22.2
1960	na	na	na	na	307	5.0	541	23.8
1970	na	na	na	na	2,958	30.1	1,082	39.6
1972	3,377	53.9	943	40.8	4,320	50.0	1,163	43.3
1976	3,745	54.1	992	38.2	4,737	na	1,133	41.5
1977	3,701	51.5	1,009	37.7	4,710	47.8	1,081	39.6
1982	3,579	48.9	1,066	37.4	4,645	45.7	1,040	38.0
1987	3,733	47.5	1,221	39.7	4,954	45.3	na	na

Sources: federal: Troy and Sheflin (1985), Table 3.92; state and local, 1933–1970, ibid.; state and local, 1972–1987: U.S. Department of Commerce, Bureau of the Census (June 1991, May 1985, October 1979, November 1974a).

The American public sector, however, cannot be viewed as a single, uniform labor market. It is a compilation of almost 83,000 governments, which employed more than 18 million people in 1996. Local governments employed almost 11 million people (60 percent), followed by the state and federal governments at 4.3 and 3.1 million employees respectively.

Membership in local government employee organizations increased from virtually zero in the early 1960s to more than 3.7 million by 1976, when 54 percent of full-time local government employees were members of an employee organization (a density well above the 1953 private sector peak of 35.7 percent). Over the subsequent decade, membership remained about the same, but density had declined slightly to 47.5 percent by 1987 (Table 1.2).

In 1960, 60 percent of the membership in public employee organizations was from the federal sector; by 1987 that same percentage came from the local sector. In large measure because of the growth in the local share, the federal share declined to less than 15 percent.

Membership in public sector employee organizations continues to grow (about 13 percent between 1987 and 1996) and, although data are not available to ascertain the composition of that growth, it is likely that a large share is at the local level.

The decline of over 5 million private sector union members since 1960 has resulted in an increase in the public sector share of total union membership—6 percent in 1960, 19 percent in 1970, 28 percent in 1982, and 42 percent in 1996. If this trend continues, public sector organizations will account for more than one-half of union membership early in the next century, despite comprising less than 20 percent of the workforce.

The low level of private sector unionization is very much in keeping with the emphasis that American values place on competitive individualism, as contrasted with other cultures that place greater emphasis on group outcomes. But the public sector levels are not in keeping with this tradition. Within the public sector, those who work for local governments have the highest propensity to organize. The proportion of organized local government employees was almost four times greater than that of American workers in the private sector in 1987 (47.5 compared to 13.4 percent). It is these differences that this research seeks to explore.

THE AMERICAN TAXPAYERS

America's long history of hostility toward taxation is very much in keeping with its political culture and anti-statist values. Tax revolts are as American as 1776 (Reid, 1979: 69), and during the twelve-year period that began in 1970, citizens took fiscal matters into their own hands by placing stringent and far-reaching limits on the ability of many state and local elected officials to use their discretion and judgment in the budgeting process. A so-called taxpayers' revolt occurred.

Fiscal discontent is used in this research to describe the various limitations on state or local budgets that were imposed in 33 states. While the causes and specific provisions varied, the result for many local governments in these states was fundamentally the same—less discretion for elected officials and greater competition for more limited resources.

LOCAL BUDGETING AND THE ROLE OF COLLECTIVE VOICE

Local government is a labor-intensive "industry." For some governments compensation costs may comprise 90 percent of the operating budget. Because financial resources are required to implement a government's compensation and working condition policies, the general context for this research will be the competition and choice making inherent in balancing local government operating budgets. This framework is described in Chapter 2.

Making budget choices often involves reconciling the competing priorities of three broad groups of actors—those who request services, the employees who provide the services, and the taxpayers who pay for them. In an effort to make their views known to the decision makers, each of these groups frequently will employ a strategy that relies on a "voice" option, which according to Hirschman (1970: 30) is "any attempt at all to change, rather than escape from, an

objectionable state of affairs . . . including those that are meant to mobilize public opinion . . . a basic portion and function of any political system, known sometimes as interest articulation.''

Fiscal discontent as used in this research includes an important collective
voice dimension, as the taxpayers took a direct democracy approach in making
their views known. Prior to the 1970s, voters had influenced taxes and spending
by electing or defeating politicians. With the revolts they imposed binding limits
by direct voting. It began slowly and gained momentum as the 1970s progressed.
California's Proposition 13 probably was the most dramatic of these populist
fiscal limitations. This use of collective voice by the taxpayers is examined in
Chapter 3.

Employee voice can be viewed from two broad perspectives—as a goal unto
itself or as a means for accomplishing a goal. In the former instance, employees
seek to participate, either individually or collectively, in the governance of their
organization and in the decisions that affect their daily work life. Their voice is
strengthened when they make decisions jointly with management. Employee
empowerment and participative management efforts to provide a greater voice
for employees have become increasingly common in recent years.

Employee voice also can be viewed as a strategy for accomplishing an agenda,
be it economic or non-economic. Participating in the political process is one
manifestation of that voice. Collective bargaining on wages, benefits, and working conditions is another. For this research, the activities surrounding that bargaining model represent the full use of collective voice by the employees.[2]

The advice offered by Freeman and Medoff (1979: 70) regarding trade unions
applies in the local government sector as well. ''A view of unions as organizations whose chief function is to raise wages is seriously misleading . . . unions
have significant non-wage effects . . . providing workers with a voice both in the
workplace and in the political arena.'' As Troy (1994: 132) notes in comparing
public and private sector unions, ''The structure of the New Unionism is derived
from its *political* market, in contrast to the *economic* market which produced
the structure of Old Unionism.''

RESEARCH QUESTION AND HYPOTHESIS

Why have Americans who work full-time for local governments chosen collective voice at a rate substantially higher than those who work in the private
sector?

Specifically, the hypothesis of this research is that a sustained high use of
bargaining among full-time local government employees is influenced by a need
for collective voice in the competition of the local budgeting process in an era
characterized by *fiscal discontent*. This study examines the use of a collective
voice strategy by both the full-time employees and the taxpayers in presenting
their often competing views regarding the operating budget. Fiscal discontent
imposed severe resource and political constraints on many local governments,

and in the environment of the local budgeting process, the use of collective voice increased as the competition for scarce resources increased.

AMERICAN LOCAL GOVERNMENT

A vast array of goods and services are provided to the citizens in 50 states by 82,932 local governments. This fragmentation creates a heterogeneous system, which is yet another manifestation of America's anti-statist values. Among the vast array of differences in these governments, three are germane to this research: (1) the variety of employee occupations, (2) the powers granted by the states to their local governments, and (3) the various types of local government. Taken together, numerous combinations of occupations, local powers, and local institutions are operating across the country. As this research will present, these combinations have vastly different propensities of employees to organize and bargain collectively.

Employee Occupations

More than three-quarters of the full-time local government employees work in the eight functional areas reported in the *Census of Governments*—instructional education, non-instructional education, police protection, fire protection, highways, hospitals, public welfare, and sanitation. There are substantial differences in densities among these various groups of employees, supporting the existence of so-called occupational communities. For example, nationally, those who provide instructional education and fire protection services have the highest propensities to organize (65 and 61 percent respectively in 1987); non-instructional education employees and those who work on the highways are among the lowest at about 37 percent. But these national averages based on government functions conceal large differences among the states and types of local government, and these dimensions are also presented in this study.

The States and Their Local Governments

Since local governments are creatures of their respective states, the powers and responsibilities granted them vary widely, even among those classified broadly as either Dillon rule[3] or home rule charter. A 1990 snapshot taken by the Advisory Commission on Intergovernmental Relations (ACIR) (1993) reported great variation in the degree to which states legislate in various aspects of local government operations,[4] including the collective bargaining powers granted to their local governments. As presented in Chapter 5, these state-imposed bargaining environments affect the propensity of local government employees to organize and bargain collectively.

Twenty-one states either prohibit or constrain bargaining in some fashion. In these states, 12 percent of the local government employees were represented by a bargaining unit and 26 percent were organized in 1987.

Twenty-nine states place no constraints on local government bargaining. The percentage of local employees in these states represented by a bargaining unit ranged between 23 and 90 percent in 1987. Sixteen of these states experienced fiscal discontent, and these were the states in which the largest share of their local government employees were represented by a bargaining unit (65 percent in 1987). The remaining thirteen states did not experience fiscal discontent, and one-third fewer of their local government employees were represented by a bargaining unit (42 percent in 1987). Does fiscal discontent help explain these differences in bargaining participation rates? That relationship is explored in Chapter 6.

Types of Local Government

Beyond these differences among the states, there also is great heterogeneity among the counties, municipalities, townships, school districts, and special districts that comprise local government in the United States. These 82,932 entities[5] differ from one another in myriad ways. Their missions may differ, as may the powers granted them by their states; differing missions may dictate very different workforces, as noted earlier (teachers, police officers, highway maintenance workers). But three additional differences are important for this research, namely, labor intensity, financing sources, and the propensity of employees to organize and bargain collectively.

- Labor intensity—the share of an operating budget devoted to salaries, wages, and employee benefits—differs substantially among the various types of local government. In 1986–1987, for example, two-thirds of total local government operating expenditures were devoted to employee compensation. However, for independent school districts the share was 82 percent compared to 38 percent for special districts (U.S. Department of Commerce, Bureau of the Census, 1988: Table 29).

- The degree to which own-source taxes are used to finance operating expenditures varies over a broad range. Nationally, own-source taxes represented 62, 46, 40, 38, and 20 percent of direct expenditures in 1987 by townships, municipalities, counties, independent school districts, and special districts respectively.

- The propensity of employees to organize and bargain collectively also varies greatly. For example, in the group of sixteen states cited previously in which 65 percent of all local employees were represented by a bargaining unit, the percentages by type of government were: 72 percent in municipalities, 65 percent in the counties and independent school districts, 51 percent in townships, and 44 percent in the special districts.

The differences in the propensities of local government employees to organize and bargain collectively based on occupation, state, and type of local government are analyzed in Chapter 5. The case study presented in Chapter 7 explores these differences as well.

The hypothesis of this research is that fiscal discontent contributed to the need for local government employees to undertake a collective voice strategy in an effort to have their views heard, especially in the budget process. A local government's labor intensity and the degree to which it relies on own-source tax revenues to finance its operating budget are relevant when trying to draw conclusions about the role played by fiscal discontent. An increase in the use of collective bargaining in governments that are the most labor intensive and rely most heavily on own-source taxes would lend support to the hypothesis of this research. The analysis identifies a pattern that relates higher rates of employee collective voice to the existence of fiscal discontent. These relationships are explored in Chapters 6 and 7.

CONTRIBUTION OF THIS RESEARCH

This study explores the reasons that local government employees use a collective voice strategy with much greater frequency than do their counterparts in either the public or the private sector. Private sector density continues its decline, while overall density remains stable at its relatively high levels in the local government sector.

A fiscal discontent hypothesis has been developed that links the American taxpayer revolts to an increased use of collective bargaining in many local governments. Previous research has not examined whether fiscal discontent has contributed to employee efforts to secure a stronger voice in those matters that affect their work life. If the hypothesis is supported, it adds a further dimension to the literature.

This study uses the all important choice making in the local budgeting process as the framework for the analysis. The importance of collective voice strategies to achieve budget goals is emphasized. Did the collective voice strategies of other stakeholders influence the employees to pursue a similar strategy when tax resources became less readily available? Was political voice used to advance the various economic and non-economic objectives of local government employees?

This analysis differs from previous research in two additional ways. First, it emphasizes the heterogeneity of local government and examines the use of employee collective voice not in the aggregate, but rather on the basis of occupation, state, and type of local government. Second, it distinguishes between employee organizing and collective bargaining. The latter propensities have been used when the data are available.

The ''center of gravity'' and the balance of power within organized labor has changed, reducing the dominance historically held by private sector unions (Troy, 1994: 29). To offset losses in membership, many private sector unions have moved into the public sector, creating so-called joint unions such as the

Teamsters and the Communication Workers of America. Others, such as the American Federation of State, County, and Municipal Employees (AFSCME), the American Federation of Teachers (AFT), and the International Association of Fire Fighters (IAFF), existed prior to the 1960s and are affiliated with the AFL-CIO, so-called "proto-unions" (ibid.). Many have adjusted their policies over time to accommodate the differing goals of the employees in the two sectors, and this research seeks to provide additional insights regarding these differences.

Since it seems likely that fiscal discontent will be with many local governments for the foreseeable future, knowing if it has influenced their employees to pursue a collective voice strategy would be important in several additional arenas—employee relations, public management (quality of work life, privatization, and TQM and other participative management policies), public budgeting, intergovernmental fiscal relationships, and economic development.

NOTES

1. Examples include: 84 to 18 percent in construction, 80 to 27 percent in transportation, and 42 to 17 percent in manufacturing (Troy and Sheflin, 1985; U.S. Department of Labor, Bureau of Labor Statistics, *Current Wage Developments*, February 1997).

2. In contrast to the private sector, organizing, unionizing, and collective bargaining should not be used interchangeably in the public sector context. Organizing as a professional association, for example, or discussing proposals with management under a meet-and-confer process where the final decisions remain with management provide much weaker levels of collective voice for the employees.

3. The Dillon rule is named after Judge John Dillon, who established the principle of limited city government powers. Since local governments are creatures of the state, they have only those powers specifically granted to them by the state constitution, the state legislature, or the state charter.

4. The ACIR examined six major categories: form of government, annexation and consolidation, local elections, administrative operations, personnel management, and financial management. Of the 201 items examined in the survey, Ohio had legislated the most with 113; other states with more than 100 items were Florida, Montana, Utah, Louisiana, Nevada, Kentucky, Oregon, Wyoming, Colorado, and Kansas. At the other end of the spectrum were Rhode Island and Vermont with 47, followed by Connecticut (51); Delaware, Hawaii, and Maine (61); Alaska (65); and Georgia and New Hampshire (69).

5. Excluding the District of Columbia, there were 26,269 special districts, 19,226 municipalities, 16,685 townships, 14,710 special districts, and 3,042 counties in 1987.

2

The Framework

Ten million people were employed by 53,483 local governments operating in the United States in October 1987.[1] The monthly payroll was $17.5 billion plus an additional $4 billion for employee benefits.[2] The annual "people cost" was $236 billion, about two-thirds of local operating expenditures.

As these figures demonstrate, a local government's personnel policies, employment levels, and compensation package are important matters on the agenda for balancing the operating budget. For many governments, decisions about these matters emerge as policy choices by elected officials and are not a function of the economic realities of a marketplace, as is frequently the case in the private sector.

In their study of public employee union activities in San Francisco during the 1970s, Boehm and Heldman (1982: 29) noted,

No other expense came anywhere near the proportion spent on employee compensation . . . payroll was ever more decisively the biggest expense over which local political officials could exercise significant control. In turn, it exerted by far the greatest pressure on the local tax structure. . . . Public employee labor relations is far from an esoteric single issue in local government. The relationship to the tax structure is crucial because most tax dollars go for personnel costs. And the tax structure, in turn, can play a vital role in many sectors of a city's private economy. Moreover, the tax structure/public service tradeoff can be a volatile issue in the local political environment.

Since financial resources are required to implement a government's compensation and working condition policies, the general framework for this research is the competition and choice making inherent in balancing local government operating budgets.

A LOCAL BUDGETING MODEL

Budgeting is choice making, and making the choices that allocate scarce resources is largely a political act (Rubin, 1993; Wildavsky, 1992; Kettl, 1992; LeLoup, 1988). It "is perhaps the central political act . . . the process of deciding who wins and who loses" (Kettl, 1992: 90).

Public budgeting is a collective decision-making process requiring thousands of judgments by numerous people about priorities among an array of infinite choices. Rubin (1993) summarizes well five unique features of public budgeting: the separation of taxpayers from decision makers, the numerous constraints, the openness to the environment, the variety of actors involved, and the need for public accountability. Since there is no marketplace for joining the payers and deciders, answers emerge as policy choices.

Local government operating budgets must be balanced, and a high level of competition, both financial and political, underlies their approval. As Wellington and Winter (1971: 1) note, "municipal budgets are inadequate to meet the political claims made upon them." As Rubin (1993: 128) says, "when programs or departments are forced to compete with one another for resources, they develop a variety of strategies to improve the priority of their spending goals."

Budgeting in the last quarter of the twentieth century has been described as *super-budgeting* (Caiden, 1988: 48).

Super-budgets are conceived less as documents or even autonomous processes than as systems, interacting with other systems . . . including the intergovernmental system, the economic system, and the political-bureaucratic system. . . . Budgets express societal decisions regarding the levels and sources of revenue. . . . Budgetary discussions come to incorporate the philosophical values of what should be financed publicly, and at what level. Budgeting becomes *super-budgeting*, whose primary concern is who should benefit and who should pay.

The framework used in this study is an adaptation of Rubin's model (1993) for budget decision making (see Figure 2.1).

This chapter describes the mosaic of this framework in the context of this study of American local government during the 1970s and 1980s. The chapter's final section describes the research design for this undertaking.

AMERICAN VALUES

A century and a half ago, in comparing the United States to Europe, Alexis de Tocqueville coined the phrase "American exceptionalism" (Lipset, 1991: 1) to describe America's values and institutions. This value system has been referred to as "the American Creed" and has been described in five terms: liberty, egalitarianism, individualism, populism, and laissez faire (Lipset, 1996: 19). Numerous studies have compared these values with those of other countries and

Figure 2.1
Adaptation of Rubin's Model

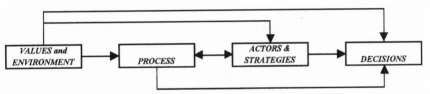

Source: Adapted from Rubin (1993): 24.

almost without exception show that Americans believe more strongly in liberal, egalitarian, democratic, and individualistic values than people in other societies (Huntington, 1981: 42). In America "what is exceptional is the alliance between egalitarianism and individualism" (Wildavsky, 1991: 121).

Egalitarianism in America emphasizes competitive individualism and the equality of opportunity and of respect, as contrasted with other cultures that place greater emphasis on outcomes for groups and the equality of result or condition.

A system of values does not just happen. America's beginning was unique in that it was ideological and not historical. The American Creed reflects the absence from its history of monarchies and aristocracies and feudalism; it incorporates the traits of classical liberalism that favor meritocracy and distrust of the state.

American values are reflected in the institutions and public policies that touch our daily lives—for example, the social welfare system, the public education system, and our political system. In the United States, the percentage of government spending to support social welfare benefits is consistently the lowest when compared to other democratic countries, while public funding for education is among the highest, emphasizing the importance of a common education available to all. The American system of federalism is decentralized, has divided power, and therefore government is relatively weak; it is replete with checks and balances and adversarial processes—the executive, legislative, and judicial branches; the federal, state, and local levels; and numerous elected officials with staggered terms of office.

The American Creed describes the nation's tendencies and relates this culture to that of other countries. It is not practiced universally by all Americans or under all circumstances. Public policy has deviated from the Creed on two notable occasions when the inequality of results was deemed unacceptable—during the New Deal of the 1930s and during the focus on ethnic, racial, and gender rights in the 1960s and beyond (Lipset, 1991: 40).

American policies regarding racial minorities and women have tended to emphasize equal results for groups, as opposed to opportunity for individuals. However, the policies and programs have contained elements of individualism and equal opportunity. Many Great Society programs focused on education and training to "remove the chains to compete equally," thereby giving an individual the means to compete based on merit. Special preferences have been used, but they have not been the sole focus; there is an Equal Employment Opportunity Commission.

The United States is the only industrialized country without an electorally viable socialist, social democratic, or labor party. Walter Dean Burnham summarized one explanation: "No feudalism, no socialism" (Lipset, 1989: 33). Michael Harrington, an American socialist theoretician, observed that "America was too socialist for socialism" (ibid.: 27). In 1988, he said that "social relations among the classes are more egalitarian and socialist-like in America than in other societies, including Sweden and Canada" (Lipset, 1990: 27).

Lipset (1989: 32) notes that the issue of American political exceptionalism must be expanded beyond asking why socialism is less developed in America than elsewhere, to asking why the organized labor movement is so weak. The organized labor movement in the United States, when compared to those in other democratic societies, has been weak and is becoming even weaker. However, as noted earlier, this has not occurred uniformly across all segments of the American labor force. Many local government workers are organized at levels much closer to those in several Atlantic Community countries. It is these differences among various groups of American workers that this research seeks to explore.

THE ENVIRONMENT

The economy of the 1970s and 1980s included economic recessions in 1974–1975 and 1981–1982, the latter the deepest since the 1930s. Oil embargoes led to energy shortages and dramatically higher prices. These were years of economic stagflation—double-digit rates of inflation accompanied by high levels of unemployment.[3] Interest rates rose to double-digit levels. Productivity gains slowed.

Population, industry, and jobs were moving either to new regions (for example, the Sunbelt), or to the burgeoning suburbs. "We created vast new urban job centers in places that only thirty years before had been residential suburbs or even corn stubble" (Garreau, 1991: xx). Many central cities lost a share of the employment base, which led to a loss in tax base; their socioeconomic character changed as well.

Demographic changes also were underway. The changing demography had profound impacts for K–12 education budgets, the largest expenditure for most localities. Steadily rising enrollments after World War II imposed great budgetary demands, followed by declining enrollments in the 1970s, which were also difficult to deal with (a 3.7 million decline over the decade that ended in 1982). The population was also growing older; the median age increased from 28 years in 1970 to 32.8 in 1990. The number of persons age 65 and over increased by more than 55 percent from 20 million in 1970 (9.8 percent of the population) to 31 million in 1990 (12.5 percent of the population).[4]

Beyond these economic conditions and demographic changes, virtually all local governments were dealing with a number of other circumstances that characterized the environment during these years: Intergovernmental assistance that peaked and began to decline, unfunded intergovernmental mandates, stringent financial markets, demands to improve the efficiency and effectiveness of programs and services, technological change, and recommendations to upgrade the public service. In addition, many localities experienced fiscal discontent, the voter-initiated, stringent limits placed on the ability of elected officials to use their discretion and judgment in the budgeting process.

Intergovernmental Revenue

Local government reliance on intergovernmental revenues began to increase in the mid-1960s, peaking at 44.7 percent of local general revenue in 1979 (from 31.4 percent in 1965); by 1992 it had declined to 37.7 percent (ACIR, 1992: 119). Of this seven percentage point decline, six points took place in non-education assistance (from 22 percent of general revenue in 1979 to 16 percent in 1992).

A new era of intergovernmental fiscal relationships emerged in the early 1980s with then-President Ronald Reagan's commitment to "reducing the size of government and decreasing federal involvement in state and local affairs" (Ladd, 1994: 219). Federal assistance to local governments peaked in 1978, and by 1990 it had declined by $1 billion, to $18.5 billion (a 58 percent decline in real per capita terms). General Revenue Sharing and Urban Development Action Grants were eliminated in 1986. Housing subsidies and various training and employment programs were reduced over 45 percent between 1980 and 1988 while other programs such as wastewater treatment construction, mass transit grants, and Community Development Block Grants were cut by more than 20 percent (ibid.). Moreover, grant programs directed toward cities tended to be harder hit than those to states. Many narrowly defined categorical programs were consolidated into block grants, and the states were designated as the recipients. Of the 77 grants that were consolidated into block grants in 1981, 47 had delivered federal funds directly to localities (ibid.).

Much, but not all, of the decline in federal assistance was offset by an increase in state assistance to local governments. The states, which also had experienced reductions in federal assistance, "were not in a position to help" (Ladd, 1994: 222). Medicaid and corrections increases limited the amount that could be devoted to other programs (Gold, 1990: 13). Budget demands in the states created pressures to reduce local assistance programs, thereby exacerbating the difficulties for local governments. These changes in intergovernmental fiscal relationships and the resulting need for local governments to rely more on their own-source revenues were occurring when taxpayers in many states and localities were in the midst of a revolt over tax burdens—the fiscal discontent described in the next chapter.

Intergovernmental Mandates

The "mandate millstone" was former New York City Mayor Edward Koch's characterization of the requirements that one government places on another without providing the resources necessary to implement them. States and localities were confronted with an ever-increasing number of these mandates at a time when intergovernmental financial assistance was being cut back.

During the 1970s and 1980s much attention was being paid to the burden of federal mandates. "For state and local governments, the 1980s were not . . . a golden age of intergovernmental deregulation. . . . The end result was an accumulation of new requirements roughly comparable to the record-setting pace of the 1970s" (Conlan, 1991: 44).

By the late 1980s and into the 1990s, mandates continued as a major issue, and local officials also had to deal with an increasing number of state mandates (MacManus, 1991: 59). By 1990, only fifteen states required themselves to remunerate localities for the costs of state mandates (nine were constitutionally based); all but one of these requirements were enacted between 1973 and 1984. Eighteen other states considered but rejected such requirements (ibid.). "One legacy of Ronald Reagan's New Federalism has been a shift of certain intergovernmental fiscal tensions into the state-local arena" (ibid.).

Tighter Financial Markets

In March 1975, credit markets were closed to New York City when major participants in those markets came to doubt that the city could redeem its securities (Shefter, 1985: 127). When that happened, "the fiscal problems of U.S. cities hit the national headlines" (Ladd, 1994: 211). Other local governments felt the impact as credit became more difficult to obtain. Investors demanded improvements in financial management and reporting. Taxpayers became more reluctant to approve bond referenda (ibid.: 218).

By the early 1980s further turbulence emerged in municipal financial markets as interest rates escalated to double-digit levels (11.57 percent on a high grade tax-free municipal bond in 1982) (ibid.: 225).

Efforts to Improve Efficiency and Effectiveness

A "more pronounced emphasis on the performance and productivity of public services and public employees" also emerged (Lewin, Feuille, Kochan, and Delaney, 1988). Efforts were directed toward improving the efficiency and effectiveness of government. "Reinventing"[5] and "revitalizing"[6] became themes, to include creating competition, focusing on customers and offering them a choice, public sector deregulation, enhanced executive leadership, and decentralized service delivery. In one form of decentralization, some suggested returning to a more traditional system of American federalism—sorting out responsibilities and devolving certain ones to the states and ultimately to the localities.[7] Each of these changes potentially affects the manner in which local governments deliver services and, in so doing, has ramifications for their employees.

Changing Technology

"In toto, the effects of technological change on state and local governments require the greatest adjustments for public service since the reform movement of the early twentieth century" (Perry and Kraemer, 1993: 232). Technological advances have been accelerating, and their implementation has contributed to increased productivity. The process has affected many organizational relationships as well as redefining the nature of the work itself.

Technological change is transforming public service in state and local governments. The transformation is an evolutionary process. . . . Despite the early stage, many of the implications . . . have become apparent, such as worker displacement; creation of entirely new job classifications; skill transformation; redefinition of the temporal, physical, and social meaning of public service; and technology-induced stress. (ibid.: 242)

Improving the Public Service

"There is evidence on all sides of an erosion of performance and morale across government in America. Too many of our most talented public servants . . . are ready to leave. Too few of our brightest young people . . . are willing to join" (National Commission on the Public Service, 1989: 1). To address these problems the so-called Volcker Commission proposed strengthening executive leadership, broadening the government's talent base, and placing greater emphasis on quality and performance by, among other things, building a competitive pay system and recognizing employee performance and productivity.

The National Commission on the State and Local Public Service (1993: 12) made a similar, but somewhat more far-reaching recommendation.

Create a learning environment by (1) restoring employee training and education budgets; (2) creating a new skills package for all employees; (3) basing pay increases on skills, not time in position; (4) insisting on a new kind of problem-solving public manager, not merely a paper passer; and (5) encouraging a new style of labor-management communication.

The National Commission on Excellence in Education (1983) found that "too many teachers are being drawn from the bottom quarter of graduating high school and college students" and recommended that "the salaries for the teaching profession should be increased and should be professionally competitive, market sensitive."

Elementary and secondary school teachers constitute almost 40 percent of the full-time local government workforce, and thus their compensation represents a large share of local operating budgets. While "the average daily wage of instructional staff increased from $34 in 1890 to $83 in 1940 to more than $183 in 1990 (all expressed in real 1990 dollars), teachers' earnings have generally declined relative to other similarly skilled workers" (Hanushek, 1994: 32). Further,

Because of rapidly expanding opportunities for women elsewhere in the workforce, the decline in the relative attractiveness of teaching did not reverse itself in the 1980s, as it did for men. Although more than 40 percent of female college graduates were teachers in 1970, only 19 percent were in 1990. More starkly, only 11 percent of female graduates ages twenty to twenty-nine were teaching in 1990, compared with 41 percent of the same age group two decades earlier. (ibid.: 34)

To attract more able college students into teaching, many school districts increased the overall salary schedule, but this approach increased salaries regardless of skills and abilities (ibid.: 80). Some systems attempted to link salaries directly to a teacher's performance, but "designing a workable system of merit pay has proved elusive" (ibid.: 95). Many teachers and their representatives resisted merit pay "in part because of concerns about a school's ability to separate a specific teacher's contribution to a student's performance from the contributions made by other teachers or the student's family" (ibid.: 96).

THE PROCESS

The budgetary environment just described, along with the emergence of fiscal discontent, contributed to "reorienting budgeting from a growth process to one which emphasizes the conservation of resources" (Schick, 1986: 124). Macrobudgeting became increasingly prevalent. Spending and revenue targets or guidelines were established before the start of budget preparation. A new "prepreparation" process emerged that created the framework for the subsequent microbudgeting.

Prepreparation has several defining characteristics (ibid.: 131). It "front loads" key decisions on fiscal objectives and spending levels so that overall budget contours are shaped much earlier in the budget cycle. It is a centralized, top-down process, not the decentralized, bottom-up process used in many organizations to claim resources. It is a more integrated, less fragmented process focusing on tradeoffs and rationing scarce resources. It often entails high level political activity dealing with issues such as the size and role of government, social and economic directions, and overall budget priorities. Many of these macro guidelines are used "to dampen future budget expectations . . . be political statements concerning the future orientation of government policy . . . give notice to the spending agencies, interest groups, and the public-at-large that the budget is being reoriented . . . exert downward pressure on spending demands (ibid.: 126).

Prepreparation is "where the action is" for many local governments. When macro targets are being established, resource demands have to be "on the radar screen," at least in general terms. Within the context of this research, for example, a legally binding collective bargaining agreement would accomplish this. The more traditional public participation processes—town meetings or public hearings—occur at the latter stages of the microbudgeting cycle, frequently too late to be meaningful for the budget under consideration.

THE ACTORS

This research identifies three groups of budget actors: those who request services, the employees who provide services, and the taxpayers. Each group seeks to make its views known to the appointed and elected decision makers who establish the macro guidelines and make the final choices allocating the resources.

Those who claim resources frequently encompass a vast array of interests within a community. Brecher and Horton (1988: 153) describe a competition among the business community, the dependent poor, the citizens who seek public services that are not highly distributive, and the civil servants; each has distinct interests to pursue in local politics, and these interests are associated with distinct fiscal preferences. For this research, these claimants are combined into two groups—those requesting services and the local government employees who provide services.

The third group of actors is the taxpayers who provide the resources needed to pay for the choices made. Taxpayers are drawn from the same groups described by Brecher and Horton (ibid.).

ALTERNATIVE STRATEGIES

Hirschman (1970) delineates two "equally important" options available to those wishing to convey their point of view—exit and voice. The options reflect the "more fundamental schism between economics and politics. Exit belongs to the former realm, voice to the latter" (ibid.: 19).

Exit and Voice

Exit has been accorded an extraordinarily privileged position in the American tradition. . . . The American idea of success confirms the hold which exit has had on the national imagination. . . . With the country having been founded on exit and having thrived in it, the belief in exit as a fundamental and beneficial social mechanism has been unquestioning. (Hirschman, 1970: 106–112)

Voice is the opposite of exit. It is a far more "messy" concept because it can be graduated all the way from faint grumbling to violent protest; it implies articulation of one's critical opinions. . . . Voice is political action par excellence. (ibid.: 16)

"While exit requires nothing but a clearcut either-or decision, voice is essentially an art constantly evolving in new directions. This situation makes for an important bias in favor of exit when both options are present. . . . The presence of the exit alternative can tend to atrophy the development of the art of voice" (ibid.: 43). While the effectiveness of voice is strengthened by a credible threat of exit, it would be wrong to conclude that one "who has 'nowhere to go' is the epitome of powerlessness" (ibid.: 70).

Collective Voice

There is obviously no purpose in having an organization when individual, unorganized action can serve the interests of the individual as well as or better than the organization. . . . But when a number of individuals have a common or collective interest . . . individual unorganized action . . . will not be able to advance that common interest at all, or will not be able to advance that interest adequately. (Olson, 1965: 7)

Often it is possible to create entirely new channels of communication for groups . . . which have had notorious difficulties in making their voice heard, in comparison to other interest groups. . . . The propensity to resort to the voice option depends also on the general readiness of the population to complain and on the invention of such institutions and mechanisms as can communicate complaints cheaply and effectively. (Hirschman, 1970: 42–43)

Voice is costly. There are direct costs "as members of an organization spend time and money in an attempt to achieve changes" as well as the opportunity costs of foregoing the exit option (ibid.: 39).

The political science literature includes competing theories to explain collective voice. The debate about interest group political participation and behavior focuses on the "logic of joining" (Moe, 1981: 531) and includes a range of perspectives including: a pluralist argument (Dahl, 1961), a rational perspective argument (Olson, 1965), and a hybrid model offered by Moe (1981).

The pluralist view challenges the existence of an all-powerful ruling elite that must consent before a community implements any change. There is no one elite that is "a ruling group, but simply one of many groups out of which individuals sporadically emerge to influence the politics and acts of city officials" (Dahl, 1961: 72).

Pluralists argue that the primary reason for forming interest groups is the existence of shared interests "that can be advanced through collective action

... for the transmission of [those] interests into the political system. The interests are primary, the groups secondary'' (Moe, 1981: 532). "There is an almost exclusive focus on the political'' (ibid.: 543).

Olson (1965), on the other hand, disagrees with pluralism's logic. He argues that individuals are motivated by economic gain, the nonpolitical dimension. "Agreement with group goals is ordinarily insufficient to induce individuals to join'' (ibid.: 533). Because of the collective nature of many of the benefits provided by an interest group, there is a free-rider problem; this is especially true for more broadly based groups.

Olson argues that groups that provide widely diffused benefits to a large number of people will be unlikely to attract significant support, since the benefit to any single member is likely to be small. Only groups that represent narrow special interests will be effective in influencing the political process. Efforts that focus on obtaining large benefits for a less diffuse, narrowly focused group can garner support that can make an effective lobbying program possible.

[Small groups] may very well be able to provide themselves with a collective good simply because of the attraction of the collective good to the individual members. In this, small groups differ from larger ones. The larger the group is, the farther it will fall short of obtaining an optimal supply of any collective good. (Olson, 1965: 36)

Moe's "revised model'' (1981) argues that "both political and non-political considerations can be integral components of organizational incentive structures and both must be taken into account'' (ibid.: 543). More than economic self-interest is involved. Individuals may perceive that their "contributions can make a difference for political outcomes. [They] may have perception of efficacy'' (ibid.: 536). In addition, they may be motivated to join by such non-economic incentives as "solidarity'' or "purposiveness.'' The former derive from such incentives as friendship, status, or social acceptance; the latter from ideological, moral, or religious principles. These may be important considerations for certain occupational communities, as will be discussed in Chapter 5.

For this research, it is important to realize that "although the competing theories offer different explanations for collective political action, each explicitly recognizes that unions actively seek to affect political outcomes'' (Delaney, Fiorito, and Masters, 1988: 618).

THE ACTORS USE COLLECTIVE VOICE

The decision makers who make the final choices must balance an almost infinite array of competing demands in order to produce an adopted budget. It would be reasonable to assume that they would want there to be

a high probability that an active and legitimate group in the population can make itself heard effectively at some crucial stage in the process of decision. To be "heard'' covers a wide range of activities . . . [by] effectively I mean more than the simple fact that it makes a noise; I mean that one or more officials are not only ready to listen to the noise, but expect to suffer in some significant way if they do not placate the group. (Dahl, 1956: 145)

The challenge for the budget actors is to present a convincing case in a way that will be heard by those decision makers. What strategy to follow? The hypothesis of this research is that they have chosen voice and, more important, collective voice.

Lobbying as practiced in America is virtually unheard of in other democratic societies since its methods do not work well with the cabinet form of government found in parliamentary systems (see, for example, Gotlieb, 1991). But in the current era of doing the public's business in the United States, the use of organized groups has become a frequently used strategy for getting one's agenda heard. "Although Americans call them special interests and often impugn their tactics, the idea that everyone should be heard in every statehouse and in tens of thousands of local communities is very American" (Nathan, 1994: 158).

While America is a relatively mobile society,[8] for many actors, leaving one's job, the exit option of the labor market, is not a viable alternative, at least in the short run. Additionally, certain local government employees (for example, firefighters, police officers, schoolteachers) may be working in monopsonistic markets that afford them only limited employment alternatives if they choose not to relocate. Thus, for a variety of reasons, many actors remain and seek to make their views heard through voting, discussion, bargaining, and the like.

The voting booth is available to most of the individual actors. For many, "it is in the voting booth that the taxpayer and consumer sides of our nature must come to grips with each other" (Fosler, 1980: 285). We have to "work through" an issue and resolve conflicting values within ourselves; we have to "come to public judgment" (Yankelovich, 1991).

But, "In the context of local public affairs, voting is . . . perhaps one of the less significant forms of citizen participation" (Sharp, 1990: 72). Typically, local elections draw only about 25 to 30 percent of eligible voters to the polls; voting is even lower in governments that have a nonpartisan or council-manager form of government. In more specialized elections (school board, for example), the turnout is likely to be even less (ibid.). However, with low levels of voter turnout, an organized group with sufficient members can have an impact on election results.

Beyond the individual voice of the voting booth are a number of collective voice alternatives to which the various groups have turned. Participation by citizens requesting services has been ongoing and growing since the 1960s. Taxpayers turned to other strategies to reduce their tax burdens. Many public employees have turned to the institutions of labor-management relations to voice their views. As Hirschman (1970: 86) notes, the detail of institutional design can be important for the balance of exit and voice; however, there is no prescription for an optimal mix (ibid.: 124).

The Voices of Those Requesting Services

No single organization typically represents the multiple interests of those requesting public services (Brecher and Horton, 1988: 153). Rather there are numerous organizations representing a broad array of constituencies. Some have very narrow interests; others are somewhat broader; few are general interest organizations (the League of Women Voters, for example). Constituencies may include the business communities, the education communities, the elderly, the disabled, low-income citizens, the homeless, crime prevention, transportation, environment, and libraries. Within these various groups there may be even narrower, competing interests; for example, in the K–12 education community there may be district-wide Parent Teacher Associations, local PTAs, parents of gifted and talented students or disabled students, and those interested in interscholastic sports or computer education, to name a few.

Beginning in the late 1960s, citizen participation underwent fundamental change.

The civil rights movement and its legacy constitute a central theme. So does the role of the national government. . . . The tremendous growth of federal programs . . . and the evolution of federal requirements for citizen participation. . . . There has been a pattern of expansion followed by routinization of citizen participation in urban politics. (Howard, Lipsky, and Marshall, 1994: 154)

The advent of citizen advisory committees, mandatory public hearings, and other routine forms of participation furnished bureaucracies with important mechanisms of political input, which became the bureaucratic equivalent of periodic elections. Even if the value of these mechanisms was primarily symbolic, they in fact functioned to organize political participation. (ibid.: 174)

Many of the federal requirements were undertaken in the context of community development and the "war on poverty" programs. For example, the Economic Opportunity Act of 1964 required, among other things, that participating local governments establish Community Action Agencies to achieve "maximum feasible participation," mainly by low income groups, which traditionally had been underrepresented.

The number of local governments subject to public hearing requirements expanded greatly as a result of the requirements of the federal government's General Revenue Sharing program. By 1978, 55 federal grant programs mandated that local government recipients hold public hearings to ensure citizen participation in deciding on the uses of funds (ACIR, in Sharp, 1990: 79).

Rehfuss (1979) cites two common themes that emerged from a 1977 survey assessing the impacts of citizen participation in the local budget process. One was an increased apathy among the general electorate toward the day-to-day details of fiscal matters. Genuine broad-based participation is difficult to muster. A second theme was the domination of public hearings by special interest groups. "The budget process is at best an imperfect means of eliciting citizen participation and, at worst, a means of highlighting the demands of special interests" (Rehfuss, 1979: 88). However, over 40 percent of the cities and counties responding to the survey answered affirmatively when asked if citizen participation had a measurable effect on setting priorities within their general budget. The two most frequently cited types of organizations attending budget hearings were social services organizations and senior citizen groups (the survey did not include public school districts). Attendance at budget hearings also was found to increase when a proposal directly affected a group or individual.

From an institutional design perspective, the public hearing process has been criticized in the literature. Hearings often occur too late in the decision-making process and can be inconvenient and inhibiting in format. They are, in the words of Kweit and Kweit (1987: 30), "often plagued by low attendance. They also may become a forum for a few dissidents who do not represent the community. While many groups may be represented, each is usually playing an advocacy role, and tradeoffs between groups are usually not considered."

But public hearings are used extensively by local governments, and their impact on the local budgeting process cannot be ignored. As Sharp (1990: 82) states, "In the hands of motivated individuals and mobilized groups, these devices have been effectively used. They have transformed the local level into a much more open and accessible context than are state and federal government processes for the typical citizen."A variety of additional mechanisms for fostering citizen participation have emerged as well, including neighborhood empowerment strategies[9] and additional open government policies.

Many states have mandated open-meeting (sunshine) laws for multi-member public bodies as well as freedom of information laws to make public documents available to those who wish to review them. The introduction of government access channels on local cable television systems and the cablecasting of many public meetings (the local legislative body or school board, for example) "exemplifies the marriage of the open-government trend with the telecommunications revolution" (Sharp, 1984: 499). Respondents to a survey conducted by Cigler and Sharp (1985) believed that a community's interest groups monitor public meetings on the cable channel. VCR technology has enhanced the ability of these groups to monitor debates, including those about fiscal matters.

Neighborhood empowerment involves the "arrangements for the formal involvement of neighborhood organizations in the planning and budgeting processes" of local governments, mainly in American urban centers (Sharp, 1990: 86). "Neighborhood organizations have become institutionalized channels for citizen input into policy making. . . . [They] are important vehicles for getting citizens involved in activities that have been overlooked by those concerned exclusively with the policy making side of local government'' (ibid.: 90).

Again, many are critical of the institutional design and its contribution to a plethora of citizen organizations. Yates (1977: 23) refers to ''street fighting pluralism.''

These diverse, fragmented citizen interests have produced a bewildering array of street-level community organizations that seek to give voice to one neighborhood demand or another. Typically, they represent highly segmented and crystallized political interests: any neighborhood is likely to have scores of these small, competing community organizations.

However, these neighborhood groups are viewed by many city officials as one, if not the most important, of the various urban interest groups (Sharp, 1990: 87). Some are quite sophisticated, others less formal; for example, in Portland, Oregon, there is an annual ''neighborhood needs'' process by which each neighborhood communicates its priorities to every city department.

The Voice of the Taxpayers

One of the defining differences between private sector and public sector budgeting is that, in the latter, those who provide the resources are not those who decide how to spend them. One set of judgments is substituted for another.

Taxpayers as a class tend to be among the least active political constituencies in terms of persistent and direct political lobbying (Fosler, 1980: 284). In Olson's lexicon (1965), this would be a group attempting to provide widely diffused benefits to a large number of people.

Their collective voice, as resource providers, frequently has been underrepresented in the traditional public participation processes. Rehfuss (1979: 90) reports that homeowner organizations attended budget hearings in about one-quarter of the governments replying to a survey. Taxpayer organizations attended in about one-third of the municipalities and one-half of the counties reporting. The survey does not report what their concerns were when they did appear.

Unable or unwilling to exit, the citizens exercised their voice option during the 1970s and early 1980s, when they called for more stringent limits on the fiscal powers of their local governments. These successful efforts to petition measures to the ballot or to urge their legislators to enact them are at the heart of the fiscal discontent employed in this research.

The major lesson of Proposition 13 in California ''lies in the process of taking matters into their own hands. Whatever taxpayers want changed, they must change through the ballot box. There is little evidence that elected officials are willing or able to reduce programs and costs without direct actions'' (Dworak, 1980: 85). As one ''revolt'' leader said, ''Our fight is not mainly about money.

It's about control. They have to learn once and for all it's our government."[10] The taxpayers' use of the collective voice strategy is explored in Chapter 3.

The Voice of Local Government Employees

> Unionism has two "faces" . . . one, which is the fore in economic analysis, is that of a monopoly; the other is that of "a voice institution," i.e., a socio-political institution . . . the key question for understanding unionism in the United States relates to the relative importance of these two faces. (Freeman and Medoff, 1979: 74–76)

Under the monopoly view, unions reduce output by increasing wages, thereby causing a misallocation of resources; in addition, employee productivity is reduced by limiting output. However, Freeman and Medoff argue that unions may also increase productivity by opening an important communication channel between employees and management. They can serve as the employees' agent (Faith and Reid, 1987: 41), thereby providing the employer with relevant labor market information during the negotiating process; assisting with governance services by administering such contract provisions as employee grievances; and communicating employee preferences regarding compensation and other human resource policies.

In the workplace, Freeman and Medoff (1979: 72) argue, employees must use collective voice since individual voice will not be effective for two main reasons. First, many aspects of a workplace are "public goods" that have an associated free-rider problem, thereby reducing the incentives for any individual to invest time and effort to express preferences about matters that would benefit all employees. Second, those "who are not prepared to exit will be unlikely to reveal their true preferences . . . workers acting collectively are protected from managerial retaliation, but an individual acting alone is not" (ibid.). Collective voice provides employees with a channel for expressing themselves to management.

By and large, local government employee bargaining units are not large groups;[11] they certainly are not large national unions. In Olson's model (1965: 67), they may well be those smaller groups with narrow special interests well positioned to provide themselves with collective goods, including higher wages, shorter hours, and better working conditions. Smaller units may have further advantages "stemming from the fact that they can be meaningful social and recreational units, and thus offer noncollective social benefits that attract members" (ibid.).

THE EMPLOYEES' POLITICAL VOICE

> Employment in the public sector has unique characteristics which exert a significant influence on the growth of organized labor. A prime considera-

tion is the participation of public employees in the hiring of their own employer. (Dalton, 1982: 164)

Particularly in local and state situations, the labor movement often plays a very important part in the election process (Bakke, 1970: 24). "The average turnout in municipal elections is only 30 to 50 percent of the registered voters. With the ratio of state and local government workers to the total workforce approaching one in six, the potential for tipping election results is readily apparent" (Zagoria, 1972: 172). This can be especially important when there is some "battle cry" for employees to rally around.

Since management is beholden to an electorate that includes public sector workers and politically active unions, management may be less adversarial than private sector managers who are accountable to stockholders (Freeman and Ichniowski, 1988). From the employees' perspective, "it is an almost impossible break the union leader must make from political support to economic adversary" (Gotbaum, 1972: 85). When labor has supported a candidate it is difficult "to then turn on him and accuse him of being a bad negotiator and an exploiter of the people you represent" (ibid.).

Employees also are constituents, and thus they both supply and demand services. Dunlop's "monopoly" union characterization is not representative of union behavior in the local public sector (Zax and Ichniowski, 1988: 328). Their objectives include many aspects of employment conditions in addition to compensation. "The process of public policy formulation is frequently responsible for many of the working conditions specified for public employees" (Macy, 1972: 11).

"For voice to function properly it is necessary that individuals possess reserves of political influence which they can bring into play when they are sufficiently aroused" (Hirschman, 1970: 71). And as Valletta (1989) says, political channels are open to municipal unions as long as membership is large enough for a substantial voting bloc and pressure group to exist. Groups such as police, firefighters, and teachers would meet this test. Research also has found a positive relationship between the proportion of female members in a union and its involvement in politics (Delaney, Fiorito, and Masters, 1988: 638).[12] "If female members are more willing to support union political activities than male workers have been traditionally, then unions may become more successful in the political arena in the future" (ibid.).

Different labor organizations emphasize different political strategies; there is no consistent or monolithic approach. They engage in a host of political activities—voter registration, get-out-the-vote activities, political education, and grassroots lobbying (Masters and Delaney, 1987: 222). Also, an organization's "demographic, economic, and internal political characteristics affect its external political activity" (Delaney, Fiorito, and Masters, 1988: 638). The International City Management Association in unpublished data identified seven techniques— candidate endorsement, candidate financial contributions, manpower or in-kind campaign contributions, mismanagement disclosure threats, publicity campaigns, state-level lobbying, and taking issues to referendum (O'Brien, 1994: 324).

In his study of 81 police and 72 fire unions, O'Brien (1994: 328) found that the most popular activities (used by more than 40 percent of the unions) were those that involve the politicians directly—candidate endorsement, financial contributions, and state-level lobbying. Other approaches that require mobilizing public opinion "appear to be used less for achieving union objectives." Since local governments are creatures of their states, local employees also may benefit from pressuring state officials regarding a range of matters—increased fiscal support or autonomy, laws regulating public employment, and pension statutes are examples.

Multilateral Bargaining

Bargaining in the public sector is not the bilateral model commonly found in the private sector. Contracts are seldom solely negotiated by labor and management. Rather, bargaining is best conceptualized as a multilateral process in which contracts are "negotiated within a context created by people and groups whose wishes cannot be ignored . . . [who] influence negotiations even though they never come near the bargaining table" (Coleman, 1990: 103).

"It is axiomatic that some form of pressure tactics will accompany collective bargaining" (Love and Sulzner, 1972: 25). "Both before and during bargaining, rallies and demonstrations are frequently used to embarrass and harass elected and senior appointed officials" (Spero and Capozzola, 1973: 127). Organizational alliances also may be formed to increase the pressure.

In the public sector, the possibility of an "end run" is much greater because the principals on management's side are . . . susceptible to political pressure. . . . One teacher representative rated "extra bargaining procedures" as "more important than the table talk."
. . . School board members are "very political" people for whom the board is often a stepping stone to further political office and who therefore often support the union's position in return for future political support. (Derber, Jennings, McAndrew, and Wagner, 1973: 60)

In the 1970–1971 labor negotiations in New York City with the uniformed employee groups, "almost nothing was done at the table; instead both sides took to television, advertising, and loud and dramatic press releases. Mayor Lindsay made his first major offer not at the table but over television" (Gotbaum, 1972: 83).

Multilateral bargaining may manifest itself in many ways.

In one form public officials intervene . . . a council rejects an agreement. Another form . . . the end run . . . [unions] bypass negotiations and deal with the people who have power to make decisions. . . . Finally, the public has many reasons to pressure the parties . . .

when its interests are threatened. . . . A wage increase . . . competes with other causes. (Coleman, 1990: 104)

One aspect of multilateral bargaining includes the participation of any individual or group capable of imposing a cost (economic, political, or otherwise) on at least one of the direct parties to the agreement (McLennan and Moskow, 1968: 228). This focus on community interest groups and community participation has been institutionalized in sixteen states by some form of open meeting or sunshine law regarding collective bargaining; eight require open negotiations (Alaska, Florida, Minnesota, Texas, Kansas, Montana, Tennessee, Maryland) (Chandler, 1989: 92). In other states, however, keeping the community informed about negotiations can result in an accusation of "bad faith bargaining" (Livingston, 1972: 66).

A second dimension of multilateral bargaining for local governments is the "interest conflict within management" (Kochan, 1975: 90). Many local governments are designed in the anti-statist American tradition of fragmentation and separation of powers. Consequently, a number of independent elected and appointed officials (mayors, council members, city managers, county clerks, various criminal justice officials, negotiators, administrators) share the management role in dealing with public employee organizations.[13] The action of these officials "is strongly affected by the need to weigh and balance divergent interests of major groups among the citizens they represent" (Macy, 1972: 11).

When conflicts within management are not resolved internally, they tend to get carried over to the bargaining process (Kochan, 1975: 100).

One cannot ignore the important role in many jurisdictions played by the legislative body. Union power could be focused with far greater effectiveness upon sympathetic and responsive elected officials than upon the managers with whom they dealt in the regular employer-employee relationship . . . legislators control the ultimate power in the appropriations of funds to convert agreements into dollars in the pay envelope or pension fund. (Macy, 1972: 10)

The separation of powers in government between the executive and legislative branches makes it necessary to clarify where bargaining authority is vested. The executive bargains, the legislature approves it; the executive only; or the legislature only. The authority to commit to a bargaining agreement may be dependent upon other statutory powers or constraints as well: fiscal powers, referendum requirements, or budget deadlines are examples.

In a 1989 survey conducted in 181 cities with a population of 100,000 or more, 44 percent of the budget and finance officers perceived that the influence of the municipal legislative body in the budget process had either increased or increased significantly; 48 percent perceived no change (Botner, 1989: 41). The factor most frequently cited was that the members of the legislative body were more interested, more involved, and better qualified. The reduction in federal revenues and fiscal stress were also considered significant.

"The dispersion of power . . . provides public sector unions the opportunity to maneuver among and within segments of management in the furtherance of union interests" (Kochan, 1975: 90). But for this avenue to be available to the employees, the union must possess sufficient political resources to influence city officials (Kochan, 1974: 530). As discussed, it must have political access and take an active role in elective politics within the community (ibid.: 531).

One arena in which this is notably present is in the context of local public school systems governed by locally elected school boards, which frequently function both as executives and legislative bodies, in many cases with the power to levy taxes.[14] In many states, the school budgets, including the funding for negotiated agreements, must go directly to the voters for approval (Livingston, 1972: 66).

In many communities, there can be an "unusually close and direct relationship" between teachers and parents and children. "A clever teachers' union can utilize this relationship during negotiations to put enormous pressure on a school board to accede to its demands" (ibid.: 71).

Multilateral bargaining is much less pronounced at the state and federal levels. For local governments, however, this research hypothesizes that multilateral bargaining techniques are among the tactics used to achieve favorable budgetary outcomes for local government employees in an era characterized by fiscal discontent.

Lobbying

The ability of public employees to alter demand through the use of political influence over the budget process is the most important of the unique features of public sector unionism in the United States (Valletta, 1989: 430). Public sector unions devote substantial lobbying energies to expanding budgets (Zax and Ichniowski, 1988). This influence is likely to be more significant at the municipal level, where employee unions can exercise a combination of lobbying and multilateral bargaining power (Valletta, 1989). Complementing bargaining with political and lobbying activity may work to the employees' advantage since the objectives of other groups may be more widely dispersed (à la Mancur Olson).

Freeman and Ichniowski (1988) distinguish the varying incentives and constraints that operate in many political environments. First, the voters must not oppose paying the tax bill needed to support the budget decisions. In the context of this research there must be no fiscal discontent. Second, since political influence depends, in part, on the size of the group one can muster, public sector unions tend to place weight on employment outcomes as well as compensation. They argue that unions can be an important ally in convincing the electorate, or the legislature, of the need to expand budgets not just for compensation but also for desired public services provided by members. As constituents, union members may have important influence with their fellow citizens (voters) who respect their expertise; again, police, firefighters, and teachers are examples (Zax, 1989: 22). This aspect of the relationship also may tend to reduce the adversarial nature of the bargaining.

A "key source of power" in collective bargaining negotiations "is information about budget problems and potential sources of funds" to finance agreements (Toulmin, 1988: 620). The national labor unions employ staff to review budgets to counter the argument that the government is not able to pay for a given contract proposal. Toulmin notes that "several unions, particularly AFSCME and SEIU, urge their locals to go beyond the short-term strategy of analyzing the budget by getting involved early and deeply in the budget process." They have recognized the importance of the prepreparation phase and the use of a collective voice strategy. Building coalitions with other organized groups, testifying at public hearings, and meeting with community leaders are cited by Toulmin as oft-used tactics.

O'Brien (1994: 337) attempts to measure the relative effects of the collective bargaining process versus union political power on department and municipal expenditures. Using data for police and firefighter unions, he found that "collective bargaining has no effect on the wage bill while political activities have a positive significant effect." These outcomes result from two very different dynamics.

Collective bargaining increases wages significantly, but this is offset by a significant reduction in employment; thus there is no increase in the wage bill. This suggests support for the demand-constrained model of collective bargaining—that is, bargaining outcomes occur along, or are constrained by, the employer's labor demand curve. Political activity, in contrast, has an insignificant effect on wages, "but a positive, significant effect on employment, thereby raising the wage bill." Thus political activities shift out the demand curve. This differs from the efficient-bargain model of collective bargaining, which argues that bargaining outcomes lie to the right of the labor demand curve along a contract curve.

O'Brien also found that "associations have no economic impact" and that "political activities are only effective in a collective bargaining environment." Thus, "bargaining would appear to be a necessary condition for union political effectiveness" (ibid.: 342).

Impasse Resolution

Closely related to an organization's lobbying efforts and the ability to have its position prevail is the manner in which an impasse is resolved. A strike, a temporary collective action that "combines the characteristics of exit with those of voice" (Hirschman, 1970: 86), is one extreme; other tactics include work slowdowns, "sick-outs," and publicity campaigns. One side of the debate argues that collective bargaining cannot be effective unless employees have the right to withhold their services.

The opposing point of view (for example, Wellington and Winter, 1971) argues that market forces are not always present to limit union power in the public sector and that providing the right to strike "would institutionalize the power of public employee unions in a way that would leave competing groups in the political process at a permanent and substantial disadvantage" (ibid.: 30). They argue that numerous government services are necessary for the public health, safety, and welfare and, further, that the demand for many government services is relatively inelastic and no close substitutes are available. Such actions would constitute "strikes against the community" (Zagoria, 1972: 165).

Zack argues (1972: 101) that the successful illegal strikes such as those in New York City in the late 1960s (transit workers in 1966, sanitation workers and teachers in 1968) "became powerful proof that the power to strike was a far greater relevance than the right-to-strike . . . the increasing militancy of public sector employees was a powerful catalyst for change." New York State's Condon-Wadlin Act enacted after a 1948 teachers' strike became a casualty of the 1966 transit strike because its "penalties were so draconian no official could enforce them" (Raskin, 1972: 131).

A union's efforts, however, "to improve professional status will have to be great to overcome the loss of status in the public mind by those who gain personally by withholding essential services from the public" (Bakke, 1970: 24). An August 1981 Harris poll (taken after the federal Air Traffic Controllers' strike) compared to a mid-1970s poll showed less support for the right to strike of both public and private workers. For local government–type jobs, between 1976 and 1981, the percentage endorsing the right to strike declined for transit workers (57 to 45 percent), sanitation workers (51 to 45 percent), and police officers (44 to 36 percent) (Lipset and Schneider, 1987: 204).

In many Western European countries the strike is used "to register grievances" and usually lasts "only a day or so" (Zagoria, 1972: 167). "The short-term cessation of services is a way to educate taxpayers of the value and importance of public service without antagonizing them to the point of retaliation rather than reward" (ibid.).

Currently, the statutory provisions in ten states grant certain local government employees the right to strike (Alaska, Hawaii, Illinois, Minnesota, Montana, Ohio, Oregon, Pennsylvania, Vermont, and Wisconsin); most limit this right to those not responsible for public safety and welfare (Pynes and Lafferty, 1993: 177). The remaining states either have a general or a selective prohibition (ibid.).

Early in his organizing efforts Jerry Wurf would state that he could "shut down a city." However, after the 1968 experience in Memphis surrounding the sanitation workers' strike and the assassination of Martin Luther King, Jr., he changed his strategy from "right to strike" to "fair arbitration by a truly independent body" (Goulden, 1982). The belief that government employees should not have the right to strike has spurred the public sector to develop many new procedures for impasse resolution (Freeman and Ichniowski, 1988). "In sharing sovereign authority . . . New Unions have pushed well ahead of the Old in innovating and changing industrial relations systems" (Troy, 1994: 63).

METHODOLOGY

A two-pronged analytical approach is used in this research—an analysis of aggregate local government statistics for each of the 50 states, supplemented by a case study of the agencies in one local jurisdiction.

While we may have "entered the age of unenlightenment" (Burton and Tho-mason, 1988: 46) regarding public sector labor-management relations data, the *Census of Governments* collected reasonably consistent, high quality data during the 1970s and 1980s for local government labor relations in each of the states. This data is relied on extensively for three main reasons: (1) it supports the longitudinal design of this research; (2) it "increases the sample size, its rep-resentativeness, and the number of observations that could lead to more encom-passing generalizations" (Frankfort-Nachmias and Nachmias, 1992: 294); and (3) there are no available alternatives. Unfortunately, the latest comprehensive data are for October 1987; labor-management relations information for local governments was not collected for the *1992 Census of Governments*. Data pub-lished by Troy and Sheflin (1985) supplement the earlier census data.

While the data may have some historical inconsistencies and data from dif-ferent sources may not be perfectly compatible, these problems do not impede analyzing trends or the orders of magnitude of change as this research seeks to do. The data, however, should not be used to derive precise numerical calcu-lations.

The data for international comparisons present several problems, not the least of which is a consistent definition for the public sector, since the public sector abroad often is very different from the American version. Troy (1988) has pre-sented data that compare union density in the public and "market" sectors for the Atlantic Community countries for the year in which the most recent data were available. The "market" sector includes the private sector plus the na-tionalized industries in goods and services. Although there are limits to this information, it can be used to delineate patterns important for this research.

Information regarding the various tax and expenditure limitations that were imposed on local governments in the various states (fiscal discontent) have been reported in various publications of the Advisory Commission on Intergovern-mental Relations (ACIR), most notably its annual *Significant Features of Fiscal Federalism*.

One is "obviously limited to what exists" (Babbie, 1992: 332), and while the aggregate state-by-state data provide a useful overlay, they do not present the interrelationships between the two movements under study—fiscal discon-tent and collective bargaining by full-time local government employees. Even if the aggregate data provide support for the pattern in the hypothesis, they may not tell the full story.

Neither of these collective voice movements occurred overnight. There was no big bang. Rather a series of events over a period of years culminated in these major changes in the local government arena. The use of collective voice by the employees evolved through several stages over the years—they organize, they move to a meet-and-confer process, and finally they achieve full collective bargaining on wages, benefits, and working conditions. A case study is used to provide a deeper understanding of events by "examining the subtle nuances of attitudes and behaviors . . . [and] processes over time" (ibid.: 305). That study is presented in Chapter 7. Regarding fiscal discontent, three additional case studies are presented in Chapter 3 to examine its evolution over time.

While general trends can be garnered from the aggregate data, an in-depth case study of the interrelationship of these events is used to "investigate [the] phenomenon within its real life context" (Yin, 1989: 23) and to take advantage of "the opportunity for a holistic view of a process" (Gummesson, 1991: 76). An important objective "is to examine some relevant 'how' and 'why' questions about the relationship of events over time, not merely to observe the time trends alone" (Yin, 1989: 120).

The goal of the case study is analogous to the one cited by Castles (1989: 13) in his discussion of comparative public policy analysis.

[to] contribute to an iterative process by which single case analysis uncovers qualitative variables which may ultimately be refined in such a way that they can be utilized as components of mainstream comparative analysis. Filling in particular gaps in our knowledge may, in other words, lead to reduction in "unexplained" variance in the universe of discourse as a whole.

Case studies can "tap a depth of meaning" (Babbie, 1992: 307) that other techniques cannot reach, thereby providing a higher level of validity. Using a case study provides, at relatively low cost,

an opportunity to use many sources of evidence . . . [which] far exceeds that in other research strategies. . . . The most important advantage [of] using multiple sources of evidence is the development of converging lines of inquiry, a process of triangulation. . . . Construct validity can potentially be dealt with because there are multiple measures of the same phenomenon. (Yin, 1989: 96–97)

However, case studies are not without their weaknesses. There are potential problems with both reliability and generalizability (Babbie, 1992: 308–309). But, for this research, care has been taken to guard against these problems. The benefit of probing the various rationales for employee actions with those who have participated in the events is crucial to understanding the dynamics that were at work.

The case study strategy employed here "follows the theoretical proposition that led to the case study" (Yin, 1989: 106). Case studies "like experiments, are generalizable to theoretical propositions and not to populations or universes" (ibid.: 21). "A fatal flaw in doing case studies is to conceive of statistical generalization as the method of generalizing the results of the case. . . . [T]he method of generalization is "analytic generalization," in which a previously developed theory is used as a template with which to compare the results of the case study" (ibid.: 38).

A single case study of one jurisdiction, Montgomery County, Maryland, was undertaken to supplement the analysis for each of the 50 states. Is a single case sufficient? Yin argues that a replication logic must be used to answer that question, not a sampling logic (ibid.: 54–55).

The theory has specified a clear set of propositions as well as the circumstances within which the propositions are believed to be true. To confirm, challenge, or extend the theory, there may exist a single case, meeting all of the conditions for testing the theory. The single case can be used to determine whether a theory's propositions are correct, or whether some alternative set of explanations might be more relevant. (ibid.: 47)

SUMMARY

This research explores the use of collective voice by full-time local government employees in the local budgeting process to help explain why they have chosen to bargain collectively at rates far higher than their counterparts in the private sector. With little abatement in the pressure by citizens to control taxes on the one hand, and with numerous groups lobbying and pressuring local elected officials to preserve or expand their program on the other, collective voice may be one avenue that local government employees have to ensure that their points of view are at least heard, if not ultimately accepted.

NOTES

1. Thirty-five percent of local governments (29,451 of 82,932) had no paid employees.

2. Assumes the average rate for all local governments of 22.4 percent of payroll.

3. Annual percentage increases in the Consumer Price Index for All Urban Consumers were 11.0 in 1974, 11.3 in 1979, 13.5 in 1980, and 10.3 in 1981. Unemployment rates for all civilian workers were 8.5 percent in 1975, 9.7 percent in 1982, and 9.6 percent in 1983 (U.S. Department of Commerce, Economic and Statistics Administration, November 1994).

4. By 1994 the median age was 34 years; there were 33.2 million persons age 65 and over (12.8 percent of the population).

5. See, for example, Osborne and Gaebler (1992).

6. See, for example, National Commission on the State and Local Public Service (1993).

7. President Reagan presented a "swap and turnback" initiative in 1981; Rivlin (1992) made a proposal to "divide the job" whereby the states would assume responsibility for the "productivity agenda."

8. In 1987, 44 million Americans moved (19 percent): 28 million of these moved within their county of residence; 16 million moved outside of it (U.S. Department of Commerce, Bureau of the Census, April 1989: 2).

9. Sharp (1990) suggests additional forms of citizen participation: (1) information-gleaning devices (surveys, ombudsmen, goal-setting activities, etc.) and (2) co-production strategies that bring citizens into working with government to deliver services. Howard, Lipsky, and Marshall (1994: 177) identify (1) direct action to pressure existing institutions and (2) creating alternative institutions (neighborhood crime watch, for example).

10. Barbara Anderson, Executive Director of Citizens for Limited Taxation, regarding Proposition 2½ in Massachusetts (in Citrin, 1984: 7).

11. In 1982, 42 percent of the bargaining units had fewer than 25 members; 77 percent had fewer than 100 members.

12. By 1987, 60 percent of the local government workforce was female, compared to 43 percent of the remaining civilian labor force.

13. In 1987, there were 479,021 local popularly elected officials in the United States (U.S. Department of Commerce, Bureau of the Census, September 1988, Table 6). "Not only are more offices open to election, but elections are much more frequent than in any other modern society . . . including primaries and counting all offices, well over one million such contests occur in every four year cycle" (Lipset, 1991: 10).

14. In 1987, there were 14,721 independent school districts and 1,492 dependent school systems (concentrated in ten states—Hawaii, Alaska, Connecticut, Maine, Massachusetts, Rhode Island, North Carolina, Maryland, Tennessee, and Virginia). All school districts had a combined total of 86,772 elected officials.

3

The Voice of the Taxpayers

During the decade of the 1970s the American taxpayers undertook a collective voice strategy in an effort to impose limits on the discretion available to their elected officials in the local budgeting process. This chapter examines this *fiscal discontent* movement, which succeeded in thirty-three states.

Two dimensions of this undertaking are important for this research, and each is explored in this chapter. First, this study assumes that actions taken by local government employees did not bring about fiscal discontent, and the validity of that assumption is documented here. Among the various hypotheses offered in the literature to explain these revolts, no evidence has been found to support attributing fiscal discontent to the collective voice of local government employees. In fact, as will be discussed in Chapter 6, employee collective bargaining rights have been limited in about one-half of the thirty-three states that experienced fiscal discontent.

Second, this chapter examines the events that ultimately led to the action to limit the discretion of elected officials in the budget process. As the case studies demonstrate, these revolts built up over a period of years, with various events along the way. Understanding the evolution and timing of events as well as their interrelationship is important. If the use of collective voice were more subtle than a one-time "big bang," examining only a narrow window of time could provide a distorted picture. For example, it is conceivable that the employees undertook efforts to counteract the voice of the taxpayers before a fiscal discontent proposition was presented to the voters for final decision.

To gain a better understanding of both the reasons for and the timing of fiscal discontent, three case studies are presented. The taxpayers' revolt was ignited by California's Proposition 13 (Pfiffner, 1983: 46); since it probably has been the most widely studied of the numerous expressions of fiscal discontent, it will be examined here. The limitation movements in Massachusetts and Michigan are also reviewed.

These tax revolts were a bicentennial reenactment of the Boston Tea Party (Shapiro, Puryear, and Ross, 1979: 1). They were not tidy, reform minded affairs. Passions ran high, and there was considerable anger at the politicians who had failed to address the problems. Their outcomes may not have been precise, but they served as "shock therapy" for the politicians (Susskind, 1983: 263).

The limitation movement was not confined to state and local governments. Between 1975 and 1983, 32 state legislatures approved resolutions calling for a Constitutional Convention to amend the United States Constitution requiring a balanced federal budget. Candidates for national office promised balanced budgets and tax relief as well. The 1980 election of Ronald Reagan as president and a Republican majority in the United States Senate reflected these attitudes.

Using a Richter scale analogy to examine the importance of various changes in the world of local finance, John Shannon concluded that the New York City fiscal crisis was a category 5 or 6, while Proposition 13 in California and the 1980 national election results both rated at least a 9 (in Sbragia, 1983a: 4).

Despite the rhetoric and action of these revolts, American taxpayers contributed a smaller percentage of Gross Domestic Product to taxes than did almost all other industrialized nations.[1]

FISCAL DISCONTENT

The concept of fiscal discontent describes the events that culminated in the externally imposed limitations on state or local revenue or expenditures approved over the twelve-year period that began in 1970. Thirty-three states experienced it.

An important dimension of this era of fiscal discontent was the use of voice by the taxpayers, who imposed binding limits by direct voting. Previously, they had influenced taxes and spending by electing or defeating politicians. With the revolt they dealt directly with a matter of concern to them. It began slowly and gained momentum as the 1970s progressed. The causes and specific provisions varied state to state, but the result for many local governments in these states was fundamentally the same—less discretion for elected officials and greater competition for more limited resources.

Fiscal discontent differs from other concepts found mainly in the urban finance literature. An array of labels has been used—there is fiscal "instability" (Fuchs, 1992), "stress" (Levine, 1980), "distress" (Stanley, 1980), "strain" (Clark and Ferguson, 1983), "crisis" (Fuchs, 1992; Stanley, 1980; Shefter, 1985), and "pressure" (Woman, 1980); there is "poor fiscal health" (Ladd, 1994); "running in the red" (Rubin, 1982); "relaxed, chronic, acute, and total scarcity" (Schick, 1980); "long-term decline" and "cities in trouble" (Stanley, 1980). Each has its own definition, and there is only limited agreement about how widespread the problems may be.

Stanley's distinctions (1980: 95) between fiscal distress, fiscal crisis, and long-term decline are illustrative. Fiscal distress is the everyday struggle of even affluent communities to balance the budget without raising taxes or cutting services; fiscal crisis is the condition of near bankruptcy in which the government has neither cash nor credit to meet near-term expenses; long-term decline is a situation in which the economy, social conditions, and the general enjoyment of life are slowly deteriorating. Ladd (1994) distinguishes between financial condition and "fiscal health." The former examines budget deficits or surpluses and short-term cash needs; the latter is a more fundamental issue of being able to provide services at reasonable levels of taxation.

Fiscal discontent may have contributed to these other conditions by providing less flexibility for fiscal authorities and making it more difficult to adapt to changing circumstances. "It was an ongoing tug of war between populist impulses toward tax minimization and local governments' needs to protect their revenue base" (Sharp, 1990: 165).

This limitation movement began to diminish in the early 1980s. The tax reduction focus shifted to the federal government (Merriman, 1987: 29). Between 1981 and 1989, when North Dakota voters rejected tax increases passed by the legislature, no major tax cutting initiative or referenda succeeded and many were rejected (Gold, 1990: 35). Furthermore, in legislative sessions in 1982 and 1983 a majority of states raised tax rates, 34 and 38 states respectively (Citrin, 1984: 20). Many limited the increases to minor taxes; five had major increases in their personal income tax rates and another five had major sales tax expansions. There were no broad tax reductions (Peterson, 1982: 192). However, in November 1983, voters in two Detroit-area cities recalled state senators who had supported a 38 percent increase in the state's income tax (Stanfield, 1983: 2568).

THE STATES AND THEIR LOCAL GOVERNMENTS

In the fiscal arena, states have long regulated local government taxing and borrowing powers, how those resources are spent, and the manner in which financial affairs are managed and controlled.

There have been three "waves" of activity during which most of the tax and expenditure limitations in United States history have been passed—the last quarter of the nineteenth century, the Great Depression, and the 1970s and early 1980s (Merriman, 1987).

Pre-1970 Fiscal Limitations

Limitations on local property taxation began at the time of the financial panic of 1873. Twenty-four states adopted them during the last quarter of the nineteenth century; Rhode Island (1870) and Nevada (1895) were the first to enact statutory limits (ibid.: 13). Their primary purpose was to shield property owners from large tax rate increases and to limit local expenditures.

A new impetus occurred during the Great Depression of the 1930s, when property values plummeted, assessments lagged behind the drastic reductions, and tax delinquencies soared. In some cities delinquencies exceeded 50 percent. In 1932 and 1933 alone, sixteen states and numerous localities enacted property tax limitations. Organized tax-resistance movements also took place throughout the country; in Chicago there was a virulent tax strike that lasted from 1930 to 1933 (O'Sullivan, Sexton, and Sheffrin, 1995: 1).[2]

Little changed between the end of the Depression and 1970. By the 1950s, many of the tax and spending limitations were viewed as "relics of the Great Depression" and there was activity in many legislatures to ease them (Merriman, 1987: 13).

In the related arena of municipal finance, the states also have been regulating local governments since the late nineteenth century, when a number of cities defaulted on their bonds. During the Great Depression, about 8 percent (1,434) of incorporated municipalities defaulted (Fuchs, 1992: 18). Between 1940 and 1969, there were relatively few defaults, mainly among small municipalities and some special districts. By the 1970s and early 1980s there were over 300 general purpose government bond defaults, most notably in New York City (ibid.).

The Fiscal Discontent of the 1970s

A third "wave" of fiscal limitations emerged during the 1970s, when local governments in 33 states had to deal with fiscal discontent. Local governments in the other seventeen states did not have to confront it directly, although it is likely there were spillover effects.

A local government experienced fiscal discontent if it was within a state in which one or more of the following limitations were imposed between 1970 and 1981. Table 3.1 provides a summary.

1. A state constitutional amendment or a voter approved state statute limiting the state government's discretion to tax or expend moneys. Fifteen states did: Alaska, Arizona, California, Colorado, Delaware, Hawaii, Idaho, Michigan, Missouri, Nevada, Oklahoma, Oregon, Tennessee, Texas, and Washington. Five states enacted legislative limits, but these are not included (Louisiana, Montana, New Jersey, Rhode Island, and South Carolina).

2. A state imposed or voter approved limit on local government property tax revenues. Fifteen states are added to the list: Alabama, Arkansas, Indiana, Kansas, Kentucky, Louisiana, Massachusetts, Minnesota, Mississippi, Montana, New Jersey, New Mexico, Rhode Island, South Carolina, and Wisconsin. Ten of the fifteen states that imposed limits on the state government implemented this as well (Colorado, Delaware, Oklahoma, Oregon, and Tennessee did not).

3. A state imposed limitation on the overall revenues or expenditures of local governments. One state, Maryland, is added to the list. Maryland's two largest jurisdictions also experienced fiscal discontent when citizen initiatives succeeded in imposing prop-

erty tax limits on those governments in 1978. One of these counties is the subject of the case study presented in Chapter 7. Eight states enumerated earlier also enacted this limitation.

4. A state imposed system of fiscal controls that tightly regulated fiscal actions in the state's major cities because the situation had deteriorated into one of "total scarcity" (Schick, 1980). Two states, New York and Pennsylvania, are added to the list.

Four New England states have no history of limits—Connecticut, Maine, New Hampshire, and Vermont. Thirteen other states either acted prior to 1970 using relatively weak limitations on property tax rates or acted after 1970 with even weaker disclosure requirements or assessment limitations—Florida, Georgia, Illinois, Iowa, Nebraska, North Carolina, North Dakota, Ohio, South Dakota, Utah, Virginia, West Virginia, and Wyoming. Ten of these states have provisions in their state constitutions permitting citizen initiatives. Indeed, limitation measures were defeated at the polls in Florida and Nebraska in 1978, and in South Dakota and Utah in 1980 (International City/County Management Association, 1979: 36). In 1983, Ohio voters rejected two proposals to repeal a 90 percent increase in the state's income tax (Stanfield, 1983).

There is no consistent pattern between the fiscal discontent targeted at the state and local governments and the call by 32 state legislatures for a Constitutional Convention to amend the Constitution to require a balanced federal budget. As portrayed in Table 3.1, twelve of the 33 fiscal discontent states did not call for a Constitutional Convention, while eleven of the seventeen non–fiscal discontent states did.

The first state in this third wave, Kansas, enacted stringent limits in 1970: no property tax revenue increase except for new construction, personal property increases, or annexations (Merriman, 1987: 26). In 1972, voters in the state of Washington approved a referendum limiting the property tax to 1 percent of assessed value (Saffell, 1984: 278). Others among this earliest group were Midwestern states: Iowa (1971), Minnesota (1971), Indiana (1973), and Wisconsin (1973). New Jersey followed in 1976 (Gold, 1981: 79).

By 1978, fiscal consciousness raising had blossomed, as 44 tax and expenditure proposals were initiated in seventeen states (Eribes and Hall, 1981). Between 1979 and 1984, there were more than 58 separate ballot measures (O'Sullivan, Sexton, and Sheffrin, 1995: 1).

The limitation measures in this era differed in several significant ways from those of earlier times. First was the citizen's use of voice, with many of the amendments placed on the ballot either by citizen initiative or referral by the legislature to the voters.[3] Second, many of the limitations were couched in constitutional rather than statutory terms, thereby making them more difficult to amend or eliminate. Third, the override provisions varied, but generally they were more stringent. Some required a simple majority of the legislature, others a super majority, and still others required approval of those voting in an election or of those registered to vote. Fourth, the limitations began to "draw the fiscal

Table 3.1
Fiscal Discontent, by State, 1970–1982

State	Government Limit	Property Tax Revenue Limit	Revenue (R) or Spending (E) Limit	Assessment Limit or Full Disclosure	Rate Limit Pre-1970	Rate Limit after 1970
FISCAL DISCONTENT STATES						
Alabama*		X			X	X
Alaska*	C	X				X
Arizona*	CV	X	E	X		
Arkansas*		X			X	
California	CV	X	E	X		
Colorado*	SV		E	X	X	
Delaware*	C	X				X
Hawaii	CV			X		
Idaho*	SV	X			X	
Indiana*		X			X	
Kansas*		X	Es		X	
Kentucky		X		X	X	
Louisiana*	S	X		X		X
Maryland*			R	X		
Massachusetts		X				
Michigan	CV	X		X	X	
Minnesota		X	RE		X	
Mississippi*		X			X	
Missouri*	CV		R		X	
Montana	S	X		X	X	
Nevada*	SV	X			X	
New Jersey	S	X	E		X	
New Mexico*		X		X	X	X
New York		X		X	X	

42

State	Type			
Oklahoma*	C			X
Oregon*	SV		X	X
Pennsylvania*				X
Rhode Island	S	X	X	X
South Carolina*	S	X	X	X
Tennessee*	CV		X	X
Texas*	CV	X		X
Washington	SV	X R		X X
Wisconsin	SV	X		X

NON-FISCAL DISCONTENT STATES

State	Type			
Florida*			X	X
Georgia*				Xs
Illinois			X	X
Iowa*			X	X
Nebraska*				X
North Carolina*					X
North Dakota*				X
Ohio				X
South Dakota*				X
Utah*			X	X
Virginia*			X	
West Virginia				X
Wyoming*				X
Connecticut				X
Maine				
New Hampshire*				
Vermont				

*State legislature called for constitutional convention to balance the federal budget (32 states).

C = Constitutional; S = Statutory; V = Voter Approved.

43

noose" (Citrin, 1984: 6) more tightly by placing restraints on revenue collections or expenditure levels rather than merely limiting tax rates or assessment levels. Overall, the novelty of these measures was in their severity.

Restraints on revenue collections limit the increase in revenue from one year to the next to some specified benchmark, such as inflation or personal income. They apply to overall revenue collections or to some specific revenue, frequently the property tax.

Restraints on appropriations or expenditures operate in much the same way as those on revenue yields. Their effectiveness in ultimately affecting tax burdens depends on the proportion of expenditures subject to control—for example, some exclude debt service or pension costs. On average, approximately 44 percent of state appropriated funds are excluded from state expenditure limitations. For example, Oregon excludes 71 percent; in Idaho and Colorado it is 60 percent (Howard, 1989: 87).

These "third wave" constraints were markedly different from the earlier limits on property tax rates, which lost much of their effectiveness as tax control measures when property assessments increased rapidly in the 1970s.

Two additional revenue limitation techniques first appeared in the 1970s, but they are relatively weak in their ability to restrict rising tax burdens. One limits assessment increases. A second, "truth in taxation" measures, requires governments to advertise proposed tax increases and provide citizens an opportunity to comment. By 1985, six states had implemented the former, and sixteen the latter. These weaker measures designed to limit tax rates, limit assessment increases, or require full disclosure are not included in this definition of fiscal discontent.

Selected State Interventions

New York and Pennsylvania did not impose statewide limitations on the budget powers of their local governments during the 1970s, but they did intervene in the fiscal affairs of the largest and most dominant local governments within their borders—New York City and Philadelphia.

These localities were among those confronting what Schick (1980) describes as "total scarcity"—the inability to garner the resources needed for financing ongoing programs, the heavy reliance on "escapist budgeting," and ultimately an inability to honor financial commitments. When these cities became unable to meet their financial obligations, the states ultimately intervened. As Bahl (1979: 283) notes, "the fiscal affairs of New York State cannot be examined apart from those of New York City."

In late 1975 and early 1976, several major cities were either excluded from the tax-exempt market or forced to pay very high rates of interest to borrow. New York City and Yonkers got most of the headlines, but Buffalo and Philadelphia, among others, had worrisome episodes (Petersen, 1980: 186). In July 1976, Moody's Investors Service downgraded the General Obligation debt rating for three of New York's major cities: New York to Poor (Caa), Yonkers and Buffalo to Speculative (Ba).

If New York City had defaulted on its $11 billion in outstanding debts in 1975, serious damage might have been done to the national and international banking systems (Shefter, 1985: 128). In response, the state established a new set of institutions to supervise the city's finances: the Municipal Assistance Corporation, the Emergency Financial Control Board, and the Office of the Special Deputy Comptroller for New York City; the Office of New York City Finance was formed in the U.S. Treasury Department.

The Municipal Assistance Corporation was established to oversee and revamp the city's finances. A majority of its directors were selected by the governor. It was authorized to sell the city's bonds; to assure investors that the debt would be repaid, the legislature converted several city taxes into state taxes. The Emergency Financial Control Board was granted plenary authority over the city's finances. Five of its seven members were appointed by the governor. Its legislative mandate was to balance the city's budget within three years. It had the power to review and reject, if necessary, the budget, the financial plan, all borrowing, and any collective bargaining agreements.

THE LOCAL FISCAL LANDSCAPE IN THE 1970s

The voice of the taxpayers became an overlay on the existing budget and fiscal landscape. Numerous factors had created a complex mosaic within which local governments were operating. While each locality may have had its own set of peculiar circumstances, most were confronting an array of social, economic, and structural dynamics, as reviewed in Chapter 2.

Challenges to the system of education finance also emerged. State policies toward education assistance became inextricably bound up with their policies toward property tax relief. As a result of court decisions involving litigation between rich and poor districts, fourteen states enacted major school finance reforms. Property tax rate limits and expenditure controls on school district budgets were an integral part of these reforms. However, regulating the tax and expenditure options of local school districts had equalization as a major goal, not control. Intertwined with the goal to balance school finance was the need to achieve racial balance between and within school districts, placing further demands on the financing requirements for K-12 public education.

A Fiscal Profile of Local Governments

There is great variation among the states in the spending and revenue patterns of their local governments. A 1977 snapshot for nine fiscal indicators covering taxes, expenditures, and employment at the time that fiscal discontent was underway is presented in Table 3.2. No patterns emerge between the discontent voiced by the voters and the level of taxation or spending measured relative to

Table 3.2
Local Government Fiscal Indicators, 1977: Taxes, Expenditures, Employment, and Fiscal Capacity

	Per Capita				Percent of Personal Income		
State	Property Taxes	Own-Source Taxes	Direct General Expenditures	State	Own-Source Taxes	Local Payroll	Direct General Expenditures
Fiscal Discontent States							
New York	$445	$650	$1,351	New York	8.25	7.49	17.14
California	454	533	879	Massachusetts	6.51	6.60	11.00
New Jersey	465	516	877	New Jersey	6.17	6.22	10.49
Massachusetts	488	491	829	California	6.03	7.46	12.13
Alaska	348	442	1,484	Montana	5.45	6.29	11.05
Colorado	321	423	879	Colorado	5.35	6.24	11.10
Oregon	375	406	857	Oregon	5.13	6.20	10.83
Nevada	271	401	974	Arizona	4.89	8.04	12.51
Maryland	244	375	933	Maryland	4.65	6.19	11.59
Montana	348	362	733	Rhode Island	4.50	5.11	8.16
Arizona	281	344	879	Michigan	4.36	6.58	10.72
Michigan	315	344	846	Kansas	4.28	5.26	9.59
Rhode Island	317	320	579	Nevada	4.19	5.38	10.17
Kansas	298	316	709	Pennsylvania	4.00	5.20	8.79
Pennsylvania	195	294	646	Missouri	3.97	5.21	8.30
Wisconsin	286	290	898	Wisconsin	3.96	6.32	12.30
Minnesota	275	287	961	Minnesota	3.79	6.43	12.71
Texas	240	280	645	Texas	3.73	5.65	8.49
Missouri	195	279	585	Alaska	3.42	6.25	11.50
Washington	179	256	774	Tennessee	3.42	6.00	9.26
Indiana	235	244	603	Indiana	3.36	4.94	8.32
Idaho	214	220	635	Louisiana	3.20	5.67	9.71
Tennessee	146	215	580	Idaho	3.15	5.28	9.11

46

Hawaii	172	215	461	Washington	3.11	5.93	9.43
Louisiana	100	205	620	Oklahoma	2.95	4.81	8.28
Oklahoma	142	203	569	Hawaii	2.58	2.60	5.56
Delaware	135	159	654	Kentucky	2.42	4.36	7.26
Kentucky	103	153	459	South Carolina	2.35	5.22	7.72
South Carolina	130	139	456	Mississippi	2.32	5.80	10.27
Alabama	53	131	528	Alabama	2.19	5.42	8.82
New Mexico	104	127	633	Arkansas	2.05	4.47	7.63
Mississippi	119	126	558	Delaware	2.00	4.60	8.23
Arkansas	110	121	449	New Mexico	1.98	5.98	9.90
Non-Fiscal Discontent States							
Wyoming	$419	$455	$972	Nebraska	5.62	6.35	10.94
Connecticut	416	420	678	South Dakota	5.48	5.09	9.16
New Hampshire	395	403	613	New Hampshire	5.44	4.35	8.29
Nebraska	368	394	766	Wyoming	5.33	6.12	11.40
Illinois	316	386	770	Vermont	5.26	4.44	8.47
South Dakota	309	341	570	Connecticut	4.89	4.59	7.90
Vermont	333	338	543	Illinois	4.57	5.84	9.12
Iowa	296	306	753	Iowa	4.17	5.56	10.28
Ohio	228	299	732	Virginia	4.08	5.40	9.01
Virginia	196	284	627	Ohio	4.06	5.41	9.93
Florida	209	247	770	Utah	3.72	5.79	9.80
Utah	202	247	651	Maine	3.70	5.06	9.23
Georgia	195	240	627	Georgia	3.69	6.12	9.63
Maine	232	234	581	North Dakota	3.66	5.60	10.19
North Dakota	224	232	644	Florida	3.33	6.25	10.38
North Carolina	135	164	617	North Carolina	2.65	6.12	9.97
West Virginia	115	141	473	West Virginia	2.24	5.12	7.56

Table 3.2 (continued)

	Personnel Indicators				Representative Tax System		
State	Employees Per 100,000 Population	Non-Instructional Earnings	Instructional Earnings	State	Fiscal Capacity	Fiscal Effort	Effort/ Capacity Ratio
Fiscal Discontent States							
New York	378.5	$1,155	$1,607	New York	94	168	1.794
Nevada	368.0	$1,009	$1,132	Massachusetts	95	133	1.389
Arizona	357.6	$1,021	$1,296	Mississippi	70	94	1.339
New Jersey	357.5	$963	$1,467	Rhode Island	87	114	1.300
California	353.7	$1,238	$1,635	Arizona	89	110	1.238
Massachusetts	352.9	$1,019	$1,312	Wisconsin	99	113	1.141
Colorado	345.1	$965	$1,172	South Carolina	77	86	1.125
Texas	343.1	$816	$1,028	Minnesota	100	112	1.117
Kansas	341.1	$783	$985	Hawaii	107	115	1.073
Minnesota	333.1	$1,045	$1,203	New Jersey	106	113	1.066
Tennessee	332.1	$745	$1,045	Michigan	103	109	1.060
Louisiana	331.8	$711	$1,019	Maryland	101	105	1.043
Montana	330.2	$824	$1,107	California	114	117	1.026
Mississippi	325.7	$620	$869	Alabama	77	79	1.022
Maryland	324.6	$968	$1,523	Idaho	88	89	1.016
Wisconsin	324.2	$985	$1,244	Kentucky	83	84	1.014
New Mexico	323.8	$801	$986	Arkansas	78	78	0.997
Alaska	323.1	$1,662	$2,017	Tennessee	83	82	0.994
Oregon	321.8	$1,037	$1,194	Pennsylvania	99	94	0.948
Michigan	320.0	$1,095	$1,497	Washington	100	94	0.934
Idaho	309.7	$772	$943	Montana	103	94	0.916
Oklahoma	307.3	$703	$948	Oregon	104	92	0.887
Alabama	305.1	$712	$952	Colorado	107	95	0.886

Missouri	303.2	$833	$1,075	Kansas	105	89	0.842
Washington	302.8	$1,078	$1,423	Missouri	96	80	0.841
Indiana	302.0	$752	$1,160	Indiana	100	83	0.825
South Carolina	291.8	$673	$906	Alaska	158	130	0.822
Arkansas	275.5	$603	$853	Louisiana	99	79	0.790
Pennsylvania	272.7	$963	$1,298	New Mexico	98	77	0.781
Delaware	263.3	$957	$1,190	Oklahoma	101	72	0.715
Rhode Island	254.0	$912	$1,388	Delaware	120	80	0.663
Kentucky	239.4	$737	$973	Texas	112	68	0.611
Hawaii	141.5	$1,186	na	Nevada	148	62	0.418
Non-Fiscal Discontent States							
Wyoming	396.0	$819	$1,077	Maine	82	100	1.217
Georgia	376.1	$712	$950	Vermont	93	104	1.121
Nebraska	370.1	$877	$1,011	Georgia	84	89	1.058
Florida	354.3	$889	$1,120	North Carolina	83	87	1.054
North Carolina	322.9	$719	$1,101	Utah	88	91	1.032
Iowa	315.2	$864	$1,105	Nebraska	101	98	0.965
Illinois	310.5	$1,120	$1,417	Virginia	91	88	0.958
Virginia	302.8	$822	$1,042	South Dakota	91	87	0.955
Ohio	301.3	$934	$1,175	Connecticut	112	103	0.920
South Dakota	293.9	$732	$1,212	West Virginia	90	80	0.893
West Virginia	281.8	$716	$1,033	North Dakota	99	88	0.891
Connecticut	278.0	$982	$1,273	Iowa	105	90	0.863
Maine	277.1	$740	$974	Illinois	112	96	0.859
Utah	269.0	$882	$1,097	Ohio	104	78	0.755
New Hampshire	263.8	$801	$972	Florida	101	73	0.724
North Dakota	261.4	$829	$1,212	New Hampshire	102	73	0.715
Vermont	241.1	$784	$931	Wyoming	154	82	0.531

Data Source: Advisory Commission on Intergovernmental Relations (1992c).

either population or personal income. There is great variability among the states that experienced fiscal discontent, as well as similarities with those that did not. Own-source taxes in the discontent states ranged from about 2 percent of personal income in New Mexico, Delaware, and Arkansas to over 8 percent in New York and over 6 percent in Massachusetts, California, and New Jersey. However, other states with relatively high levels of own-source taxes did not experience fiscal discontent (Nebraska, South Dakota, New Hampshire, Wyoming, and Vermont).

Local government employment relative to population was almost 50 percent higher in New York, Nevada, Arizona, New Jersey, California, and Massachusetts than it was in Kentucky or Rhode Island. Wyoming, Georgia, Nebraska, and Florida had high employment levels, but did not experience discontent. Local government payrolls relative to personal income reveal no consistent patterns as well.

Additionally, no patterns emerge between the existence of fiscal discontent and the hypothetical capacity of a state to bear those taxes. Table 3.2 also displays the 1977 fiscal "capacity" and "effort" indices developed by the Advisory Commission on Intergovernmental Relations (1992: 268–269). Effort exceeded capacity in less than one-half of the states that experienced fiscal discontent (16 of the 33). Effort exceeded the national average in only one-third of the discontent states (12 of the 33); capacity was above the national average in about one-half of these states (17 of the 33).

One pattern does emerge in the seventeen states that did not experience fiscal discontent—in twelve of these states, tax effort was below capacity, and in three additional states the difference was within 6 percent. Only in Maine and Vermont was the effort well above the capacity.

WHY THE REVOLT?

Taxation is an important link of the citizen to the political system. . . . There is nothing abstract about the payment of taxes. . . . Theoretically, the payment of taxes and voting on tax referendums are important indices of approval of the political system. Indeed, voting on revenue issues is a more refined index of political support than voting for leaders. . . . When the choice between leaders is not much of a choice, referendums are a concrete and specific way of giving or withdrawing support. (Meltsner, 1971: 3)

Media attention focused on California in 1978 and Massachusetts in 1980, but the pressure for fiscal control was underway in a large number of states. For example, in California's neighboring states of Arizona, Idaho, Nevada, and Oregon expressions of discontent were also taking place in 1978. These latter examples were "hardly the model of taxpayers' revolt environments described by the *American Political Reporter*" (in Eribes and Hall, 1981: 112): "large welfare rolls, a relatively large bureaucracy, burdensome environmental regulation and controversial educational sociology (controversial busing orders, egalitarian school district finance). Anger seems strongest where these characteristics coexist—as they usually do—with high tax burdens.''

Why did the citizens turn to the "heavy artillery along the lines of Proposition 13?'' (Citrin, 1984: 4). What diseases led them to opt for powerful, inflexible cures? (Courant, Gramlich, and Rubinfeld, 1980: 2). Why did the revolt erupt in a relatively short period of time? The research exploring the reasons for the voters' support is limited; much of it examines individual states. As the following overview demonstrates, prior research does not provide definitive answers to these questions. One can reasonably conclude that the confluence of a large number of factors came together in varying combinations in each of the 33 states.

There are two general schools of thought regarding the reasons for this wave of limitation measures. One focuses on identifying generic explanations applicable in all states—the unpopularity of the property tax, a dislike for taxes in general, an excessively large and inefficient government, rapid inflation and stagnant real income, excessive public employee compensation, and self-interest. A second group sees the circumstances of the individual states as providing important variations. As concerns varied from state to state, some specifically attacked the property tax, others targeted revenues in general, and still others focused on expenditures.

The Property Tax as Target

The revolts should be viewed as reactions against perceived abuses of the property tax (O'Sullivan, Sexton, and Sheffrin, 1995: 1). Whether the property tax was the intended target or not, the result of the limitation efforts was to constrain local property tax collections in most states. But why?

"One of the great arts of the tax game is to design revenue sources so that people will not know that they are paying taxes. Taxes should not be seen nor felt only paid'' (Meltsner, 1971: 38). For most people the real estate tax does not meet this test. It is levied on what most Americans regard as an essential component of success and security—owning their own home. California's Proposition 13 was advertised as a campaign to save the American dream (O'Sullivan, Sexton, and Sheffrin, 1995: 1).

The real estate tax is based on accumulated wealth, not income or transactions. The property is not necessarily sold, nor does it necessarily produce income in proportion to its value; unrealized capital gains are taxed. It requires that property values first be estimated and then be taxed, frequently by elected officials at a rate that can change from year to year. The tax bill may bear little relationship to a homeowner's ability to pay, but it may be a reasonable measure of benefits received from the government.

The local property tax consistently shares the "distinction'' of being the least fair tax with the federal income tax; 45 percent of respondents in 1972, 32 percent in 1978, 30 percent in 1982, and 24 percent in 1987 chose the property tax (ACIR, 1992a).

As property taxation is regulated by the states, there are at least 50 different systems in the United States. Local governments collect more than 95 percent of property tax revenue, the balance by the states. However, it constitutes a shrinking share of overall local revenue (68 percent in 1927, 50 percent in 1946, 36 percent in 1972, and 25 percent in 1987). The United States constitutional requirement for apportionment of any direct tax makes a federal property tax highly unlikely[4]; to achieve apportionment would require a high rate in poor states and a low rate in wealthier states.

Land taxation has enjoyed support for two independent reasons. At least since Henry George advocated it in 1879, appreciation in land values has been held fit for taxation because such gains are created socially, not by the efforts of their owners. In addition, economists have favored land taxes as perhaps the only practical major tax available that does not distort economic decisions. A land tax would not fall on improvements, and unlike the conventional real property tax, it would not deter any investment whose gross returns exceed costs. (Aaron, 1975: 87)

George articulated this distinction between taxing land and taxing improvements. Unlike improvements on the land, which are produced by labor, land "is a part of nature" and all have an equal right to its value (George, 1879: 337). Taxing land's value is

the most just and equal of all taxes. It falls only upon those who receive from society a peculiar and valuable benefit, and upon them in proportions to the benefit they receive. It is the taking by the community, for the use of the community, of that value which is the creation of the community. It is the application of the common property to common uses.

General property taxation emerged in the middle of the nineteenth century as an effort to reduce complicated sets of special taxes of colonial origin to one general levy and to apply that levy to all forms of privately owned wealth—tangible and intangible. The words "general" and "uniform," which were used in many constitutions and statutes, connoted fairness and equity. But this proved unworkable. Assessors were under pressure to keep assessments low and unchanged; some assets escaped taxation entirely. Most state provisions have been amended over time to reflect these realities; exemptions and property classifications are now common.

The property tax was suited to financing local government in a large, developing, diverse country populated by people with a very strong sense of independence and a distrust of centralized bureaucracy. Property was largely tangible, visible, and immobile. Small overlapping units of government could be financed with little addition to administrative cost. Viewed from a political systems perspective, there was a formal structure of universal, uniform, ad valorem property taxation that transferred difficult decisions from state legislators to local officials. The fragmented nature of the administrative responsibility and the subjective nature of property values made it possible for the tax to be adapted to local political pressures in a way that made the tax tolerable, but not popular (Fisher, 1981).

However, "No major fiscal institution, here or abroad, has been criticized at such length and with such vigor; yet no major fiscal institution has changed so little in modern times" (Netzer, 1966: 1). The tax's unpopularity was discussed in 1907 at the First Annual Conference of the National Tax Association (Fisher, 1981: 42).

The general property tax . . . is a survival of the system . . . adopted under more primitive economic conditions, when property was relatively homogenous . . . and constituted an approximately fair test of the ability to bear the public burden. The conditions which rendered it tolerable have however long since passed . . . it has become utterly inadequate to afford a just and reasonable system . . . during the past thirty years constantly increasing evidences of dissatisfaction and protest have appeared on every hand.

During the period that began in the 1920s and continued into the years of the Great Depression, the states developed other sources of revenue, primarily the general sales and income taxes. These changes relieved the pressure on the property tax, but local governments continued to rely on it (ibid.: 46).

But the property tax remained unpopular. In the early days of the Great Depression, Jens Peter Jensen wrote: "One searches in vain for one of its friends to defend it intelligently. It is even difficult to find anyone who has given it careful study who can subsequently speak of its failure in temperate language"(ibid: 42).

The 1970s witnessed growing concern in the states about the burden of the property tax, evidenced by the widespread enactment of tax relief programs, the state takeover of certain local government expenditure categories, provision of additional state aid to localities, and statutes enabling local governments to use sales, income, or other forms of taxation. But "relief means getting the same people to pay with less pain" (Meltsner, 1971: 6).

By the late 1970s all states had approved some measure of relief for homeowners. Targeted programs or "sniper fire tactics" (Citrin, 1984: 4) included (1) circuit-breakers; (2) homestead exemptions; (3) narrower definitions of taxable property—farmland preferences, industrial preferences, and personal property exemptions; and (4) differential treatment for residential and non-residential properties. General property tax relief also was provided by amending assessment practices, such as rollbacks and timing changes. "The concern for political tranquillity by banking the fires of homeowner discontent emerged as the major operating principle. In many states it superseded the older doctrines of local fiscal autonomy and property tax uniformity. Preferential treatment for home-

owners and curbs on tax and spending powers became the legacy of the inflationary 1970s'' (Shannon, 1981: 233).

The data presented in Table 3.2 suggest that high property tax burdens are
not a sufficient cause for passing radical fiscal limits. On a per capita basis the
1977 range was $53 in Alabama to over $400 in Massachusetts, New Jersey,
California, and New York. In addition, the property tax was not the only target.
In state legislative actions, 23 cut the individual income tax, twelve on more
than one occasion, for a total of 36 cuts; seventeen reduced the general sales
tax, five more than once for a total of 22; nine indexed the income tax (ibid.:
236).

Furthermore, targeting the property tax was not consistent with reducing those
expenditures that public opinion seemed to oppose. For example, police and fire
protection, which seemed to enjoy wide public support, were mainly or entirely
financed with property tax receipts. In contrast, the share of welfare and other
income support programs financed by property taxes was either small or non-
existent in most states. It is not clear whether people were expressing a distaste
for the property tax regardless of the kinds, qualities, or quantities of public
services supported by it or were expressing a preference for lower levels of
government expenditures (Brazer, 1981: 23).

It may be that states and local governments were easier targets to attack since
the federal government is so far removed from direct citizen access (Phares,
1981: 165). There is some evidence that local elections are used as psychological
punching bags by some voters; they are a means of protest not just against the
local political system but also against the citizen's general deprived condition
(Meltsner, 1971: 259).

Was there more than just a strong dislike for the property tax? The next
section examines some alternative explanations offered in the literature.

Other Generic Explanations

Other general explanations rely heavily on the economics paradigm and have
as their foundation the Public Choice School's models of government. The tax
revolt coincided with the development of a number of these theories, which
examine the generic relationship, in general terms, between the institutional sur-
roundings of a government and its spending patterns. Several theoretical models
were developed regarding excessive spending, which could be attributed to: (1)
exploitation (Brennan and Buchanan, 1979), (2) the expansionary motives of
bureaucrats or politicians (Niskanen, 1994), or (3) monopolistic labor market
bargaining (Tullock, 1974). Tax limitations were hypothesized to be the voters'
way to restrain these spending patterns.

The major intellectual conflict was between the median voter and the Leviathan view of public choice. In the former view, the mix of government goods
and services in any community is that demanded by the median voter. In the
latter view, that same mix of government goods and services is viewed as a

response to the wishes of the bureaucrats (William Oates, quoted in Shapiro, Puryear, and Ross, 1979: 1). But when government is responsive to the median voter, a substantial portion of the electorate may believe that levels of taxes and/or expenditures are too high (Brazer, 1981: 22).

Brennan and Buchanan (1979) argue that tax limitation amendments by voters are a means through which the individual citizen can avoid

exposing himself to gross exploitation by government—exploitation in the form of disastrously excessive tax burdens. It is a constitutional affair which did not emerge out of normal political processes and is designed to prevent government from taking actions which citizens believe they would have taken. These constraints either supplement or operate in lieu of normal electoral processes.

Niskanen (1994) provides a second line of reasoning. There is an agency problem in the relationships among voters, politicians, and bureaucrats. He assumes that bureaucrats act to maximize their discretionary budget, defined as the difference between the total budget and the minimum cost of producing the output expected by the political authorities. Bureaus are inefficient suppliers of government services as measured by the interests of the general population; most of the problems often attributed to bureaus are more fundamentally caused by the structure and decision rules of the legislature. There is an inherent difficulty in attributing the shares of total waste in government services to the separate effects of politics and the bureaucracy.

People were not seeking tax cuts, but were expressing a frustration about government waste (Gold, 1990: 35). They were dissatisfied with government and its bewildering nexus of regulations, an increasing tax burden, inflation that erodes their standard of living, and a crazy quilt federal system that seems to defy comprehension (Phares, 1981: 165). The voters concluded that the legislative branch of government was no match for all the special interests and that they could impose their will only by slashing government revenues or fixing iron lids on spending (Davenport, 1979: 135).

Tullock (1974) offers a third hypothesis, arguing that public employee wages exceed competitive levels. The structure of most modern bureaucracies is such that large improvements in the returns to individuals are difficult to achieve without a considerable increase in the total number of individuals employed. As the number increased, however, it would become possible to use more of their power to directly increase wages. Expansion becomes an investment.

Brennan and Buchanan, Niskanen, and Tullock provide no empirical evidence to support their hypotheses. Niskanen "confesses" that he does not know how to pose a testable hypothesis about the shares of the total waste. Tullock admits that his hypothesis is hard to test, but that neither proves nor disproves it. But, "there is hardly evidence of a growing governmental Leviathan" (Shapiro, Puryear, and Ross, 1979: 1).

Boskin (1979) provides a fourth general explanation. The cause was more fundamental than an unpopular tax or spending category such as welfare. It was more than just something "in the air." Fundamental economic and demographic features in large measure explained the growing discontent. The total tax burden and the aggregate amount of spending at all levels of government were the concerns. Most important, it was caused primarily by a complete lack of growth in real private income, which was either eaten by inflation or went into government spending. The changing age structure of the population and the shift from unemployment to inflation and higher taxes as the major economic problem suggested a changing perception of government from private economic ally to private economic antagonist.

A fifth group of explanations is the rational decision making models—the utility maximizing aspects of voter behavior (Sears, Lau, Tyler, and Allen, 1980: 670). Self-interest is defined as gains from tax reduction or public employment. However, polling data that show that people supported limits even if they believed others would benefit most raise doubts about this explanation (Lowery and Sigelman, 1981: 970).

"Symbolic politics" contrasts with self-interest (Sears, Lau, Tyler, and Allen, 1980: 671). People acquire stable preferences through conditioning in their pre-adult years, with little calculation of the future costs and benefits of these attitudes. Policy preferences may reflect an earlier political socialization that was not considering present self-interest.

Tax limitation may have been a "style issue" as opposed to a "position issue" (Lowery and Sigelman, 1981: 972) and therefore cannot be explained by any of these models. They cite polls showing that "most Americans have been unhappy about taxes for a long time." The displeasure had to be activated and channeled toward a goal. Howard Jarvis's antipathy toward discussing details and his emphasis on such symbols as "lazy bureaucrats" and "lying politicians" should be viewed as key elements in the origin and diffusion of the tax revolt. When coupled with the prevailing public frustration over a number of tax related issues, the effort of a charismatic leader spearheading a massive effort provided a sufficient condition for the revolt. "States that had hitherto not been known for discontent over taxation suddenly became caught up in the contagion of Howard Jarvis's revolt" (Rabushka and Ryan, 1982: 189).

"Micro" Explanations

"The political and tax contours of individual states make all the difference in the world. So it's a misnomer to say a tax revolt is sweeping the nation."[5]

Like bands of a guerilla army, state and local units of tax rebels sprang up independently and operated with relatively little coordination. Indeed, the tax revolt never developed a central command structure. It was led by political outsiders and recruited mainly from groups on the fringe of the dominant institutions in American society. They were arrayed against a coalition of establishment forces comprising most elected officials, public employees, the trade unions, and the large corporations (Citrin, 1984: 3).

Measures enacted in 1978 represented one more step in a series of fiscal control attempts initiated earlier, whereas others were first time events, directly stimulated by Proposition 13 (Eribes and Hall, 1981: 111). The consideration of Proposition 13–like measures was more a reflection of an attempt to replicate California's "success" with voter induced tax reduction than a response to similar fiscal pressures (Oakland, 1979: 388).

Some of the conditions found in California in 1978 existed in many states (Brazer, 1981: 26). Others were more or less peculiar to California. Inflation was everywhere, but skyrocketing housing values and a large state surplus were known only in California. Only in Massachusetts and New Jersey did the property tax exceed California's per capita level.

Regarding Proposition 13, whether it attracted voters as a means of attacking Big Government and taxes in general or as a way of protesting the heavy overload of the property tax was simply not clear. Nor is it clear whether one should pursue a "tax limitation hypothesis" or a "tax shift hypothesis" (Break, 1979: 43).

The purpose of this research is not to ascertain the precise causes for the fiscal discontent, but it is important to have confidence that it was not the wages or actions of local government employees that explicitly led to this use of the taxpayers' voice. To enhance the confidence of the causal relationship that underlies the hypothesis of this research, fiscal discontent in three states—California, Massachusetts, and Michigan—is examined in further detail.

These case studies illustrate that the events that led voters to impose these limitations had built up over a period of years. This timing is an important consideration as one examines the use of collective voice by the employees, as presented in subsequent chapters. Snapshots at particular points in time should not be analyzed in a simple "before and after" manner.

CALIFORNIA

On June 6, 1978, 65 percent of those who voted in the California primary election approved Proposition 13, a 389-word initiative petitioned to the ballot in a campaign led by Howard Jarvis and Paul Gann. They gathered 1.25 million signatures by the deadline, well above the 500,000 required; 300,000 signatures were added shortly thereafter. About 43 percent of the eligible voters turned out, the highest rate in a statewide primary in 20 years.

Seventeen months later, in November 1979, 76 percent of the voters in the general election approved a constitutional amendment to limit expenditures by the state and all local governments. Proposition 4, called the "Spirit of 13," limits expenditure increases to the growth in population and inflation or to the growth of personal income, whichever is lower.

Seven months after that, in June 1980, 60 percent of the voters defeated

Proposition 9, a constitutional amendment to cut income tax rates in half. Voter turnout was the lowest since 1960. Lipset and Schneider (in Pfiffner, 1983: 52) argued that this defeat did not signal the end of the tax revolt so much as prompt the voters' realization that further cuts in tax revenues would directly lead to reductions in services or to other taxes being raised. According to public opinion polls, many who had voted for "13" but against "9" believed they had been correct in voting for "13."

And it was not the end! In June 1982, by a 2-to-1 margin, voters passed initiatives to fully index the state's personal income tax (overriding the governor's veto of similar legislation) and to repeal the inheritance tax.

Proposition 13

Proposition 13 did the following: (1) limited the maximum real property tax rate to 1 percent of full cash value (in 1977, on a typical California home it had averaged about 2.6 percent); the only exception was to repay bonded indebtedness approved by the voters before July 1978; (2) rolled assessments back to their 1975–1976 levels; (3) limited increases in assessed valuations to the rate of inflation, but not more than 2 percent per year. If property ownership transferred or if there were new construction, the assessment would change to market value (a "Welcome, Stranger" provision); (4) prohibited any new tax levies on real property and required any new local government tax levy be approved by two-thirds of the qualified electorate; and (5) required two-thirds approval in each house of the legislature to increase state taxes, but prohibited any new taxes on real property.

The immediate financial effect was to reduce, about three weeks before the start of the fiscal year, local government property tax revenue by approximately $7 billion of the $12 billion projected, equivalent to 22 percent of budgeted expenditures.

The breakdown of property tax saving was estimated as follows: 33 percent for homeowner-occupants; 27 percent for commercial and industrial properties; 17 percent for owners of rental property; 13 percent for agricultural land and uses; and 9 percent for the state in the form of reduced deductions (May 1978 California Legislative Analyst, in Congressional Budget Office, 1979: 110). Utilities and transportation companies were large beneficiaries; Southern Pacific, the state's largest landowner, realized a property tax reduction from $35 million to $19 million (Quirt, 1979). The federal government received $2.7 billion in increased revenue for the reduced deductions on the income tax (Heller, 1979).

On June 6, an alternative measure, Proposition 8, which would have provided property tax relief solely to homeowners, was defeated (47–53 percent). Schneider (1979: 114) argues that the voters understood the limitations of Proposition 13 but viewed it as a stronger measure. Proposition 8 probably would have provided more relief for the homeowner, but it was more complicated, "supporting the maxim that simpler is more passable."

Proposition 13 was not a spontaneous phenomenon, but the latest inning in a biennial event, a restitching of numerous earlier initiatives (Levy, 1979: 74). Between 1968 and 1976, there had been numerous attempts to reduce taxes or expenditures by initiative. Many never qualified for the ballot. Those that did in 1968, 1972, and 1973 were rejected by the voters.

A 1968 ballot question to limit the property tax to 1 percent of value, sponsored by Los Angeles County Assessor Philip Watson, was defeated 2 to 1. A modified version of the Watson question failed 2 to 1 in 1972. In 1973, Proposition 1, the so-called Reagan initiative, was defeated 46–54 percent and lost in 47 of the 58 counties. It included a property tax limitation, a state income tax reduction, and a ceiling on expenditures pegged to personal income.

Clearly there was a change in the views held by California voters between 1973 and 1978. By May 1978, a California Poll found that 94 percent of the voting public was aware of Proposition 13. The reasons most often cited for its success seem to fall into three broad categories—assessment reform, inflation, and public cynicism.

Assessment Reform

State legislation enacted in 1967 required assessors to use and maintain 25 percent of market value. This was reform legislation responding to newspaper stories regarding elected assessors receiving campaign contributions to "review and adjust" business assessments. Its immediate impact was to increase home-owner assessments, thereby shifting the tax burden to that sector. Paradoxically perhaps, it was the state's efforts to improve the administration of the property tax through continual reassessment that ultimately led to an amendment severely restricting its use.

Inflation

Dworak (1980: 71) cites inflation as the number one factor. "Inflation injects high octane fuel into the fires of local property tax discontent" (Shannon, 1981: 223). The 1970s were boom years in the real estate markets, and the assessors did a good job of accurately reflecting market values. Values in the single family residential market rose at a faster rate than those on commercial and industrial property, and these residential increases were rising faster than the incomes of homeowners. Those with limited liquidity faced the prospect of having to sell their homes.

Between 1977 and 1978 the average value of owner-occupied single family homes increased 20 percent, while the value of all other property increased 10.5 percent (California Office of Legislative Analyst estimate, in Levy, 1979). In some counties the increases averaged 40 percent. Since local jurisdictions had to tax all properties at the same rate and since the overall assessable base changed very little, tax rates could not be reduced if revenues were to be maintained, resulting in tax bill increases that paralleled the skyrocketing assessment growth. The average combined tax rate declined about 1.2 percent per year, not nearly enough to offset the average 20 percent assessment increases faced by homeowners (California Office of Legislative Analyst estimate, ibid.).

The combined effect of the assessment reforms and the inflation was that over the decade that ended in 1978 the share of property tax revenue from residential properties increased from 33 to 43 percent.

Inflation also contributed to producing a large $6.8 billion state surplus, which would have reached $10 billion if Proposition 13 had not passed. Much of the surplus resulted from an economy that was recovering from recession and from the inflationary increases in nominal incomes, which led to higher revenues because of the bracket-creep associated with the state's steeply progressive personal income tax.

Further increasing the state's surplus was the structure of its foundation grant program for elementary and secondary education. The formula presupposed static economic conditions. When local real estate assessments were rising everywhere, every district appeared richer and so all districts lost state aid. Thus increases in a school district tax base were offset by declines in state aid, thereby increasing the local share and leaving the district unable to reduce tax rates (Levy, 1979: 77).

Public Cynicism

The voters perceived that the legislature was not taking their demands for property tax relief seriously. This despite the fact that over the previous decade, the legislature had enacted nineteen property tax relief measures, including exemptions for homeowners, disabled veterans, and businesses. But two years of debate in the legislature prior to Proposition 13 failed to produce a program for further relief. Jarvis and Gann began circulating their petition only after legislative efforts to pass property tax relief collapsed in 1977 in "an atmosphere of acrimony and disarray." There were disagreements over the amount and targeting of the relief; with statewide elections approaching, apportioning political credit for a tax cut became a bitterly contested issue (Citrin and Levy, 1981: 7). Only after Proposition 13 qualified for the ballot did the legislature propose a competing measure (O'Sullivan, Sexton, and Sheffrin, 1995: 1).

"Proposition 13 was a classic example of an initiative surmounting a paralyzed state legislative process" (Kirlin, 1979: 85). It was "a political shock wave of an overwhelming rejection of the policy direction of the legislature and the governor" (ibid.: 70). As the campaign came increasingly to be portrayed as a struggle of the people against the politicians, voting for Proposition 13 provided a vehicle for expressing frustration with government for reasons unrelated to the property tax (Citrin and Levy, 1981: 6). Jarvis and Gann "railed against dishonest politicians, bloated budgets, bureaucratic waste, and big government" (Pfiffner, 1983: 49). "If the proponents went beyond the bounds of reason in their campaign rhetoric, the opponents went just as far in the other direction" (Dworak, 1980: 73). Public employee organizations waged a massive campaign in opposition; they were joined by local government officials, the academic community, and an assortment of special interest groups dedicated to protecting local services.

While there was deep cynicism about government operations, the survey evidence suggests that voters did not want large scale service cutbacks. They sought to eliminate waste and inefficiency. A June 1978 California Poll found 89 percent believed the federal government was inefficient; 69 percent, 70 percent, and 62 percent saw state, county, and city inefficiency, respectively. On the eve of the vote, 38 percent of the California electorate felt that the state and local governments could provide the same services with a 40 percent reduction in budgets (Citrin, 1979: 115). Schneider (1979: 114) cites an election day poll that revealed two reasons for favoring Proposition 13—high property taxes and waste in government; only 22 percent believed the government provided unnecessary services. Seventy-four percent of those who voted yes thought there would be no significant reductions in local services.

The Immediate Impact of Proposition 13

After Proposition 13 passed, the voices resonated throughout the state.

The pressure on state legislators . . . was fierce. Schools, cities, counties, and special districts were vying for a larger share of the limited resources. Program advocates were seeking protection by legislation, while local governments pleaded for maximum flexibility. Local employee groups in each district made sure each member heard from home. Leaders of the revolt made known they would not accept tax increases, they wanted essential services maintained, and the fat cut. (Kirlin, 1979: 70)

On June 23, 1978, the legislature passed, and on June 25 the governor signed, SB154, the Bailout I plan, which allocated $4.2 billion of the state surplus in fiscal year 1979 to replace a large share of the $7 billion in revenue lost by local governments. The net resulting shortfall represented about 10 percent of total revenues from all sources (Levy, 1979: 85). A longer term plan, Bailout II, was enacted in July and provided $4.9 billion and $5.5 billion for fiscal years 1980 and 1981 respectively. Four major issues were covered in these actions—the sharing of local revenues, K–12 education funding, expenditure reductions, and personnel issues.

First, a system of tax-base revenue sharing was created at the county level to live within the 1 percent limit. This effectively removed from local governments the power to set property tax rates. Revenues were divided among the governments within each county, including the independent tax authorities, on the same percentage basis that existed prior to Proposition 13's passage.

Second, the state provided $2.1 billion in fiscal year 1979 for K–12 education funding to guarantee 90 percent of the fiscal year 1978 amount. The state share of K–12 funding increased from 38 to 71 percent in that one year.

Low spending school districts were required to achieve a 9 percent budget reduction, while a 15 percent reduction was required of the high spending districts. This was designed to comply with court decisions regarding the financing of public education, most notably the 1971 California Supreme Court ruling in *Serrano v. Priest* that the system of school finance made "the quality of a child's education a function of the wealth of his parents and neighbors" and thus violated the equal protection clause of the Fourteenth Amendment of the U.S. Constitution.

The price for additional state financial assistance was a loss of local autonomy, which had consequences for home rule, as did the revenue sharing within the counties. The centralization of power at the state level was an unanticipated and, to many, an unwelcome consequence of Proposition 13.

Third, the cities and counties could not reduce levels of police and fire protection. Citrin (1979) cites surveys showing that people "favored more rather than less spending on police, fire departments, mental health programs, and education while demanding cuts in spending on welfare, public housing, and the government's own administrative services." Elected officials listened to public opinion and to the organized power of the police and firefighter unions (Citrin, 1984: 29).

Service reductions generally were in programs that lacked support from well-organized and well-financed special interest groups, such as libraries, parks, and recreation. They had no collective voice! The areas that taxpayers were unhappy with were untouched compared to the cuts suffered by these discretionary activities (Dworak, 1980: 96). The California Poll consistently found that the budget reductions occurred in the "wrong" places, with the most common complaints being that schools were cut too much and "bureaucracy" too little (Citrin, 1984).

Most of the local personnel cutbacks resulted from the elimination of unfilled positions and voluntary resignations. Those with alternative employment opportunities left, leaving behind workers who were less productive (May and Meltsner, 1981: 176).

The principal vehicle for personnel reductions was to eliminate CETA positions (Levy, Shimasaki, and Berk, 1982: 282). Reductions in the cities were concentrated in libraries, parks, recreation, and general government, which had many CETA positions. County reductions were spread more evenly, "but neither the cities nor the counties showed evidence of dismantling the personnel changes which had occurred over the prior 15 years" (ibid.). "Avoiding layoffs of regular staff was a paramount objective in most jurisdictions and departments. . . . Lower wage settlements also contributed, as employees frequently chose, however reluctantly, to trade off pay for jobs" (Citrin, 1984: 41). Most employees "could be sanguine about keeping their jobs even as the rate of unemployment in California soared" (Citrin and Green, 1985: 17).

Fourth, salary and wage increases for local government employees could not exceed the increases for state employees. After the passage of Proposition 13, the governor had frozen the salaries of state workers and imposed a hiring freeze. This was "political dynamite causing no end of trouble with the powerful employee associations'' (Dworak, 1980). Local government employees were shocked when the 1979 legislative session prohibited any cost-of-living salary increases for them (Kirlin, 1979: 67).

Two additional impacts are noteworthy. User fees were increased for a broad array of services. Second, sweeping changes took place in property assessment practices. The ad valorem system was replaced with an acquisition-value system. Two properties of identical market value could have sharply different assessed values if one were sold after March 1975. While this may not seem equitable to many, it has survived a constitutional challenge (U.S. Supreme Court: 1992 decision in *Nordlinger v. Hahn*).

Over the longer term, Reid (1988) found that the effects of the constraints varied tremendously across the various types of local government in large part because of the differences in taxing and spending authority vested in local governments. Counties and school districts having limited local options became more dependent on state funding; cities were better able to reduce their dependence on outside sources.

Why Did It Happen?

> Proposition 13 emerges as a unique California phenomenon. The combination of factors which gave it birth are unlikely to be matched in any other state. The same can be said of its consequences. The surplus mitigated its potentially disruptive impacts. (Oakland, 1979: 405)

Proposition 13 was a battle with homeowners incensed over soaring tax bills (Quirt, 1979: 105; Rabushka and Ryan, 1982: 206). It was not a vote to fire all the bureaucrats, sharply cut services, or totally abolish welfare and other programs for the needy (Rabushka and Ryan, 1982: 206). Citrin and Levy (1981: 6) cite survey data that point to the tax burden as well. In a 1963 Harris Poll, 49 percent thought taxes were too high. In a 1976 poll, 72 percent thought so. In a June 1977 California Poll, 60 percent of the sample answered an open-ended query about which taxes they paid were too high by naming the property tax. No other tax received more than a 20 percent response.

"The average taxpayer saw Proposition 13 returning $870 straight off" (Reid, 1979: 75). It was self-interest (Schneider, 1979: 114). Households that owned a home and included no public employees voted 81 percent for Proposition 13 and 80 percent against Proposition 8. Households that included public employees and lived in rental units voted 80 percent for Proposition 8; 28 percent voted for Proposition 13. Proposition 13 failed to carry in only three of 58 counties: San Francisco had many renters; Yolo had many state employees; and Kern, a wealthy agricultural community, had not experienced large property tax increases. Voters in the high self-interest category (homeowners with no public employees) gave Proposition 13 a majority of their votes, whether they were liberal, moderate, or conservative (ibid.: 115).

Proposition 13 does not seem at odds with the median voter model. The vote reflected a preference for some form of financing local public services other than the residential property tax (Shapiro, Puryear, and Ross, 1979: 5).

Dworak (1980: 80) argues that the voters wanted more than a property tax reduction. "It was a message sent by the people to their elected officials . . . more direct and powerful than any that could have been transmitted through the normal procedure of election and reelection of public officials . . . concern over government performance was the major message of the 13 vote . . . unhappy with the fiscal operations of the state." It was "as much a frustrated electorate's reaction to bad government as a reasoned response to a bad tax. . . . It is not the property tax, but the local political process which is the culprit" (Inman, 1979: 159).

By March 1983, only 15 percent of the public in California complained that property taxes were too high, compared to 60 percent in late 1977; 75 percent of homeowners credited Proposition 13. One month before the Proposition 13 vote, 49 percent of Californians believed that budgets could be reduced 20 percent with no service impact; by August 1982, 22 percent felt there was that much "fat" (California Poll cited in Citrin and Green, 1985: 18).

The results of the Proposition 13 vote are a good example of a political feedback loop (ibid.: 15). A dissatisfaction with high property taxes stimulated protest that led to a change, which in turn assuaged discontent by more closely aligning opinion and policy.

MASSACHUSETTS

In the November 4, 1980, general election, 59 percent of those who voted in Massachusetts approved Proposition 2½, an Initiative Law limiting the real estate tax levies of cities and towns to 2.5 percent of the fair market valuation or the 1979 rate, whichever was less. Local governments were required to reduce their levies by 15 percent per year until that limit was reached. Annual growth was limited to 2.5 percent. It also reduced the motor vehicle excise tax rate from $66 to $25 per thousand of valuation (for a local revenue loss of $150 million). Further, it prohibited unfunded state mandates, abolished the autonomy of local school committees, eliminated compulsory and binding arbitration with public employees, and allowed renters to deduct one-half of their rent payments from state taxable income.

Just two years after the 1978 rush of voter approvals, it was the only measure that succeeded at the polls; others tried, but were defeated.

The state legislature considered, but did not approve, any alternative to Proposition 2½. Polling data showed that voters would have preferred a more moderate alternative, but none was available. The vote was "2½ versus the status quo." An alternative measure was placed on the ballot by the Massachusetts Teachers' Association, but they did not actively campaign for it; they focused on opposing 2½ (Ladd and Wilson, 1982: 122). There was a vigorous campaign with thorough media coverage, and the voters seemed well-informed about the issues (ibid.).

As in California, Proposition 2½ was not an overnight phenomenon. It had been proposed initially in 1936, but it did not qualify for the ballot (O'Sullivan, Sexton, and Sheffrin, 1995: 4). For the next 40 years there were failed efforts to reform the state's tax structure and provide property tax relief (Citrin, 1984: 45). The final push began after Proposition 13 passed in California.

In November 1978, the voters approved by a 2–1 margin a constitutional amendment calling for the differential taxation of property by class. A similar provision had been rejected 2 to 1 just eight years earlier. Two intervening events seem to have changed the voters.

First, the state supreme court's 1974 Sudbury decision reaffirmed the same ad valorem rate for all properties within each city and town. That decision established a mechanism that shifted the property tax burden from commercial and industrial to residential property (Avault, Ganz, and Holland, 1979: 289). This was an outcome very similar to the California experience, albeit in California tax administration had been highly rated while in Massachusetts it was described as poor. Prior to the court's decision, local officials had been able to assuage protest through a system of abatements and selective assessment procedures that protected residential property owners. The "informal" political system of residential tax relief broke down with the court's ruling (Citrin, 1984: 45).

A second intervening event also occurred in the November 1978 election. Voters passed an advisory resolution petitioning for a property tax reduction and an increase in state aid to localities. The governor and legislature responded by adopting a "loose tax cap" that, for the next two fiscal years, limited increases in the property tax levy to 4 percent of the previous year's amount. The limit excluded school budgets and was often overriden by votes of town meetings and city councils (ibid.). In the last days of the 1978 session, the legislature narrowly defeated a proposal that would have limited taxation to 2.5 percent of property value (Avault, Ganz, and Holland, 1979: 301).

Proposition 2½ reduced overall local tax revenues $486 million (about 14 percent) between fiscal years 1981 and 1982; property taxes declined by more than one-third in many parts of the state. In the first year, 182 of 351 cities and towns were required to reduce property tax levies (Bradbury and Ladd, January 1982: 15); 101 had a revenue loss in excess of 10 percent (Bradbury and Ladd, March 1982: 52). About 40 percent of the larger cities and towns had to reduce levels 15 percent in the second year as well (ibid.: 55).

Residential property taxes would have been reduced an estimated 15 percent in one year if Proposition 2½ had been implemented as written (Citrin, 1984: 46). As originally drafted, there were no exceptions for inflation, population growth, or new construction; the legislation that implemented the measure relaxed these limitations. The levy limit could also be overriden only by a vote of the relevant electorate; however, because of the election cycle, that was not a viable option in the first year (Bradbury and Ladd, 1982: 15). As of September 1983, 74 of 100 attempts to override had been defeated (Citrin, 1984: 51).

Drastic cuts in local services were avoided because several sources replaced the lost revenue—the reevaluation of existing property, which had been ordered by the courts; new construction; increased user fees; and increased state aid. State assistance to localities increased $265 million in fiscal year 1982 and $550 million in fiscal year 1984 (ibid.: 47). State spending was reduced to offset these increases; although the state did not have a large surplus as had existed in California, Proposition 2½ did not restrict the state from raising revenue.

The increased aid to local governments resulted from pressure by local officials and required more than six months of debate. A middle ground emerged between the governor's $37 million proposal, which argued that the state was not responsible and that the problem was for local governments to solve, and a $360 million "share the pain" bill, which distributed funds in proportion to lost local revenue (Bradbury and Ladd, 1982: 20). The final state aid distributions were based on a formula that did not cushion the loss equally.

Local employment was reduced about 12 percent (about 30,400). State employment fell 6.2 percent (about 6,200). About half of the local workers who lost their jobs were laid off; many, as in California, were CETA workers (Citrin, 1984: 47).

Budget reductions were much the same as those made by local governments in California. In deference to public opinion, police and fire departments were cut substantially less, despite evidence they were staffed at higher levels than their counterparts in other states. Departments with smaller and less vocal constituencies, such as recreation and libraries, endured the deepest cuts in percentage terms. Partly because of the forced withdrawal of municipalities from the bond market, there were enormous cuts in capital projects. Schools (47 percent of local expenditures) and health departments were targets. Advocates for public schools complained that education had been unfairly treated (ibid.: 48).

The changed process of local budgeting considerably enhanced the power of central executives. Local school committees were abolished except in Boston (Bradbury and Ladd, 1982: 15). The loss of autonomy for school communities and the end of compulsory arbitration increased the ability of central executives to control personnel costs.

In several surveys conducted prior to the vote, respondents indicated they were satisfied with local officials and services. Many expressed apprehension about service cutbacks (Susskind, 1983: 4). Voters believed its passage would eliminate waste and inefficiency and not affect service levels (O'Sullivan, Sexton, and Sheffrin, 1995: 1).

Proposition 2½ was caused not by dramatic increases in assessments, but by persistent reliance on the property tax. By 1980, the property tax was 70 percent above the national average and provided virtually all of the revenue for cities and towns. Massachusetts ranked forty-second in the nation in the balanced use of taxes. The voters were frustrated with high taxes and a legislature that did not enact tax relief or reform. The vote was a "chance to gain control" of the budget (Susskind, 1983: 5).

Survey results indicate that the vote was much more an attempt to obtain lower taxes and more efficient government than to reduce service levels (Ladd and Wilson, 1982). Over 80 percent believed state and local spending could be reduced 5 percent or more with no change in quality or quantity; 60 percent believed local spending could be cut 15 percent with no effect (ibid.: 128). A majority wanted to maintain or increase service levels; welfare was the only service a majority wanted to see reduced.

Another survey found that Proposition 2½ was supported by 63 percent of homeowners and 46 percent of renters. Seventy percent of households that included local public employees voted "No"; 50 percent of those with a state employee did so. Gender, race, religion, occupation, education, and political orientation also mattered; women, non-whites, and Jews were more likely to have opposed the measure (Ladd and Wilson, 1983: 256).

MICHIGAN

In November 1978, 52 percent of Michigan voters approved the so-called Headlee Amendment to the state constitution, which limited the state's revenue to a share of its personal income, limited increases in the assessed valuation of existing properties to inflation growth, and prohibited the state from placing mandates on local governments (as in Massachusetts).

Two other amendments were defeated in that same election. One targeted local governments and would have required a large reduction in the assessed valuation of property; it also would have limited the state income tax rate. A second amendment would have established a voucher system for financing local K–12 education. These failed with 36 percent and 25 percent of the vote respectively. Two years later, in 1980, 56 percent of the voters defeated a proposal to reduce the maximum assessment to market value ratio from 50 to 25 percent.

In their study of the Michigan vote, Courant, Gramlich, and Rubinfeld (1980) surveyed voters. Their "most striking empirical result" was that voters were satisfied with current levels of state and local services. "With the exception of spending on welfare programs, there is a decided sentiment for expansion (and a stated willingness to pay for expansion) in all the program areas for which responses were elicited" (ibid.: 3). To the extent there was a taxpayer revolt, it seemed to be a revolt against welfare spending.

The strongest support for the Headlee Amendment came from those who felt it would increase government efficiency or voter control of government. "It appears that voters are perceiving that their own taxes will be cut without expenditures being cut, either because of supposed efficiency gains, greater uncertainty about the spending side of the budget, or an unending search for a free lunch" (ibid.: 19).

Very few voters felt the amendment would have as its most important impact the limitation of future government wage increases. "There does not appear to be a strong desire to punish public employees. . . . [It] does not appear to be seen as an attempt to alter the income distribution between public and private employees" (ibid.).

Among private sector voters there appears to be little resentment directed against the high wages of government employees, and little occasion to vote for tax limitation on that account. Whether this result would obtain in other states is uncertain: perhaps the union solidarity is very strong in Michigan. . . . The public employment findings also demonstrate the non-punitive feelings of private sector voters. Among those who felt the amendment would reduce government employment, voters were neutral to or against the amendment even if they felt public employees worked less hard than private employees. (ibid.: 14)

CONCLUSION

Why did the citizens in some states raise their voices during this period? Why weren't voices raised in others? Neither the literature nor the fiscal data provide a clear answer to that question. It is not likely there is one. Overall, a majority of voters in the case studies examined wanted to rein in government taxing and "wasteful spending." However, placing a complex matter on a ballot for a simple Yes-No vote makes it difficult to ascertain all of the ingredients that went into the "legislative sausage" in each of 33 states. The complexity and nuance get lost.

One plausible hypothesis is that a confluence of factors merged in varying combinations, from state to state. If this were a multiple-choice question, the answer might well be "all of the above"—the nation's political culture and the anti-government protests of those times, the economic and political conditions, perceived government waste and inefficiency, excessive spending, high levels of welfare spending, high or rising taxes, burdensome residential property taxes, self-interest, large budget surpluses, and good marketing by charismatic sponsors or opponents.

The research does suggest that voters were generally satisfied with the overall level of government services. More important for this research, there is virtually no evidence to attribute the voters' discontent explicitly to the compensation levels of local government employees. Indeed, the survey results in Michigan found that this was not a reason for supporting the limitation. So did Straussman and Rodgers (1979: 438), who concluded that unions "do not contribute to an explanation of differences in the fiscal condition of states as measured by the change in tax effort from 1960 to 1971."

Might employee issues be subsumed in some of the other often cited reasons? Possibly! But no direct link has been established in any of the studies reviewed for this research. And, as presented in Chapter 6, the collective bargaining rights of local government employees have been constrained in sixteen of the 33 states that experienced fiscal discontent. Thus, the relationship underlying the hypothesis for this research is supportable.

The case studies also support an assumption in this research that the decisions to limit the discretion of elected officials were not overnight phenomena, but rather were actions that had been building over a number of years. While June 6, 1978, and November 4, 1980, were the action days for Proposition 13 and Proposition 2½ respectively, the case studies suggest that their lives began well before those dates—as much as a decade earlier in California, when the 1968 Watson question first appeared on the ballot, and six years earlier in Massachusetts, with the 1974 Sudbury decision. Since there was no "big bang," using a research design that examines a situation only "before and after" election day could produce misleading conclusions. This matter of timing is examined further in the case study presented in Chapter 7.

But what is the relationship of the use of collective voice by the taxpayers to its use by local government employees? The next chapter begins to examine that question.

NOTES

1. In 1987, tax revenues as a percent of Gross Domestic Product for selected OECD countries were as follows: Sweden 56.0 percent; Denmark 51.8 percent; Netherlands 48.4 percent; Norway 47.8 percent; Belgium 46.1 percent; France 44.8 percent; Austria 42.4 percent; Germany 37.7 percent; United Kingdom 37.2 percent; Italy 36.2 percent; Canada 34.9 percent; Spain 32.5 percent; Portugal 31.5 percent; Australia 31.1 percent; Japan 30.1 percent; United States 30.1 percent (Advisory Commission on Intergovernmental Relations, 1992c: Volume 2, Table 2).

2. Many of these earlier controls remain "on the books" in 25 states: Alabama (1875 and 1916), Missouri (1875), Texas (1876 and 1883), Arkansas (1883), Wyoming (1890 and 1911), New York (1894), Utah (1898 and 1929), Nebraska (1903 and 1921), Kentucky (1908), Colorado and Idaho (1913), Arizona (1913 and 1921), New Mexico (1914), South Dakota (1915), Oregon (1916), Ohio and North Dakota (1929), Nevada (1929 and 1936), Oklahoma and Michigan (1933), Illinois and West Virginia (1939), Pennsylvania (1940), Washington (1944), and Georgia (1945) (ACIR and Indiana Center for Urban Policy and the Environment, 1995).

3. Since only 23 states provide for citizen initiatives in their constitutions, this opportunity was not available everywhere.

4. Article I, Sec. 9[4].

5. Dean C. Tipps, Executive Director of Citizens for Tax Justice (in Stanfield, 1983: 2568).

4

The Voice of the Employees

Public sector employees in the United States have joined together to create a collective voice with greater frequency than have their private sector counterparts. Within the public sector, full-time local government employees have the highest propensity to organize—in 1987, at 47.5 percent, compared to 13.4 percent in the private sector. This low level of private sector unionization is very much in keeping with American exceptionalism and with the attitudes expressed by the American public regarding unions and their leaders. The local government levels are not consistent with these values, and in some instances resemble more closely those in other countries of the Atlantic Community.

This chapter examines various aspects of the use of collective voice by local government employees as it evolved over the years. The early years of the 1960s and 1970s are examined, when state enabling legislation was enacted, when the courts were ruling on the right of employees to organize, and when the employees aligned their voices with those of the civil rights and other protest movements. In the decade of the 1980s new issues emerged, notably pay equity and privatization, and their roles in motivating local government employees to use collective voice also are examined.

Finally, this chapter presents previous research that explores specific reasons that local government employees organize. Many studies focus on the economic, as opposed to the political, marketplace, and many analyze the various economic benefits gained by using collective voice—the effects on wages, employee benefits, and/or employment levels.

PUBLIC ATTITUDES TOWARD UNIONS

The trend in private sector union membership in America, outlined in Chapter 1, seems to have followed the change in public attitudes toward unions and their leaders. When private sector density was at its 1953 peak, the favorability rating for labor unions was high; a Gallup Poll showed 75 percent approving of them. From 1967 to 1980 both declined appreciably (Lipset and Schneider, 1987: 353). The average percentage expressing "a great deal of confidence" in the leaders of ten institutions between 1966 and 1981 ranked organized labor last, with 15.3 percent of those polled. Congress ranked ninth, with 18.8 percent; medicine was first, with 50.5 percent; and the Supreme Court was in the middle, at 31.8 percent (ibid.: 68).

In most polls, unions were found to be the least trusted major institution in American life, despite having the largest mass membership of any American organization. Americans show an ambivalence toward unions similar to their contradictory feelings about a number of other institutions, that is, approval of their function accompanied by condemnation of their behavior (ibid.: 199). For example, in a December 1976 Harris poll a majority of the public agreed with every pro-union and every anti-union statement. Unions protect employee interests and are socially progressive, but they also are seen as self-interested and too powerful (ibid.: 218).

In a 1984 Harris Poll conducted for the AFL-CIO, nearly half of all non-union workers indicated they would join an association, but most of those surveyed said they would not vote for a union to serve as a bargaining agent (Ichniowski and Zax, 1990: 191).

Stephen Hills (1985), using surveys from 1977 and 1980, found major differences in attitudes between two groups of men aged 28 to 38: 87 percent of those covered by a union contract would vote for union representation; 27 percent of non-union workers would do so. Among workers in government, pro-union attitudes were more widespread than in other industries and were consistent with the membership trends: 54 percent of non-organized government employees supported representation, and 92 percent of organized workers in government supported representation.

The proportion of blacks favoring unionism was nineteen percentage points higher than that of whites (Hills, 1985). Blacks also showed more confidence than whites in the people running organized labor (Lipset and Schneider, 1987: 122). Democrats showed consistently greater sympathy for labor. However, the beliefs of the younger, more Independent left have apparently tended to counteract the traditional pro-labor bias of the left (ibid.: 328).

AN INTERNATIONAL PERSPECTIVE

As a percentage of the workforce, membership in both public (36 percent) and private (13 percent) sector employee organizations (density) in the United States is well below that of other Atlantic Community countries (Table 4.1). This relatively weak union experience in the United States highlights those values emphasized in American exceptionalism.

In the public sector, the United States density was the lowest, while the high-

Table 4.1
Density: Market and Public Sectors, Twelve Atlantic Community Countries, 1980s and 1970s

| Country (Year) | 1980s | | | 1970s |
| | Public/Market Density Ratio | Density | | Public Density |
		Market*	Public	
Norway (1980)	1.90	50	95	87
Sweden (1985)	1.13	77	87	70
Denmark (1984)	1.01	81	82	na
Great Britain (1985)	2.13	38	81	82
Austria (1985)	1.37	52	71	84
Canada (1987)	2.44	27	66	59
Switzerland (1985)	2.44	25	61	68
W. Germany (1985)	2.07	28	58	61
Italy (1985)	1.26	39	49	45
Netherlands (1985)	2.71	17	46	60
France (1975)	3.23	13	42	na
United States (1987)	2.77	13	36	32

*The "market" sector for the Atlantic Community countries includes the private sector plus the nationalized industries in goods and services (Troy, 1988).
Source: Troy (1988): 11, 19.

est densities were in the Scandinavian countries and Great Britain. Since the 1970s, gains in public sector unionization have taken place in five countries—Norway, Sweden, Canada, Italy, and the United States. Other countries had declines—the Netherlands, Austria, Switzerland, Germany, and Great Britain. Trend data for Denmark and France are not available.

Table 4.1 also presents a ratio of public to "market" densities, to illustrate that, in these countries, the propensity of public sector workers to organize is greater than that of those in the market sector. The American ratio of 2.77 is higher than that of seven countries and very similar to that of Canada, Switzerland, the Netherlands, and France.[1]

Changes in the public sector's share of both union membership and total employment have occurred in most countries of the Atlantic Community. The strength of these unions relative to private unions has increased. In the United States the large change in public share resulted largely from the decline in private sector unionization.

In contrast, Great Britain did not experience a large increase in public unionism. Great Britain, like Austria, Switzerland, and West Germany, began to pursue a policy of privatization during the 1980s that may have contributed to the decline in public sector density.

In Great Britain, 81 percent of the public sector workforce was unionized in 1985. The more than 500 local governments or authorities employed 2.9 million workers, about 14 percent of the workforce. Since 1945, local government collective bargaining has been characterized by centralized negotiations at the national level and standardized employment conditions among all local authorities (Sheldrake, 1988: 57). This is very different from the decentralized American model. However, in recent years, Britain has been moving away from a centralized negotiating process, with national entities assuming an advisory role to local authorities (Roberts, 1988: 87).

In Canada, virtually all municipal corporations with more than 50 employees and a population above 10,000 have a collective bargaining agreement with at least one employee unit. Collective bargaining is also practiced on a wide scale by health and education workers.

In 1962, the United States and Canada had public sector densities that were virtually equal (23.3 and 24.3 percent respectively). During the 1960s and early 1970s, Canada amended its national and provincial statutes to make wages subject to bargaining and to legalize strikes. Canada broke new ground in public sector labor relations when it granted municipal workers (not police or firefighters) the same rights as private sector workers, including the right to strike (Goldenberg, 1988: 267). Historically, the resistance had been rooted largely in the principle of sovereignty of the state. However, in 1965 the government of Quebec granted the first broad collective bargaining rights to civil service employees, and a new era began.

By 1987 Canada's public sector density was 66 percent, compared to 36 percent south of the border. The fact that Canada's public sector density was almost double that of the United States reflects that "[t]he American social structure and values foster the free market and competitive individualism, an orientation which is not congruent with class consciousness, support for socialist or social democratic parties, or a strong union movement" (Lipset, 1986: 452).

Meltz (1989) notes that the differences in public sector union density among the Canadian provinces are much less than those among the American states (2:1 and 6:1 respectively). These density differences are attributed to differences in legislation and support for labor-oriented political parties (Meltz, 1989: 143). However, this analysis makes no distinction between state and local or full- and part-time workers; such aggregation conceals important variations, which are analyzed in this study.

LOCAL GOVERNMENT EMPLOYEES ORGANIZE: THE 1960s AND THE 1970s

While prior to 1960 there was relative stability in local government labor relations, the history of workers organizing predates that time. In the pre–Civil

War days of the 1830s, local government employees were organizing craft-type units of "laborers, workmen, and mechanics" in municipal public works. Local police benefit societies and fraternal groups were also formed. The National Education Association (NEA) was established as a professional organization in 1857, and its predecessor, the American Institute of Instruction, had been established a quarter century earlier. Most were "sporadic, limited, and relatively ineffective" efforts to organize (Spero and Capozzola, 1973: 15).

It was not until the early twentieth century that these groups began to "turn to activities designed to advance and protect their interests as employees" (ibid.). For example, police officers and firefighters in New York City worked for amended work hours and for a decent burial (Maier, 1987: 20). Early efforts by the American Federation of State, County, and Municipal Employees (AFSCME) were aimed at preventing encroachment on the civil service system by political patronage (ibid.).

Samuel Gompers, writing in 1912, expressed support for the right of government employees to organize.

The American Federation of Labor is working out its destiny within the law and will contest the assumption by Government officials of the right to dictate to the employees of the government to which organizations they shall or shall not belong. The American people are not yet ready to take the position that because an individual accepts employment from the Government he thereby forfeits the rights guaranteed to him by the Constitution of the United States. (Gompers, 1969: 48)

Gompers also expressed support in a 1914 article for public school teachers seeking to use a collective voice strategy.

Because the Cleveland school board had refused requests for higher wages, because no other methods remained, the Cleveland grade teachers organized a union. A union secures results in proportion to the power it can wield. . . . Teachers throughout the country are reaching the conviction that they must help themselves if they wish better things. (Gompers, 1971: 127)

Until the late 1960s, except for teachers, the AFL-CIO expressed little interest in, and provided little financial support for, public employee unions. The United Auto Workers was the only national union to provide financial assistance for local government employee efforts to organize (Maier, 1987: 14). Other unions led the drive to organize—AFSCME, the International Brotherhood of Teamsters, the Service Employees International Union (SEIU), the Laborers International Union.

In 1962 George Meany was quoted as saying it is "impossible to bargain collectively with the government" (Goulden, 1982: 184). History has shown that to be wrong! "The speed of changeover, measured against the backdrop of labor history, is almost breathtaking—public unions and employee associations have attracted a larger proportion of their share of the workforce in ten years than the industrial unions have been able to do in thirty'' (Zagoria, 1972: 1). ''In effect, a new union movement was established in a relatively short time and it was accomplished with an ease which contrasts sharply with the rise of the CIO in the 1930's'' (Troy and Sheflin, 1984: 16).

''The metamorphosis transcends a quantitative alteration. The change has also marked a shift in what unions do and why, their philosophy. These changes have given birth to a new union movement, the New Unionism'' (Troy, 1994: 1). This New Unionism differs from the Old Unionism in several ways (ibid.: 2). First, it is made up of professional and other white collar employees who are in a stronger position than were the blue collar workers of the earlier unions to shape and influence ideas, policies, and trends. Second, its base is services, not manufacturing and production; its goals often exclude ownership of the ''means of production.'' Third, its members administer government spending, which exceeds 40 percent of the national income. Further, these two movements disagree regarding the distribution of the national income; the New focuses on the distribution between the private and public economies, while the Old focuses on private parties—employers and union members (ibid.: 135).

''Only in the 1960s did there begin to be felt a massive stirring of public employees as they began to object to decades of often paternalistic treatment'' (Zack, 1972: 101). Historians and researchers cite several major events in the public policy arena that help explain the initial rapid growth of public sector bargaining: (1) the 1959 enactment in Wisconsin of comprehensive legislation that gave local (not state) employees a legally enforceable right to bargain collectively; (2) the 1962 signing of an Executive Order by President John Kennedy establishing limited bargaining rights for federal employees; (3) the Supreme Court decisions that public employees have a right to organize and that an agency shop clause in a public sector collective bargaining agreement is legal; and (4) increased funding for Great Society programs.

Wisconsin's enactment ended ''the era of unquestioned sovereignty of elected representatives in labor matters'' (Maier, 1972: 60). Following Wisconsin, a momentum began to build, and 30 states enacted collective bargaining laws during the 1960s and 1970s. The legislative reapportionment in the early 1960s, which entailed a shift from rural to urban representatives, may have facilitated some of these enactments (Cohany and Dewey, 1970: 18). Prior to 1968, the courts with near unanimity held that public employees did not have a constitutional right to unionize and, as a corollary, that legislative bodies could prohibit their employees from joining and forming a union (Shaw, 1972: 21). In 1968, however, the United States Court of Appeals for the Seventh Circuit (Illinois, Indiana, Wisconsin) held in a landmark decision in *McLaughlin v. Tilendis*[2] that ''teachers have the right of free association, and unjustified interference with teachers' associational freedom violates the Due Process clause of the Fourteenth Amendment'' (Wellington and Winter, 1971: 75). The Supreme Court in *United States v. Robel*[3] left little room for state limitations on the right of public employees to join unions. If such limitations interfere with the legitimate First Amendment rights of public employees, a state "must achieve its goal by means which have a 'less dramatic' impact" (ibid.: 81). Such avenues might include restrictions on collective bargaining or the right to strike, but not on prior association.

However, while public employees have a constitutional right to organize, the courts have uniformly held that there is no constitutional right to force a public employer to bargain collectively in the absence of legislation (ibid.: 22). The courts with near uniformity also have held that public employees do not have a constitutional right to strike and that such strikes can be legislatively proscribed (ibid.).

The structure of public sector bargaining grew both *de jure* and *de facto* (Anderson, 1972: 37). Many states enacted statutes "permitting or protecting and encouraging" bargaining; some followed with compulsory interest arbitration or, in some cases, a right to strike. Some states did not enact legislation, while others passed anti-bargaining statutes. In the absence of state legislation, there have been "executive orders issued by governors, mayors, or county executives. . . . In still other jurisdictions, the attorney general, corporation counsel, or city attorney has rendered an opinion" (ibid.). These state imposed collective bargaining environments are explored in the next chapter.

During this period there was

a consistent thread of concern that collective bargaining as we know it in the private sector is irreconcilable with the nature of government. . . . [T]he complete transplantation of traditional collective bargaining . . . would impair the decision-making power of elected officials as they seek to represent the public interest. . . . The political nature of government . . . create(s) a unique employment environment, one in which the sovereignty and nondelegation doctrines have been critical in the creation of public sector laws. (Schneider, 1988: 189)

While employees might have the constitutional right to associate, the government employer has a responsibility to protect the public interest. Collective bargaining agreements and certainly strikes were seen as "intolerable invasions of the sovereign's absolute authority to act in the public interest" (ibid.: 193). Sovereign immunity was not the only hurdle, but it was a major one.

Whether changes in public policy and statutes caused an increase in public sector employee organizing is a matter of debate in the literature. Regardless of causation, either the emergence of the public policy or the organization itself must be explained. The rapidity with which it occurred after the legislative enactments suggests there was a large pent-up demand. In Troy's view (1994), the growth of public sector unionism is not merely an extension of the private sector experience, the "spurt" theory of union growth that deals with a unitary movement, which obfuscates the fundamental differences. Rather he sees it as a unique movement of "organizing the organized," which transformed existing

public and professional associations into unions, with a choice of becoming
unions or disappearing.

The results of a 1988 survey by the International City Management Association suggest that ''a high demand existed for unionization that could be expressed by public employees after they were given legal protection to engage
in collective bargaining'' (Chandler, 1989: 86). In 51 percent of the reporting
cities, the first public employee unions or associations were organized in their
municipality between 1968 and 1977, the period during which the taxpayers had
begun to express their fiscal discontent. After one state enacted its authorization
bill, Jerry Wurf, then-president of AFSCME, said that government workers ''no
longer have to go hat in hand to beg politicians for a raise'' (Goulden, 1982:
122).

''The public employee [in 1960] was in the same position as the mass production workers in the 1930s: numerous, needed, and neglected'' (Tyler, 1972:
97). Wurf perceived that the ''broad overall problems facing municipal employees were low pay, unstructured working conditions, and lack of status''
(Goulden, 1982: 124). In later speeches, however, he would say that ''most
organizers think they're peddling better wages and working conditions, but essentially they're peddling dignity'' (ibid.: xvi). In 1966 he said that ''workers
are essentially tired of being patronized. Unions would be unable to sign up a
single employee if he . . . were treated with justice'' (ibid.: 117).

An Alliance with the Civil Rights Movement

Jerry Wurf described his first troops as the ''economic serfs who do scut
work'' (ibid.: xvi) and frequently they were blacks and Hispanics. Hospital
workers, among the first groups to be organized in New York City, were overwhelmingly black females who had not completed high school. To organize
them Wurf hired James Farmer, who said that ''the grievances were built around
two words: ''decency'' and ''dignity''—the desire to feel you were somebody
important. . . . The major issue was human dignity'' (ibid.: 125).

AFSCME organizers forged a close alliance with the civil rights movement
during the 1960s. ''Projecting the union and civil rights as a valid common
cause meant that the hospital workers could equate their own situation with the
plight of blacks elsewhere'' (ibid.: 127). ''The same women who wanted to
break down segregation laws also wanted to overcome institutionalized occupational barriers that kept black workers in low skill, low paying jobs with
disagreeable hours and little respect for administrators'' (Maier, 1987: 54).

The 1968 sanitation strike in Memphis was a similar situation. The workers
were overwhelmingly black; were paid $70 per week with no vacation, holidays,
or health insurance; and had terrible working conditions. The mayor ''understood the portion of his constituency that was redneck and he thought it was
good politics to exploit these black men'' (Goulden, 1982: 156). Wurf said,
''The only way we could win this was by mobilizing the black community to

understand what these men were going through was what the community was struggling for'' (ibid.: 158). Martin Luther King, Jr., before being killed on the eve of the march in support of that strike, had lauded the strikers and their pursuit of justice.

While not new in the 1960s, the increased militancy was a product of the times and reflected the growing acquiescence in such actions by society in general. Mass pressure to challenge authority, while inconsistent with the competitive individualism of American exceptionalism, was becoming a more acceptable way of getting action on demands that had been ignored. The examples of the civil rights movement, student protests, and the Vietnam war protests were not unnoticed by unions and public workers.

The increase in white collar, service, and university-trained positions enlarged the constituency for nonmaterialist social reform movements, such as feminism, ecology, peace, and civil rights causes. But apart from public employees, those in such pursuits showed much less interest than manual workers in labor organizations (Lipset, 1986: 423).

There also was a competition between the various employee organizations, which tended to increase militancy as they competed with one another for the most favorable contract. For example, in the New York City teachers' campaign, "the United Federation of Teachers (UFT) focused on the non-militant heritage of the National Education Association (NEA) which the UFT maintained was inherently pro-management in orientation . . . particularly embarrassing to the NEA was the continued presence of segregated locals in the South'' (Maier, 1987: 118).

Maier (ibid.: 125) notes that the civil rights movement and urban unrest created what someone referred to as an "explosive mixture" as conventional teaching became "hazardous." Educational quality became inseparable from the issue of working conditions. Every UFT contract contained some form of commitment by the New York City Board of Education to new programs.

THE 1980s

Two broad areas of concern for local government employees began to garner greater attention as the decade of the 1970s came to a close and the 1980s began. One was the emergence of the so-called pink-collar ghetto issues raised by the large number of female workers. Their list of concerns included low recognition, high stress, child care, and pay equity (Baden, 1986: 244). The second was concern about job security, brought to the fore by efforts to privatize services and downsize organizations. These will be reviewed briefly.

Pay Equity and Comparable Worth

Pay equity has been called by many "the women's issue of the 1980s." It is not the "equal pay for equal work" required by the Equal Pay Act of 1963.

Rather, it is based on a concept enunciated in the Civil Service Reform Act of 1978 that all employees should receive fair and equitable treatment, including "equal pay for work of comparable value." Compensation scales should be gender neutral, and should be equal for different jobs that require the same skills, effort, level of responsibility, and working conditions. Advocates argue that pay levels based on labor market rates cannot be relied upon since they may discriminate on the basis of gender. Thousands (the precise number is not known) of local government classification plans are now established using gender-neutral job evaluation techniques. "Comparable worth arises out of the underlying values of social equity. Viewed from an historical perspective, it is one of a series of personnel issues connected to redressing patterns of discrimination against identifiable groups, . . . though it may benefit different groups" (Klinger, 1988: 48). It is another example of determining wages or other conditions of employment without relying solely on the labor market; for example, we pay a minimum wage, refrain from hiring children, offer veterans' preferences, use affirmative action programs, and the like.

Between 1977 and 1983, 26 states enacted comparable worth legislation. The City of San Jose, California, in 1981, after a six-day strike, and the state of Minnesota in 1982 were among the first to implement comparable worth studies, appropriating $1.5 million and $22 million respectively as equity pay adjustments. In a nationally celebrated case in the state of Washington, the court ordered the state to raise the salary of 15,000 workers in predominantly female job classifications and awarded four years' back pay. The order was overturned in 1985 by the Court of Appeals, but before it could be appealed to the Supreme Court, there was an out-of-court settlement with large pay increases for the female-dominated jobs.

The rationale for comparable worth fits well within the arguments traditionally used by union organizers to recruit new members; it is simply the application of old methods in a new environment (Aaron and Lougy, 1986).

One reason for the emphasis on pay equity by local government employee organizations is that it is where women work. By 1987, women comprised 60 percent of the local government workforce compared to 43 percent in the balance of the civilian labor force—80 percent in hospitals, 70 percent in education, but less than 10 percent in public safety. From 1977, when one-half of the local government workers were female, the number of female employees increased 2.1 million to almost 6.7 million by 1987.[4] Teachers, librarians, nurses, social workers, and clerical workers are examples of female-dominated job classifications.

Another factor was that state and local workers were being unionized by AFSCME, one of the few major unions that endorsed pay equity and recruited successfully during the 1970s and 1980s (Aaron and Lougy, 1986). The AFL-CIO did not adopt a pay equity policy until 1985.

Winn Newman in 1982 testimony stated that AFSCME

used pay equity as an effective organizing tool. In two recent close elections involving 3,000 and 7,500 eligible voters, AFSCME successfully made its approach to pay equity a major campaign issue, winning each election. . . . The allegation of wage discrimination, together with the promise that discrimination can be corrected is a powerful organizing tool. (Aaron and Lougy, 1986: 39)

According to the American Nurses' Association (1986: 6), "Women workers are finding collective bargaining an effective way to pursue more equitable compensation. . . . Unions or units within unions that are predominantly female are successfully negotiating contract provisions that recognize the principle of pay equity."

Riccucci (1990) concludes that unions operating in the public sector are important, yet frequently overlooked, components in the policy processes affecting female and minority employment. She notes, however, that union support for pay equity is not unequivocal. In some cases unions facilitate the process through collective bargaining, conducting job evaluation studies, political activity, or litigation. But in other cases they oppose it or set up barriers to its implementation (for example, seniority systems). Although AFSCME at the national level may support pay equity, not all of its locals have done so. Support at the local bargaining table depends upon the gender composition of the local, the willingness of women to press for it, the local's security among its constituents, and local economic conditions (Riccucci, 1990: 151). Police, firefighter, and other uniformed service unions, affiliated with the AFL-CIO or not and with few females, have not been supportive of pay equity.

Given the role played by the local union leadership in setting priorities, the extent and position of leadership by women in the local governance structure will determine their influence over bargaining table and service priorities (Baden, 1986: 245). By 1982, 33 percent of AFSCME's local presidents and 45 percent of its officers were female (Bell, 1985: 288).

Privatization and Competition

Privatization is not new for local government. But its recent growth and current popularity are. Virtually all local governments have used its most popular form, contracting with the private sector, since the late nineteenth century (Kettl, 1993: 155). A wide range of goods and services have been provided in this way—refuse collection, highway construction, facilities maintenance, human services (especially with non-profit organizations), legal services, and clerical services are examples. In 1972 the value of contracts let by local governments to private organizations was valued at $22 billion (ibid.: 156).

By the late 1970s and into the 1980s, the use of the contracting model increased greatly, and by 1982 the value of local government contracts with private organizations had increased three-fold to $65 billion (ibid.).

"The widespread popular movement to limit taxes, spurred by Proposition

13 in California, forced state and local officials to search for tactics to deliver government goods and services at lower costs'' (ibid.: 155). They began to expand their use of the various forms of privatization—ceasing to provide a service, contracting with private operators, or using voucher systems. Further, more programs and services were added to the list of those that could be privatized—fire and ambulance services, detention facilities, libraries, and public schools are examples. Some governments also have sold their public assets—hospitals, airports, and ports, for example.

While there are supply-side and demand-side imperfections in the marketplace for the goods and services that governments provide (Kettl, 1993), many local officials felt that efficiency and effectiveness could be increased if they could create, in Osborne and Gaebler's lexicon (1992), a ''competitive government.'' The goal was not to transfer a program from one monopoly provider to another. Rather, to the extent feasible, it was to create a competitive environment—public versus private, private versus private, public versus public (Osborne and Gaebler, 1992)—in a way that achieves the appropriate balance between public and private delivery so that the government is able to maintain the public interest (Kettl, 1993: 38–40).

Saving money and resolving labor problems are the two advantages most frequently cited by local governments for contracting out (ibid.: 16); improving the quality of service does not seem to be the primary rationale. Research has found substantial savings across the range of contracted services; for example, Chandler and Feuille (1991) found savings of 29 to 37 percent for sanitation services. But, as Kettl (1993: 160) argues, ''the cost savings argument masks a genuine anti-government worker sentiment underlying the privatization prescription.''

Further, these cost savings accrue in ways that ''adversely affect the employees who had been delivering the now-contracted service'' (Chandler and Feuille, 1991: 16). ''Concern over job displacement, especially among women and minorities . . . has been the major reason for employee opposition to contracting out'' (ibid.). Lower wages, lower benefits, and the use of more flexible personnel practices (part-time workers, for example) are other commonly used ways to reduce costs (Kettl, 1993: 160).

Thus, a tradeoff is presented to decision makers between cost savings and public employee jobs, which

suggests that the implementation of contracting out depends upon the relative political power of taxpayers eager to reduce costs versus public employees eager to protect jobs. . . . When public employees are organized . . . the union may enable the employees to communicate their contracting opposition preferences to policy makers. (Chandler and Feuille, 1991: 16)

Just one of the skirmishes in the ''battle of collective voices.''

In their 1991 study of contracting for sanitation services in 1,256 cities, Chandler and Feuille (1991: 17) found that the "union's ability to function as an organized political interest group" allowed the employees to express effectively their opposition to contracting out.

The presence of a union . . . reduces the probability that a city will seriously consider contracting out. . . . Evidently the presence of a city sanitation union provides an institutional vehicle through which sanitation employees effectively may express their contracting opposition to city officials, which, in turn, results in job protection benefits that their nonunion peers do not receive. . . . The reduced incidence of contracting in unionized cities is due in large part to union-organized opposition to contracting which extends beyond the words agreed to at the contract negotiation table. (ibid.: 20)

Chandler and Feuille also found that contracting did not eliminate unions from the sanitation collection function; "many of the public sanitation services became privately unionized" (ibid.).

PREVIOUS RESEARCH

Excerpts from the goal and mission statements of AFSCME and the NEA summarize well the economic and non-economic reasons for many local government employees seeking the right to bargain collectively.

Workers organize . . . primarily to secure better wages and working conditions, . . . to participate in decisions which affect them at work . . . consent of the governed; collective bargaining is the expression of citizenship in employment . . . dedicated to exert ourselves, individually and collectively, to fulfill the promise of the American life; . . . for unions, the work place and the polling place are inseparable and the exercise . . . of citizenship is required at both. (AFSCME)

[To] reform public education and restructure public schools . . . establish public education as a basic right . . . increase the nation's investment in public education . . . improving the professional standards, compensation, and working conditions of employees . . . further the interests of . . . employees through collective bargaining, political action, litigation, and other advocacy processes . . . eliminate all forms of discrimination . . . increase the number of members. (NEA)

The literature includes numerous, sometimes conflicting, explanations for local government employees choosing collective voice. They include both economic and non-economic reasons: a tradition of low wages (Burton and Thomason, 1988); wage and benefit gains by private industry unions (Cohany and Dewey, 1970); resentment by teachers at earning less than some blue collar workers and a substantial increase in the size of schools and school systems (Saltzman, 1985); teachers wanting better physical facilities and protection from violent students (Maier); an increase in the number of young, male, and Jewish teachers (Cole, 1969, 1987); a lack of individual bargaining power, a community of interest because of skills and training, and the dependence of individual status on the status of the group as a whole (Bakke, 1970); pay equity and comparable worth (Aaron and Lougy, 1986); and policy processes affecting female and minority employment (Riccucci, 1990).

Other non-economic explanations include the intense competition of unions in the organizing process (Saltzman, 1985); public managers resisting unionization with less intensity than those in the private sector (Saltzman, 1985; Cohany and Dewey, 1970); the existence of professional and employee associations that could be transformed with relative ease into bargaining organizations, although not all made that change (Troy, 1994; Levitan and Gallo, 1989; Burton and Thomason, 1988; Troy and Sheflin, 1984); and governments controlled by Democrats and those in the larger metropolitan areas in Illinois (Wilson and Elder, 1988).

The traditional security of government employment became less attractive in an inflationary economy with tight labor markets, as existed in the late 1960s and early 1970s. Longstanding local wage relationships were being upset, to the disadvantage of the government workers. For example, Zack (1972: 101) cites the requirement to pay construction workers employed under government contracts the wages and fringe benefits that "prevail" in the locality in which the work is done (by Davis-Bacon–type laws).

In addition to compensation and economic matters, for professional employees "many demands involve job content and job responsibilities" (Gotbaum, 1972: 78). They were seeking a way to participate in the decision making from which they had been excluded—raising so-called governance issues (Cohany and Dewey, 1970).

Consider, for example, elementary and secondary public school teachers who constitute almost 40 percent of full-time local government employees and about one-half of those who have organized (their density is more than two-thirds).[5] In New York City, for example, male teachers, especially in the high schools, felt that their wages had eroded in comparison with similarly educated men; young teachers (4,000 were hired each year after 1965) who had not experienced the Great Depression were less fearful of losing their jobs; and Jewish teachers (after 1940 over 60 percent of all new teachers were Jewish) were more likely to be members of pro-union political movements (Cole, 1969: 79–109).

The larger educational institutions had a critical mass of militants and more freedom and constituted a credible strike threat; schools were more bureaucratic; and there was less personal contact between teachers and administrators, which meant that collective rather than individual bargaining could be more effective (Saltzman, 1985). In Philadelphia, for example, the teachers' contracts in the late 1960s required administrators to meet with the union to discuss "the areas of educational policies and development." The 1969 contract asserted a role for teachers in matters of "social justice" and provided for equal representation on a committee to effectuate faculty transfers to assure "quality integrated education" (Spero and Capozzola, 1973: 175).

As noted earlier, there were strong inter-union rivalries; since unions operate in a competitive market, the need to maintain and increase membership is an important organizational objective (ibid.: 31). Some unions entered into cooperative arrangements, others did not. In their study of public employee unions in San Francisco during the 1970s, Boehm and Heldman (1982: ix) noted that

the intensely political nature of the unions was one of the most powerful corrosives in the breakdown of city labor relations. . . . [The] newer unions . . . had regional and national designs for which the representation of local employees was merely a means. The basic goal was to maintain a high national profile to enhance the union's organizing efforts and to advance its political ambitions. An obvious route to these goals was for union leaders to grandstand before potential members by prying the most impressive compensation package possible from local officials.

Another factor may have been employee apathy, a reality in many of America's political elections. When the Supreme Court sustained the legality of agency shop provisions in public sector collective bargaining agreements for certain services (bargaining a contract, administering it, providing a grievance procedure),[6] all workers in an organization would be covered by bargaining if that were legislated or negotiated. To establish a bargaining unit an initial vote is generally required, but in many states only a simple majority of the votes cast in the election is needed to certify an exclusive bargaining representative; no minimum participation in that voting is required. The case study presented in Chapter 7 provides one example—of the 2,400 eligible to vote, the union was selected by the 477 of those voting ''yes'' (20 percent of the eligible voters).

HOW WELL DID THEY DO?

The literature focuses on four broad economic arenas in which employee organizations are likely to have an impact: wages, employee benefits, staffing levels, and total budget expenditures. Each is reviewed in the following sections.

Wage Effects

In general, the research supports a conclusion that local public employee organizations increased wages for their members (Ashenfelter, 1971; Ehrenberg, 1973; Bartel and Lewin, 1981; Edwards and Edwards, 1982; Moore and Raisian, 1982; Feuille, Delaney, and Hendricks, 1985; Freeman and Ichniowski, 1988; Lewis, 1988; Kleiner and Petree, 1988). Higher wages for non-union workers and for non-unionized departments of the same organization (''spillover effects'') were also realized (Freeman and Valletta, 1988; Zax and Ichniowski, 1988; Freeman and Ichniowski, 1988).

The research has found the range of differentials to be quite broad (1 to 21 percent). On average, salaries are increased 5 to 6 percent (Kearney, 1994: 89).

It is difficult to generalize about the magnitude of the wage effects since they vary according to government function (police, fire, instructional education, etc.), size of jurisdiction, time period analyzed, and research methodology used. However, public sector impacts are well below those attributed to private sector unions, which are associated with an average 15 to 25 percent wage premium (ibid.).

Among public school teachers the earnings advantages for those covered by collective bargaining agreements were as large or larger than in the private sector (Kleiner and Petree, 1988). In New York State, Lipsky and Drotning (1973) found that "unionism came to districts in which slightly higher salaries were already being paid . . . [and] the effect was to increase the favorable differential." They also found the effect was greatest at the highest salary steps. In California, however, Chambers (1977) found that bargaining may have increased starting teachers' salaries by as much as 8 to 17 percent.

Public sector union-nonunion differentials were about the same for black and white workers, but they were higher for women. In cities employing a professional manager the impact of unionism on wages was less than in those that did not (4 versus 12 percent) (Edwards and Edwards, 1982). Ehrenberg (1973) found them to be marginally lower in city manager governments.

Employee Benefit Effects

Collective bargaining had a "very large and strongly positive association with the level of police fringe benefits during the entire 1971–1981 period . . . police unions may be systematically influencing cities to contribute larger amounts to fringe benefits" than would be contributed otherwise (Feuille, Delaney, and Hendricks, 1985: 17). Benefits for police officers were significantly higher in larger and wealthier cities, in those with higher reported crime rates, and in those with a city manager form of government. Bartel and Lewin (1981) also found higher fringe benefits for police, although the differential was substantially lower (9 percent versus 31 percent in the former study). Ichniowski (1980) found higher benefits for union firefighters; Edwards and Edwards (1982) had a similar finding for sanitation workers.

Employment Effects

Public sector unions also influence demand for local public services and thus increase employment in the organizations for which they work (Valletta, 1989; Zax and Ichniowski, 1988; Zax, 1989; O'Brien, 1994). These employment effects are, in percentage terms, as large or perhaps larger than the wage effects (Valletta, 1989; O'Brien, 1994). Only among teachers have researchers failed to find a positive bargaining effect on employment, although more recent research did detect such effects (Freeman and Ichniowski, 1988). Unions also can produce job security by lowering unemployment probabilities and shortening layoff periods (Allen, 1988).

Union contracts raised wages at the expense of employment (Freeman and Valletta, 1988). However, employment and wages in otherwise identical departments are higher in those with collective bargaining contracts, supporting the notion that unions raise demand for labor as well as increase wages. For example, contracts may incorporate staffing standards—officers per beat, students per class, and the like. Woodbury (1985) found strong probabilities of substitution between teacher pay and class size.

As with wages, there are employment "spillover effects"; the effects on employment levels in non-unionized departments are consistently negative and frequently significant (Zax and Ichniowski, 1988; Freeman and Valletta, 1988; Freeman and Ichniowski, 1988).

Valletta (1989: 432) suggests that employment gains by unionized departments and workers can be "disguised as representing a union's desire for improvements in service rather than economic opportunism." Similarly it can be politically less costly for elected decision makers to be perceived as improving services rather than as giving in to a union's wage demands.

Regarding worker attitudes, Kochan (1979: 24) found that more than 80 percent of American workers either "agree" or "strongly agree" that unions improved wages and job security and protected workers against unfair practices. However, less than half (45 percent) felt that unions "give members their money's worth." A majority of union members surveyed listed handling grievances, fringe benefits, wages, and job security as their top priorities.

Expenditure Effects

Total general expenditures of a municipality are not increased by bargaining units. Rather, the funds are reallocated; expenditures are increased in departments covered by a contract and reduced in others (Zax and Ichniowski, 1988; Freeman and Ichniowski, 1988; Valletta, 1989; O'Brien, 1994). Chambers (1977) concluded that bargaining by teachers did not have a statistically significant effect on education spending. "The most important effect of union political power may not be to increase overall municipal spending, but to cause an inefficient composition of public services" (O'Brien, 1994: 343). However, Benecki (1978) did find evidence that municipal unionism increased bottom-line expenditures.

CONCLUSION

Why have so many of the people who work for local governments in the United States chosen a collective voice? To paraphrase a popular saying from a 1950s television series: There were 8 million stories in these governments; these have been some of them.

This chapter has explored an array of reasons for local government employees using collective voice. The reasons appear to have changed over the decades. Earlier concerns focused on enacting enabling state legislation permitting them to use collective voice at the bargaining table and then working to improve their compensation and working conditions. In the 1980s, the agenda expanded to include pay equity and job security. However, notably absent from these research efforts is any explicit analysis of a relationship of the use of collective voice by employees to its use by the taxpayers. Did the collective voice of the taxpayers—fiscal discontent—encourage the employees to pursue a collective voice strategy as well? That relationship is explored in the following chapters.

NOTES

1. In 1992, the U.S. ratio had increased to 3.2, likely making it nearly the highest in the Atlantic Community.

2. 398 F.2d 287 (7th Cir. 1968).

3. 389 U.S. 258 (1967).

4. In February 1996, there were 7.15 million women employed by local governments, 60 percent of the workforce. This compares to 39 percent in the balance of the civilian labor force (U.S. Department of Labor, Bureau of Labor Statistics, *Employment and Earnings*, March 1996).

5. This segment of the local government workforce was among the fastest growing in the post–World War II era—the number of teachers increased from 900,000 in 1950 to 2 million by 1969 and to 2.3 million by 1987.

6. *Abood v. Detroit Board of Education*, 431 U.S. 209 (1977). Agency shops are legal except in the right-to-work states, which have statutes banning them. The decision stated further that the spending of service fees for "political and ideological purposes unrelated to collective bargaining" violated the First Amendment rights of non-union employees.

5

Employee Whispers and Shouts

The collective voice strategy as used by two groups of actors in the local budgeting process is discussed in the preceding chapters. This chapter examines the use of that strategy by local government employees at two levels of intensity— the milder form, joining an organization, and the stronger collective bargaining model. Chapter 6 examines whether the use of collective voice by the taxpayers influenced local government employees to adopt a similar strategy, as hypothesized here.

This chapter begins with a snapshot for October 1987, the last date for which comprehensive data are available. It then examines the changes in the use of employee collective voice, beginning in the early 1970s. The propensity of employees to join an organization is explored from three perspectives—by government function, by state, and by type of local government. The propensities to use the stronger collective bargaining model are then examined, by state and by type of local government.

Chapter 6 examines the various propensities to organize and bargain in relation to fiscal discontent. Higher propensities found in the states and types of local government that experienced fiscal discontent lend support to the hypothesis of this research.

THE LOWER LEVEL OF COLLECTIVE VOICE: EMPLOYEES ORGANIZE

While nationally 47.4 percent of full-time local government employees were organized in October 1987,[1] that average conceals more than it reveals, as there are thousands of local government labor markets. To a great extent they are

Table 5.1

Full-Time Local Government Employees, Selected Functions, by Density, 1987

| | Employees | | |
Functional Area	Number (000)	Percent	Density
Fire Protection	231	3.0	64.7
Instructional Education	2,995	38.4	60.9
Police Protection	529	6.8	54.1
Sanitation	99	1.3	49.8
Public Welfare	202	2.6	45.5
Non-Instructional Education	1,230	15.8	37.2
Highways	258	3.3	36.5
Hospitals	442	5.7	27.8
All Other	1,815	23.2	34.4
All Functions*	7,801	100%	47.4

*Excludes the District of Columbia.
Data Source: U.S. Department of Commerce, Bureau of the Census (June 1991).

defined by government function, by state, and by type of local government. Each topic is discussed hereafter.

Differences among the Functions of Government

More than three-quarters of the full-time local government employees work in eight functional areas for which the Bureau of the Census reports data in the *Census of Governments*.[2] The propensity of these various groups to organize (the density) varied greatly in 1987, ranging from 64.7 percent for fire protection to 29.3 percent for public hospitals (Table 5.1). The ranking (highest to lowest) was (1) fire protection, (2) instructional education, (3) police protection, (4) sanitation, (5) public welfare, (6) non-instructional education, (7) highways, (8) other functions, and (9) hospitals. The first five functions had densities markedly higher than the lowest four.

Occupational Communities

A certain body of sociological research literature explores the theory of community. Community "as an identity-giving unit is a valuable explanatory statement in discussing the behavior of individuals in *place* communities (geographic) as well as *nonplace* communities (occupational/professional groups)" (Martinez-Brawley, 1990: xxii). These occupational and professional "communities of interest" are those in which people partially satisfy their need for identity and significance (ibid.: 46).

Community without physical locus . . . may be called a community by virtue of these characteristics: (1) Its members are bound by a sense of identity. (2) Once in it, few leave so that it is a terminal or continuing status for the most part. (3) Its members share values in common. (4) Its role definitions vis-à-vis both members and non-members are agreed upon and are the same for all members. (5) Within the area of communal action, there is a common language which is understood only partially by outsiders. (6) The community has power over its members. (7) Its limits are reasonably clear, though they are not physical and geographical but social. (8) Though it does not produce the next generation biologically, it does so socially through its control over the selection of professional trainees, and through its training processes it sends these recruits through an adult socialization process. (Goode, 1957: 194)

In an employee community of interest, identification arises through common skills and standards of performance, similarity in type and extent of training, in status in the eyes of the community, and the dependence of individual status on the status of the group as a whole. This reinforces other bases for collective organized representation. If that community of interest is exaggerated by a commonly experienced sense of being left behind or being as a group taken for granted, the predisposition is increased; this is true for teachers (Bakke, 1970). Firefighters and police officers, whose organizations are fraternal in nature, have strong communities of interest as well and are among the functional groups with the highest densities.

Police associations were started primarily as social institutions; in New York City, the Policeman's Benevolent Association was formed in 1892. In 1915, the Fraternal Order of Police (FOP), considered the first police union, was created in Fort Pitt, Pennsylvania; in 1919, the AFL reversed its policy and granted a charter to police employee organizations.

When the Boston Police Social Club was chartered, its leaders were fired under a law that prohibited police officers to unionize, thereby producing the 1919 Boston police strike. The strike was broken by then-governor Calvin Coolidge, who rose to the presidency with the lesson that "public employees are convenient stepping-stones for someone striving for higher office; if you kick them and wipe your feet on them along the way, so much the better" (Goulden, 1982: 27).

The data presented in Table 5.1 suggest that "community" may be less important for highway, non-instructional education, and hospital workers, while for welfare and sanitation employees the data are mixed.

Differences among the States

Beyond these density differences among the employees engaged in the various functions of local government, there were wide variations in density levels among the 50 states. The national average of 47.4 percent encompassed Hawaii's 95.7 percent and South Carolina's 6 percent. This research identifies three groups of states having different state-imposed collective bargaining environ-

Table 5.2
Full-Time Local Government Employees, by Group of States, 1987

	Employees		Organized		
Group of States (#)	Number	Percent	Number	Percent	Density
High Density States (16)	3,448,192	44.2	2,267,205	61.3	65.8
Moderate Density States (13)	1,454,118	18.6	677,617	18.3	46.6
Bargaining Constrained States (21)	2,898,841	37.2	756,112	20.4	26.1
All States (50) *	7,801,151	100.0	3,700,934	100.0	47.4

*Excludes the District of Columbia.
Data Source: U.S. Department of Commerce, Bureau of the Census (June 1991).

ments and distinctly different densities—twenty-one states averaged 26.1 percent, thirteen averaged 46.6 percent, and a third group of sixteen averaged 65.8 percent (Tables 5.2 and 5.3). These three groups of states are further differentiated by the degree to which their overall density levels were skewed by high rates for two occupational communities—fire protection and instructional education (Table 5.4).

• Twenty-one states had an overall average 1987 density of 26.1 percent, or 12 percent exclusive of fire protection and instructional education employees. A defining characteristic of this group is that each has some form of state-imposed constraint on local government collective bargaining—an outright prohibition, no enabling legislation, or a limitation on which employees may bargain (AFL-CIO, 1994). Thirteen had right-to-work laws. Only West Virginia, Arizona, and New Mexico had densities above 20 percent excluding fire protection and instructional education. These 21 states comprised 37 percent of the full-time workforce, but 20 percent of those who organized. States were located in various regions: eleven in the southeast (not Florida), four in the southwest, three in the Rocky Mountains (Colorado, Idaho, Wyoming), and three in the Plains (Indiana, Kansas, and Missouri). Henceforth, these will be referred to as the *BC states* (bargaining constrained/low density).

In contrast, in the remaining 29 states there were virtually no state imposed impediments to local government employee bargaining. State enabling legislation had been enacted in 28 of these states; Utah did not have state legislation, but its largest local jurisdiction, Salt Lake City, had a local collective bargaining ordinance (AFL-CIO, 1994). These 29 states are presented in two groups:

• Thirteen states had an overall average density of 46.6 percent, or 33.8 percent exclusive of fire protection and instructional education employees; only Illinois averaged more than 40 percent, excluding these latter two groups of employees. These states comprised about 18 percent both of the full-time workforce and of those organized. Seven states

Table 5.3
Density, Full-Time Local Government Employees, 1987, Number of States, by Group of States

| | NO STATE BARGAINING CONSTRAINTS | | | | STATE BARGAINING CONSTRAINTS | |
| | High Density | | Moderate Density | | Low Density States | |
Density	All Full-Time Employees	Excluding Instructional Education	All Full-Time Employees	Excluding Instructional Education	All Full-Time Employees	Excluding Instructional Education
90 Under 100%	1	1				
80 Under 90%	0	0				
70 Under 80%	2	3				
60 Under 70%	10	2				
50 Under 60%	3	10	5			
40 Under 50%			8	3		
30 Under 40%				5	10	
20 Under 30%				3	7	5
10 Under 20%				2	2	9
Under 10%					2	7
Average Density	65.8%	60.2%	46.6%	34.3%	26.1%	13.3%

Table 5.4
Density, Full-Time Local Government Employees, by State and Group of States, 1987

State	*NO STATE BARGAINING CONSTRAINTS*			
	All Full-Time Employees	Fire Protection Employees	Instructional Education Employees	Excluding Fire Protection & Inst. Education
High Density States				
Hawaii	95.7	98.7	na	95.3
New York	75.1	86.6	82.9	70.8
Massachusetts	74.8	89.8	81.2	67.5
Washington	69.1	71.8	87.9	59.2
Connecticut	68.2	84.6	76.8	57.7
Michigan	67.5	76.4	72.0	64.0
New Jersey	66.9	82.2	80.1	57.2
Rhode Island	65.6	87.1	60.2	67.3
Delaware	65.5	73.6	73.5	56.1
Minnesota	65.4	92.5	79.4	55.8
Pennsylvania	63.1	87.2	78.0	51.6
Oregon	62.8	75.6	73.2	53.8
Maryland	61.6	72.0	67.7	56.6
Alaska	59.9	70.2	67.8	54.2
Wisconsin	58.8	84.3	62.9	54.7
California	56.7	74.4	68.7	50.3
Average Density	65.8	81.3	75.6	59.1
Moderate Density States				
Maine	55.7	74.9	74.7	32.2
Utah*	54.1	57.0	68.0	39.8
North Dakota*	52.3	67.9	79.4	24.9
New Hampshire	51.9	67.2	70.4	29.3
Nevada*	51.2	83.7	72.3	38.7
Illinois	48.4	59.4	58.0	41.9
Nebraska*	47.7	88.5	73.5	28.9
Iowa*	47.5	83.0	72.9	24.9
Florida*	46.2	62.3	78.4	31.3
Vermont	45.0	54.4	62.2	16.9
Ohio	42.4	73.3	56.7	32.6
Montana	42.1	74.8	55.0	28.0
South Dakota*	41.1	81.1	62.1	16.4
Average Density	46.6	66.6	65.8	33.8

Table 5.4 (continued)

	STATE BARGAINING CONSTRAINTS			
State	All Full-Time Employees	Fire Protection Employees	Instructional Education Employees	Excluding Fire Protection & Inst. Education
	Low Density States			
Indiana	37.6	58.1	65.0	16.6
West Virginia	37.0	46.4	48.0	25.6
Missouri	35.9	71.1	57.8	17.3
Oklahoma	35.7	67.4	55.4	18.3
Idaho	35.5	63.9	62.5	11.6
Arizona*	34.8	58.5	56.6	20.4
Alabama*	33.2	37.0	56.8	17.8
Colorado	33.0	60.3	53.2	19.4
Kentucky	31.8	32.6	52.1	12.3
Wyoming*	30.9	68.4	59.0	7.8
Kansas*	29.7	50.0	51.7	11.3
New Mexico	27.4	45.2	34.2	21.6
Tennessee*	27.0	46.8	47.7	13.5
Virginia*	25.8	31.7	49.4	6.4
Louisiana*	25.7	58.8	43.0	11.7
North Carolina*	25.7	5.1	54.3	3.6
Texas*	23.0	43.2	36.3	11.5
Arkansas*	19.1	36.9	33.0	4.9
Georgia*	13.5	10.5	23.1	7.3
Mississippi*	7.9	22.0	13.5	2.6
South Carolina*	6.0	9.2	10.1	2.2
Average Density	26.1	41.2	43.7	12.0

*Right-to-Work State

had right-to-work laws. Regionally, these states were in New England (4), the Plains (4), the Rocky Mountains (2), the Great Lakes region (2), and Florida. These will be referred to as the *MD states* (moderate density).

• Sixteen states had an overall average density of 65.8 percent, 59.1 percent exclusive of fire protection and instructional education employees; all states were above 50 percent, excluding these latter two groups. Densities were five times the private sector rate. These states had 44 percent of the full-time employees, but 61 percent of the organized full-time workers. None was a right-to-work state. They were located in three clusters of contiguous states: eight from New England to the Mideast (Massachusetts, Rhode Island, Connecticut, New York, New Jersey, Pennsylvania, Delaware, and Maryland), three in the Great Lakes region (Michigan, Wisconsin, and Minnesota), and five in the Far West (Washington, Oregon, California, Hawaii, and Alaska). These will be referred to as the *HD states* (high density).

Table 5.5
Density, Full-Time Local Government Employees, by Group of States and
Government Function, 1987

Function	State Density Category			All States
	High	Moderate	Low	
Fire Protection	81.3	66.6	41.2	64.7
Instructional Education	75.6	65.8	43.7	60.9
Police Protection	77.2	50.7	22.5	54.1
Sanitation	80.4	55.1	15.8	49.8
Public Welfare	60.4	23.6	5.1	45.5
Non-Instructional Education	57.1	38.2	16.3	37.2
Highways	60.2	29.9	9.6	36.5
Other Functions	53.7	28.4	9.1	34.4
Hospitals	59.5	22.4	2.1	27.8
All Functions	65.8	46.6	26.1	47.4
All Except Fire Protection and Instructional Education	59.1	33.8	12.0	37.8

These density differences among the three groups of states are maintained when combined with the density variations in the functional categories discussed earlier. For example, as portrayed in Table 5.5, fire protection in the HD states had a higher 1987 density (81.3 percent) than police protection in the same group (77.2 percent), and each had a higher density than its counterpart in the MD states (66.6 and 50.7 percent respectively) or in the BC states (41.2 and 22.5 percent).

Differences among the Types of Local Government

The broad array of government functions is delivered to the citizens by the variety of institutions that comprise American local government: counties, municipalities, townships, school districts, and special districts. By 1987, there were 82,932 of these governments distributed among the fifty states: 29,269 special districts; 14,710 independent school districts; 16,685 townships; 19,226 municipalities; and 3,042 counties. Appendix 1 provides a breakdown for each group of states.

Between 1972 and 1987, the number of local governments in the United

Table 5.6
Density, Full-Time Local Government Employees, by Group of States and Type of Government, 1987

Type of Government	State Density Category			All States
	High	Moderate	Low	
Dependent School	76.0	85.7	40.0	61.1
Independent School	68.6	56.6	35.0	52.5
Municipality	69.2	46.4	17.6	47.4
Township	51.8	<	<	46.7
Special District	50.5	31.3	13.0	32.9
County	54.3	24.3	4.3	30.9
All Governments	65.8	46.6	26.1	47.4

< = Fewer than 10,000 full-time employees.

States increased by more than 4,700. Over those years, the number of counties remained virtually unchanged; municipalities increased; townships declined; and the number of independent school districts declined substantially (by 1,071). Special districts, on the other hand, were a growth industry—with an increase of almost 5,400 (23 percent). However, for governments with 25 or more full-time-equivalent employees, the number has been more stable.

By 1987, special districts comprised 35 percent of all local governments, but only 5 percent of the full-time workforce. The large increase in their number reflects, in part, the emergence of public authorities created by general purpose governments to finance and/or operate public facilities (housing, transportation, ports, stadiums, and economic development are examples). The Port Authority of New York and New Jersey, established in 1921, is believed to have been the first.

There was great variation among these local governments in their use of full-time employees; 29,451 had no paid employees; another 30,046 had fewer than 25 (Appendix 1). These 59,497 governments[3] (72 percent) accounted for only 2 percent of the workyears (186,764). The 3,834 governments (4.6 percent) that had 400 or more employees accounted for 71 percent of the workyears.

Densities varied greatly according to type of local government (Table 5.6). A general, albeit not perfect, pattern emerges within each group of states (highest to lowest): (1) dependent school district, (2) independent school district, (3) municipality, (4) township, (5) special district, and (6) county. In the HD states, the first three had markedly higher densities; in the other two groups, only school districts had much higher densities. The range was 4.3 percent in BC counties to over 75 percent in the HD and MD dependent school districts. No discussion of these differences has been found in the research literature.

Combining the Differences

Density differences have been portrayed among nine functional areas, three groups of states, and six types of local government. These differences, when combined, maintain the patterns that were evident in each of the individual groupings.[4] As shown in Table 5.7 for example, fire protection in the HD municipalities had a higher density (86.6 percent) than it did in HD counties (58.1 percent), and these, in turn, were higher than police protection in municipalities (80.8 percent) and counties (70.5 percent).

A Longitudinal Perspective: 1972 to 1987

The preceding section discussed various propensities of full-time local government employees to organize as they existed in 1987. But what were the changes in density during the 1970s and 1980s, the fiscal discontent era that is the focus of this research? These changes are explored below at five-year intervals for the 1972–1987 period.[5]

Differences among the States

Over this fifteen-year period, the total number of organized full-time local government employees increased by 340,000, but overall density declined from 54.1 to 47.4 percent (Table 5.8). While in both the sixteen HD and thirteen MD states, the number of organized employees increased (268,000 and 166,000 respectively), their average densities remained about the same over this entire period. In contrast, the BC states experienced a decline of almost 100,000 organized employees, and average density declined from 42 to 26 percent. The decline in these 21 BC states accounts for the overall fifteen-year decline in local government density.

Differences among the Functions

The density pattern for the state groupings continued for each government function for each of the four time periods examined—that is, the density for a given function in the HD states is higher than that in the MD states, which is in turn higher than the BC states (Table 5.9).

For many of the functions within the HD and MD states, there were only small density fluctuations over the 1972–1987 period, although by 1987 most were above their 1972 levels. There were large density increases in the police protection and sanitation functions in the MD states between 1982 and 1987. In the BC states, there were large declines in the fire protection and instructional education functions between 1972 and 1982, as well as lesser declines in most of the other functions.

Table 5.7
Density, by Group of States, Type of Government, and Government Function, 1987

Function	Municipality	County	Special District	Township
High Density States				
Fire Protection	86.6	58.1	<	<
Sanitation	84.7	<	<	<
Police Protection	80.8	70.5	na	69.4
Highways	56.5	69.3	<	53.5
Other Functions	57.1	50.5	57.1	37.5
Public Welfare	88.6	51.2	na	<
Hospitals	82.9	52.8	23.9	<
All Functions*	69.2	54.3	50.5	51.8
Moderate Density States				
Fire Protection	69.9	<	<	<
Sanitation	60.2	<	<	<
Police Protection	60.2	31.0	na	<
Highways	37.6	25.0	na	<
Other Functions	34.5	18.3	42.4	<
Public Welfare	<	22.0	na	<
Hospitals	<	36.4	4.4	na
All Functions*	46.4	24.3	31.3	13.3
Bargaining Constrained States				
Fire Protection	43.1	25.2	<	<
Sanitation	17.4	<	<	na
Police Protection	27.6	10.6	na	na
Highways	13.5	5.7	<	<
Other Functions	10.3	2.5	24.1	na
Public Welfare	<	5.6	<	<
Hospitals	2.5	2.6	1.4	na
All Functions*	17.6	4.3	13.0	na

*Excludes education employees.
< = Fewer than 10,000 full-time employees.
na = No full-time employees.

Table 5.8
Full-Time Local Government Employees, Number and Density, by Group of States, 1972, 1977, 1982, and 1987

Year	High Density States			Moderate Density States		
	Number	Organized	Density	Number	Organized	Density
1972	3,041,756	1,999,212	65.7	1,159,355	511,519	44.1
1977	3,310,311	2,290,669	69.2	1,329,819	598,665	45.0
1982	3,235,557	2,223,772	68.7	1,360,973	603,585	44.3
1987	3,448,192	2,267,205	65.8	1,454,118	677,617	46.6

Year	Low Density States			All States *		
	Number	Organized	Density	Number	Organized	Density
1972	2,016,991	850,615	42.2	6,218,102	3,361,346	54.1
1977	2,494,402	780,189	31.3	7,134,532	3,669,523	51.4
1982	2,674,052	718,776	26.9	7,270,582	3,546,133	48.8
1987	2,898,841	756,112	26.1	7,801,151	3,700,934	47.4

*Excludes the District of Columbia.

Differences among the Types of Local Government

As presented in Table 5.6, there were large variations in 1987 densities not only among the states, but also among the various types of local government within a state. The pattern presented there has existed at least since 1972: Dependent school districts have the highest densities, counties the lowest (Table 5.10). The picture is one of relative stability in the HD and MD states with several exceptions over the 1972–1982 decade—large increases in the HD and MD dependent school districts, in HD townships, and in MD municipalities. In contrast, in the BC states all government types except special districts experienced declines.

State-by-State Differences

Average densities are one indicator of what occurred in the various groups of states, but each type of government does not provide each function in every state. Thus, further insight can be gained by examining density levels for the various relevant categories within each state.

Table 5.11 reports the number of states that experienced an increase or no change in density, according to type of local government and government func-

Table 5.9
Density, Full-Time Local Government Employees, by Group of States and Government Function, 1972, 1977, 1982, and 1987

Function	High Density				Moderate Density				Low Density				All States			
	1972	1977	1982	1987	1972	1977	1982	1987	1972	1977	1982	1987	1972	1977	1982	1987
Fire Protection	84.0	86.0	83.6	81.3	71.4	71.7	70.0	66.6	59.3	50.0	40.9	41.2	74.5	71.9	66.3	64.7
Instructional Education	74.5	79.5	80.8	75.6	67.7	66.3	63.5	65.8	76.1	54.5	47.1	43.7	73.8	67.6	64.3	60.9
Police Protection	74.3	77.1	76.8	77.2	42.1	41.5	43.4	50.7	29.6	23.3	20.4	22.5	55.7	53.6	51.5	54.1
Sanitation	77.0	75.4	78.1	80.4	44.5	39.8	37.7	55.1	22.6	19.3	14.9	15.8	50.1	45.7	43.1	49.8
Public Welfare	62.5	51.5	56.6	60.4	17.6	16.3	15.0	23.6	2.5	2.7	2.9	5.1	45.8	38.4	41.1	45.5
Non-Instructional Education	52.7	64.5	63.3	57.1	29.3	39.6	33.7	38.2	14.5	20.8	17.8	16.3	35.1	44.3	40.0	37.2
Highways	53.1	59.5	59.9	60.2	22.1	28.7	30.4	29.9	11.5	9.6	8.5	9.6	33.5	35.8	35.8	36.5
Other Functions	57.7	58.3	60.2	53.7	20.9	23.8	30.6	28.4	10.1	9.3	9.6	9.1	37.9	36.9	38.7	34.4
Hospitals	58.2	60.3	36.2*	59.5	20.4	14.9	15.0	22.4	6.9	4.3	1.3	2.1	30.8	27.4	15.9*	27.8
All Functions	65.7	69.2	68.7	65.8	44.1	45.0	44.3	46.6	42.2	31.3	26.9	26.1	54.1	51.4	48.8	47.4
Excluding Fire Protection and Instructional Educ.	59.2	62.2	60.9	59.1	26.2	29.5	31.0	33.8	15.4	13.3	11.8	12.0	39.5	39.8	38.0	37.8

*This appears to be an error in the data presented in U.S. Department of Commerce, Bureau of the Census (May 1985).

Table 5.10
Density, Full-Time Local Government Employees, by Group of States and Type of Government, 1972, 1977, 1982, and 1987

Type of Government	High Density				Moderate Density				Low Density				All States			
	1972	1977	1982	1987	1972	1977	1982	1987	1972	1977	1982	1987	1972	1977	1982	1987
Dependent School	71.0	81.1	89.5	76.0	60.9	69.4	94.4	85.7	62.3	45.9	49.6	40.0	67.7	67.1	75.6	61.1
Independent School	67.8	73.3	71.3	68.6	57.0	58.8	54.1	56.6	58.7	45.6	36.2	35.0	62.1	59.9	53.8	52.5
Municipality	72.7	71.8	68.9	69.2	35.2	39.3	43.3	46.4	24.2	19.7	17.1	17.6	51.7	48.5	46.2	47.4
Township	*42.6*	*48.4*	*50.1*	*51.8*	<	<	<	<	<	<	<	<	38.3	42.8	44.4	46.7
Special District	50.7	51.8	54.9	50.5	35.5	33.9	37.5	31.3	12.4	11.9	12.7	13.0	33.2	33.8	35.4	32.9
County	*51.8*	*55.5*	*55.6*	*54.3*	16.5	15.7	20.6	24.3	12.0	3.5	3.3	4.3	32.8	30.4	30.2	30.9
All Governments	65.7	69.2	68.7	65.8	44.1	45.0	44.3	46.6	42.2	31.3	26.9	26.1	54.1	51.4	48.8	47.4

Italics indicate item is not in descending order by more than one percentage point.
< = Fewer than 10,000 full-time employees.

102

Table 5.11
Number of States Having Increased or Unchanged Densities, by Type of Government and Government Function, High and Moderate Density States, Selected Time Periods

Type of Government and Function	Total Number of States*	Number of States with Increased Density or No Change			
		1972-77	1977-82	1982-87	1977-87
High Density States					
Number of Full-Time Organized	16	15	6	8	6
Overall Density	16	12	10	4	7
Density in Municipalities (Overall)	(16)	(11)	(13)	(6)	(10)
Fire Protection	16	7	5	10	5
Police Protection	16	11	6	10	10
Other Functions	16	16	11	7	10
Highways	15	10	10	7	11
Sanitation	12	6	8	9	8
Public Welfare	9	4	7	9	7
Hospitals	8	4	4	6	6
(Subtotal for Municipalities)	(92)	(58)	(51)	(58)	(57)
Density in Counties (Overall)	(14)	(11)	(9)	(7)	(10)
Fire Protection	6	4	3	2	3
Police Protection	12	10	7	5	8
Other Functions	14	14	9	6	11
Highways	11	10	6	7	6
Public Welfare	11	6	7	7	7
Hospitals	8	4	5	4	5
(Subtotal for Counties)	(62)	(48)	(37)	(31)	(40)
Density in Townships (Overall)	(8)	(8)	(6)	(3)	(5)
Fire Protection	7	5	5	2	3
Other Functions	8	8	6	2	6
Highways	7	7	4	5	5
(Subtotal for Townships)	(22)	(20)	(15)	(9)	(14)
Density in Special Districts (Overall)	(12)	(4)	(7)	(3)	(5)
Other Functions	13	13	7	2	6
Hospitals	5	3	3	1	3
(Subtotal for Special Districts)	(18)	(16)	(10)	(3)	(9)
All except Independent School Dist.	**194**	**142**	**113**	**101**	**120**
Density in Independent School Dist.	(12)	(8)	(5)	(4)	(4)
Instructional Education	12	8	7	4	6
Non-Instructional Education	12	12	6	5	3
OVERALL TOTAL	218	162	126	110	129
Excluding Fire Protection & Instructional Education	177	138	106	92	112

Table 5.11 (continued)

Type of Government and Function	Total Number of States*	Number of States with Increased Density or No Change			
		1972-77	1977-82	1982-87	1977-87
Moderate Density States					
Number of Full-Time Organized	13	11	8	11	11
Overall Density	13	7	5	8	9
Density in Municipalities (Overall)	(13)	(12)	(11)	(8)	(10)
Fire Protection	12	4	2	5	6
Police Protection	13	9	7	9	9
Other Functions	13	13	10	7	8
Highways	12	11	4	8	5
Sanitation	5	3	2	2	2
Public Welfare	*	*	*	*	*
Hospitals	*	*	*	*	*
(Subtotal for Municipalities)	(55)	(40)	(25)	(31)	(30)
Density in Counties (Overall)	(11)	(8)	(7)	(9)	(9)
Fire Protection	*	*	*	*	*
Police Protection	11	6	6	8	7
Other Functions	12	12	8	9	8
Highways	10	8	7	6	6
Public Welfare	9	5	5	5	9
Hospitals	8	2	5	7	8
(Subtotal for Counties)	(50)	(33)	(31)	(35)	(38)
Density in Townships (Overall)	(5)	(2)	(5)	(5)	(5)
Fire Protection	*	*	*	*	*
Other Functions	*	*	*	*	*
Highways	*	*	*	*	*
(Subtotal for Townships)	*	*	*	*	*
Density in Special Districts (Overall)	(6)	(4)	(4)	(2)	(3)
Other Functions	11	10	8	3	6
Hospitals	3	2	3	2	3
(Subtotal for Special Districts)	(14)	(12)	(11)	(5)	(9)
All except Independent School Dist.	**119**	**85**	**67**	**71**	**77**
Density in Independent School Dist.	(13)	(8)	(2)	(7)	(4)
Instructional Education	13	5	5	6	6
Non-Instructional Education	13	13	9	8	9
OVERALL TOTAL	145	103	81	85	92
Excluding Fire Protection & Instructional Education	120	94	74	74	80

*Excludes those states with fewer than 1,000 full-time employees in a type of government or 200 full-time employees in a function of government, by type of government in October 1987.

tion. Excluding independent school districts, of the 194 possible combinations for the HD states, more than half had no decline in density for each of the time periods presented: 113 (58 percent) between 1977 and 1982; 120 (62 percent) between 1977 and 1987. In the MD states, the changes were similar for the 119 possible combinations—56 percent and 65 percent respectively—although at much lower density levels.

Table 5.12 portrays for the 1977–1987 decade the details for each HD state. While density did not decline in 120 of the 194 possible combinations (excluding independent school districts), the experience varied greatly among these sixteen states. In Minnesota, Hawaii, and Delaware all relevant combinations had no declines; in Massachusetts twelve of thirteen did not fall. California had the fewest increases (2 of the possible 15), followed by Wisconsin (6 of 15), Connecticut (4 of 11), and Oregon (4 of 10). Of the 74 combinations that experienced declines, 35 were in these latter four states and six each in Washington and New York.

Thus, in a majority of circumstances in the 29 states that do not constrain local government collective bargaining, the propensity of full-time employees remained stable or increased. However, while a majority in both the HD and MD states did not decline, large density differences are evident both between these two groups of states and among the various types of local government within them. This research hypothesizes that fiscal discontent can help explain some of these differences, and that association is explored in Chapter 6.

A STRONGER VOICE: COLLECTIVE BARGAINING

The analysis to this point has focused on one important aspect of employee collective voice—the propensity of full-time employees to organize. But what was the intensity of that voice? How did it manifest itself in dealing with the government employer?

Employees talk collectively with their employers in two broad types of labor relations systems: meet-and-confer and collective bargaining. Meet-and-confer provides employees a forum to meet with management and discuss proposals affecting their employment, but in all meet-and-confer jurisdictions (Pynes and Lafferty, 1993: 107) the employer retains unilateral decision authority.

Collective bargaining, on the other hand, requires an employer to negotiate with the employees' representative. Both the union and the employer are expected to come to the table prepared to compromise and reach a settlement—to "bargain in good faith." Employers are "prevented from dictating to the employees" (Chandler, 1989: 85). They must do more than consider proposals. The employees are at the table with an equal voice in decision making about the terms and conditions of their employment. Final decisions are made jointly, and a settlement is presumed to be mutually acceptable.

Collective bargaining represents a new form of "power sharing" between sovereign authority and unelected groups (employee unions, arbitrators, etc.)

Table 5.12
Density Increases, 1977–1987: High Density States, by Government Function and Type of Government, by State

State	By Government Function and Type of Government		By Government Function		By Type of Government	
	Number Applicable (18 Possible)	Number Increased Density	Number Applicable (9 Possible)	Number Increased Density	Number Applicable (5 Possible)	Number Increased Density
Minnesota	14	14	9	8	4	4
Massachusetts	13	12	9	7	5	3
Pennsylvania	16	12	9	5	5	2
Michigan	16	11	9	4	5	3
New Jersey	16	11	9	6	5	3
New York	17	11	9	7	5	4
Hawaii	9	9	5	5	2	2
Maryland	11	7	8	6	3	1
Washington	13	7	9	5	4	3
Wisconsin	15	6	9	2	5	2
Delaware	5	5	6	4	3	3
Connecticut	11	4	8	1	4	1
Oregon	10	4	8	3	4	1
Rhode Island	8	3	6	2	2	1
Alaska	5	2	7	4	2	1
California	15	2	9	0	4	0
HD States Total	194	120	129	69	62	34

By Government Function

State	Municipality		County		Township		Special District	
	Number Applicable (7 Possible)	Number Increased Density	Number Applicable (6 Possible)	Number Increased Density	Number Applicable (3 Possible)	Number Increased Density	Number Applicable (2 Possible)	Number Increased Density
Minnesota	7	7	5	5	0	0	2	2
Massachusetts	7	7	2	2	3	3	1	0
Pennsylvania	6	4	6	6	3	2	1	0
Michigan	7	5	5	4	2	0	2	2
New Jersey	7	6	5	3	3	2	1	0
New York	7	4	6	3	3	3	1	1
Hawaii	5	5	4	4	0	0	0	0
Maryland	5	4	5	3	0	0	1	0
Washington	6	4	5	2	0	0	2	1
Wisconsin	6	0	6	5	2	1	1	0
Delaware	3	3	2	2	0	0	0	0
Connecticut	7	2	0	0	3	1	1	1
Oregon	4	2	4	1	0	0	2	1
Rhode Island	4	1	0	0	3	2	1	1
Alaska	4	2	1	0	0	0	0	0
California	7	1	6	0	0	0	2	1
HD States Total	92	57	62	40	22	14	18	9

(Troy, 1994: 63). The process itself curtails sovereign authority; it is a first step in altering the nature and practice of political governance (ibid.: 71). "Collective bargaining by public employees and the political process cannot be separated. The costs of such bargaining cannot be fully measured without taking into account the impact on the allocation of political power in the typical municipality" (Wellington and Winter, 1971: 29). Thus it is important to structure a bargaining process that does not give employee groups "a substantial competitive advantage over the other interest groups in pressing its claims" (ibid.: 49).

To adopt a collective bargaining system is to adopt an explicit way of handling organizational conflict. It is an adversarial approach that neither denies nor ends conflict; it resolves it (Dresang, 1991: 259). Once established, an array of issues must be confronted regarding the bargaining structure, including its scope, the composition of bargaining units, and impasse procedures (mediation, fact-finding, arbitration).[6]

In most instances, these voice-related labor relations systems become overlays on a complex of laws and regulations pertaining to existing merit systems. Reconciling these very different approaches to managing human resources creates problems for all concerned. The unions frequently pursue a "best of both worlds" policy "to keep the protective features of the merit system but transfer position classification, wage administration, some aspects of grievance procedure, and several other unilaterally administered personnel functions to the bargaining table" (Spero and Capozzola, 1973: 209).

Scope of Bargaining

The scope of bargaining defines those subjects that are negotiable. Some statutes are very explicit, others vague. In general, topics are classified as mandatory, permissive, or prohibited. Mandatory topics must be bargained if either side requests it. A permissive topic may be subject to bargaining if there is mutual agreement between the parties, but neither side may unilaterally insist on bargaining it. An illegal topic cannot be bargained, and any agreement on such a topic would be void and unenforceable (Pynes and Lafferty, 1993: 112–113). In the public sector, frequently there are statutes that will preempt bargaining about an issue; for example, in many jurisdictions bargaining may not supersede the provisions of a civil service law, a pension system, or their education and welfare statutes. "Some unions seek through state legislative action benefits they are unable to negotiate—pensions are one example" (Hayes, 1972: 99). Often the courts must resolve disputes pertaining to the scope of bargaining.

Many issues affect both the terms and conditions of employment and involve policy choices that frequently are determined politically (examples include class size, curriculum, teaching loads, tenure, staffing ratios, shifts). Drawing the line and defining the boundaries of management rights can involve contentious debates. There are few "legal walls to keep unions from moving into the policy field and punching holes in management's rights" (Raskin, 1972: 143). In many arenas, "collective bargaining has steadily encroached on these sovereign responsibilities" (Troy, 1994: 75).

Public sector employers tend to have more discretion in exercising their management rights than private sector employers (Pynes and Lafferty, 1993: 115). "The doctrine of the illegal delegation of power . . . is a constitutional doctrine that sometimes forbids government from sharing its powers with others. . . . [It] commands that certain discretionary decisions be made solely on the basis of a judgment of a designated official" (Wellington and Winter, 1971: 38). The authority to control the mission of an agency is generally considered to be an unlawful topic for bargaining because it involves the power of the agency to govern itself. Decisions involving the size and allocation of budgets, tax rates, levels of service, and long-term government obligations are generally considered legislative and also not subject to delegation.[7]

Membership in a Bargaining Unit

Employees eligible to join a bargaining unit select their representative according to a procedure that is usually set forth in a statute. Generally, a secret ballot election provides an employee with a choice between one or more unions and "no bargaining representation." In most jurisdictions a union is certified if it wins a majority of the votes cast in the election. Some statutes, however, require a union to receive a majority of the employees in the unit rather than simply a majority of those who vote (Coleman, 1990: 81).

A brief word about levels of participation in bargaining units. Since certain employees are excluded by statute from collective bargaining in most states, it is unlikely that a given government's bargaining unit participation rate will be 100 percent. Elected and appointed officials, board and commission members, supervisory, managerial, confidential, and part-time employees are among those frequently excluded (Pynes and Lafferty, 1993: 21).

Most public employers argue that supervisors represent management and management cannot negotiate with itself (ibid.: 22). Some governments have allowed supervisors to form a separate unit that does not include subordinates; others have not. Managerial employees are considered policy makers who should operate free from the conflict of interest that would result from their inclusion in the bargaining unit. Frequently those who work directly for managers also are excluded—for example, their support staff and policy advisors. Confidential employees work closely with those who set the employer's labor relations policies and have access to confidential information—personnel, budget, and legal staffs are examples.

Differences among the States and Types of Local Government

By 1987, 41.8 percent of full- and part-time local government employees were represented by a bargaining unit.[8] The three groups of states remain essentially the same—the high, moderate, and low density states also are the high, moderate, and low bargaining states.

Again, the national average conceals more than it reveals as it encompasses Hawaii's 89.6 percent as well as Mississippi, North Carolina, and South Carolina, where virtually no employees were members of a bargaining unit. Tables 5.13 and 5.14 provide an overview of the proportion of the employees in each state that were represented by a bargaining unit in 1987, displayed by group of states and type of local government.[9]

HD States

The sixteen high density states also were the states with the highest propensities for local government employees to be represented by a bargaining unit. In 1987, 65.2 percent of these local employees were represented, virtually the same as their 65.8 percent density. Twelve states were above 60 percent. Michigan, Minnesota, and Wisconsin were above 50 percent; Alaska was at 48 percent. Exclusive of independent school district employees (both instructional and non-instructional), the proportion was 64.8 percent, although Minnesota and Wisconsin joined Alaska at rates below 50 percent. Seventy percent of all employees represented by bargaining units worked in these sixteen states.

By type of government, the 1987 rankings were (highest to lowest): municipality, independent school district, county, township, special district. Substantial differences existed between municipalities (71.6 percent) and special districts (44.4 percent).

MD States

In 1987, 42.1 percent of the local employees in these thirteen states were represented by a bargaining unit, slightly less than this group's 46.6 percent density. On a state-by-state, government-by-government basis, the patterns were erratic, although at rates of participation well below those in the HD states. Nevada, however, was at 68 percent, placing it within the range of the HD states. Florida was at 50 percent; eight states were below 40 percent. Exclusive of independent school district employees, 31.6 percent were members of a bargaining unit; only Nevada was above 60 percent, within the range of the HD states.

The 1987 rankings by type of government differed from the HD states in that independent school districts (51.1 percent) were higher than municipalities (41.1 percent); each was substantially higher than counties and special districts.

BC States

In 1987, about 12 percent of the local employees in these 21 states were represented by a bargaining unit, reflecting the state imposed constraints on local bargaining. Only Colorado and Indiana were above 30 percent, weighted by the fact that more than one-half of the independent school district employees were members of a bargaining unit. Exclusive of school district employees, 7.5 percent were members of a bargaining unit; in fourteen states, 10 percent or less of the employees were bargaining unit members.

A Longitudinal Perspective: 1972 to 1987

What changes occurred in the use of collective bargaining during the era of fiscal discontent? The bargaining propensities are now examined for the 1970s and 1980s.

Differences among the States

Over the fifteen year period beginning in 1972, the number of full- and part-time employees represented by a bargaining unit increased by 1.1 million, three times greater than the 340,000 increase in the number that organized. The proportion of employees represented by a bargaining unit increased from 35.8 to 41.8 percent (Table 5.15).

Both the HD and MD states registered twelve percentage point increases to 65.2 and 42.1 percent respectively, as the number of represented employees increased by 670,000 in the HD states and 325,000 in the MD group. Each group had increases over the fifteen years, although the largest growth occurred between 1972 and 1977. In the BC states, the number of employees represented by a bargaining unit increased about 100,000, but the percent of represented employees remained at about 12 percent, well below the averages of the other groups.

Differences among the Types of Local Government

Table 5.13 presented the bargaining unit participation rates for the employees in the various types of local government as they existed in 1987 for each group of states. Table 5.16 presents that information for 1974,[10] 1977, 1982, and 1987.

HD States. Participation increased in virtually all types of government during each time period, although the 1974–1977 period witnessed the largest growth. There was a leveling off between 1982 and 1987; special districts declined to their 1974 level.

Between 1974 and 1982, bargaining unit representation increased from 53.9 to 66.9 percent. By 1982, two-thirds of those employed by independent school districts were members of a bargaining unit; eight years earlier less than one-half had been represented. In municipalities, almost three-quarters of the employees were unit members by 1982, a ten percentage point increase over that same eight year span. The other types of government also registered increases, but to a lesser degree.

MD States. In all cases, bargaining membership rates were substantially below those in the HD states. However, there were increases in virtually all types of government over each period; the two exceptions were independent school districts between 1977 and 1982 and special districts between 1982 and 1987. Between 1974 and 1982, representation increased from 29.4 to 40.4 percent of the employees.

Table 5.13
Full- and Part-Time Local Government Employees Represented by a Bargaining Unit, by State and Group of States, 1987

State	All Full- & Part-Time Employees	Municipality Employees	Independent School District Employees	County Employees	Township Employees	Special District Employees	All Except School District Employees
High Density States							
Hawaii	89.6	93.7	na	80.0	na	na	89.6
New Jersey	76.5	82.7	71.7	93.2	61.0	33.2	80.3
Rhode Island	76.5	85.9	<	na	68.4	<	76.4
New York	72.4	79.8	65.7	73.7	36.5	47.7	75.0
Massachusetts	67.0	65.5	60.4	42.6	70.9	65.9	67.5
California	65.5	71.4	65.7	69.3	na	38.8	65.2
Maryland	63.9	83.1	na	59.2	na	29.3	63.9
Connecticut	62.2	67.4	52.1	na	59.5	53.5	62.5
Delaware	62.3	54.6	65.7	61.1	na	<	54.3
Washington	67.8	60.6	83.8	52.0	na	44.0	52.6
Oregon	64.5	48.7	71.8	54.3	na	50.5	51.1
Pennsylvania	60.0	64.4	66.5	37.9	27.8	58.5	50.7
Michigan	50.9	60.6	51.3	52.4	8.6	41.8	50.2
Wisconsin	53.8	46.9	58.4	62.6	2.7	33.5	48.8
Alaska	48.2	55.1	na	35.3	na	na	48.2
Minnesota	58.1	38.3	81.6	47.4	<	47.8	38.7
Average	65.2	71.6	65.6	65.0	50.6	44.4	64.8
Moderate Density States							
Nevada*	68.0	71.9	75.5	60.8	<	<	60.5
Maine	47.5	62.0	51.9	<	36.2	23.2	45.5
New Hampshire	41.9	58.9	49.9	34.3	7.7	<	35.8
Illinois	39.9	39.7	44.0	38.6	0.4	33.5	35.6
Florida*	50.9	46.2	65.0	33.2	na	5.8	34.9
Montana	37.5	51.5	42.0	19.5	<	<	28.8
Ohio	37.8	42.3	46.5	13.2	5.7	32.0	26.8

State							
Iowa*	38.4	29.8	45.7	22.1	<	<	26.4
Nebraska*	36.7	34.2	45.9	13.3	<	30.6	25.7
Utah*	44.8	16.3	58.4	19.4	na	31.7	18.9
Vermont	31.1	28.3	38.7	<	4.1	<	12.6
South Dakota*	32.6	22.5	48.6	8.7	<	<	12.2
North Dakota*	23.4	5.9	49.6	2.7	<	<	2.4
Average	42.1	41.1	51.1	26.8	11.0	25.6	31.6
Bargaining Constrained States							
Tennessee*	28.6	37.1	4.2	22.9	na	4.7	28.9
New Mexico	16.9	25.6	15.0	9.2	na	<	19.9
Oklahoma	26.7	27.1	32.6	0	na	0	17.8
Missouri	23.3	19.1	28.7	2.1	0.6	24.9	15.6
Indiana	34.3	25.5	51.0	0.6	na	14.2	13.1
Kentucky	16.0	15.7	17.5	4.2	0	26.6	13.0
Kansas*	24.3	17.1	34.6	3.8	na	7.7	10.0
Colorado	33.1	10.8	51.9	1.5	na	22.2	9.9
Alabama*	5.3	13.2	3.3	1.4	na	2.0	7.7
West Virginia	3.4	10.6	1.7	0.1	na	14.2	7.3
Idaho	27.7	13.7	41.7	1.2	na	6.7	6.9
Louisiana*	10.3	10.9	13.0	0.8	na	<	6.4
Arizona*	25.4	4.2	40.4	0	na	19.3	4.9
Arkansas*	9.4	8.1	12.2	0.2	na	<	4.6
Texas*	1.8	3.8	0.9	0.2	na	9.9	3.4
Wyoming*	21.9	7.8	32.9	0	na	0	3.1
Georgia*	2.1	1.3	1.4	0	na	6.7	3.0
Mississippi*	0.3	1.7	0	0	na	<	0.8
Virginia*	0.1	0	na	0	na	4.9	0.1
North Carolina*	0	0	na	0	na	0	0
South Carolina*	0.1	0	0.1	0	na	0	0
Average	11.8	11.8	16.5	3.0	0.3	9.9	7.5
All States	41.8	47.5	44.1	32.7	42.1	28.0	39.7

*Right-to-Work state; na = not applicable; < = fewer than 1,000 full-time employees in the state.

Table 5.14
Full- and Part-Time Local Government Employees Represented by a Bargaining Unit, 1987: Number of States, by Group of States

Percent Represented	NO STATE BARGAINING CONSTRAINTS				STATE BARGAINING CONSTRAINTS	
	High Density		Moderate Density		Low Density States	
	All Employees	Excluding Independent School Districts	All Employees	Excluding Independent School Districts	All Employees	Excluding Independent School Districts
90 Under 100%	0	0				
80 Under 90%	1	2				
70 Under 80%	3	2				
60 Under 70%	8	4	1	1		
50 Under 60%	3	5	1	0		
40 Under 50%	1	2	4	1		
30 Under 40%		1	6	3	2	
20 Under 30%			1	4	7	2
10 Under 20%				3	3	5
Under 10%				1	9	14
Average	65.2%	64.8%	42.1%	31.6%	11.8%	7.5%

Table 5.15

Full- and Part-Time Local Government Employees Represented by a Bargaining Unit, by Group of States, 1974, 1977, 1982, and 1987

Year	High Density States			Moderate Density States		
	Number	Represented	Percent	Number	Represented	Percent
1974	4,187,517	2,256,636	53.9	1,651,834	485,197	29.4
1977	4,298,576	2,700,034	62.8	1,729,892	691,336	40.0
1982	4,232,065	2,830,462	66.9	1,746,961	705,342	40.4
1987	4,493,117	2,927,714	65.2	1,924,615	810,855	42.1

Year	Bargaining Constrained States			All States*		
	Number	Represented	Percent	Number	Represented	Percent
1974	2,701,124	319,217	11.8	8,540,475	3,061,050	35.8
1977	3,188,910	433,006	13.6	9,217,378	3,824,376	41.5
1982	3,220,771	401,042	12.5	9,199,797	3,936,846	42.8
1987	3,530,452	418,309	11.8	9,948,184	4,156,878	41.8

*Excludes the District of Columbia.

BC States. For the entire period, the participation rates remained stable at their relatively low levels, reflecting the state imposed bargaining constraints.

State-by-State Differences

As with density, the group averages may conceal important information. Therefore, the various collective bargaining propensities are examined below on a state-by-state basis. Since the BC states have constrained bargaining, they are not included here. Appendix 3 presents the percent of full- and part-time employees represented by a bargaining unit for each state and type of local government for four different years—1974, 1977, 1982, and 1987.

HD States. The sixteen high density states also were the high bargaining states over the fifteen year period. However, unlike overall density, which remained stable between 1972 and 1987, the percent of employees represented by a bargaining unit increased from 53.9 to 65.2 percent between 1974 and 1987. Fourteen states had an increase; only Alaska and Michigan experienced declines.

For the eight years which began in 1974, all states except Hawaii experienced

Table 5.16
Percentage of Full- and Part-Time Employees Represented by a Bargaining Unit, by Group of States and Type of Government, 1974, 1977, 1982, and 1987

Type of Government	High Density				Moderate Density			
	1974	1977	1982	1987	1974	1977	1982	1987
Municipality	64.0	70.7	74.4	71.6	24.4	29.5	36.1	41.1
Independent School	49.1	61.4	67.9	65.6	38.5	54.8	51.3	51.1
County	57.0	62.7	64.8	65.0	12.1	15.9	20.9	26.8
Township	33.6	45.5	45.0	50.6	<	<	<	<
Special District	43.4	48.2	51.6	44.4	19.8	23.5	29.5	25.6
All Governments	53.9	62.8	66.9	65.2	29.4	40.0	40.4	42.1

Type of Government	Low Density				All States			
	1974	1977	1982	1987	1974	1977	1982	1987
Municipality	12.1	11.6	12.2	11.8	43.1	43.7	48.4	47.5
Independent School	16.3	21.8	17.8	16.5	35.8	46.4	46.1	44.1
County	3.8	1.3	3.2	3.0	29.0	30.1	31.9	32.7
Township	<	<	<	<	28.0	39.0	38.9	42.1
Special District	3.9	8.2	8.4	9.9	24.1	28.2	30.7	28.0
All Governments	11.8	13.6	12.5	11.8	35.8	41.5	42.8	41.8

< = Fewer than 10,000 full-time employees.

an increase in the overall percentage of employees represented by a bargaining unit; Hawaii, however, remained stable at a relatively high 82 percent.

Between 1982 and 1987, bargaining unit representation plateaued; five states experienced overall declines—Alaska, California, Michigan, New York, and Rhode Island. Special district rates declined in nine states.

There are some interesting anomalies among the propensities to bargain by type of government—a low but stable level in Minnesota's municipalities; levels below 50 percent in Oregon's and Wisconsin's municipalities as well as in Alaska's and Pennsylvania's counties; large declines in Wisconsin's special districts and Connecticut's independent school districts.

An analysis of each state on the basis of each type of local government for the various periods between 1974 and 1987 reveals that in every instance except one (special districts between 1982 and 1987), a majority of states had an increase in the percent of their employees represented by a bargaining unit (Table 5.17). Between 1977 and 1987, increases were registered in about two-thirds of the possible cases (41 of 62) (Table 5.18).

MD States. The percent of employees represented by a bargaining unit increased in these thirteen states from 29.4 to 42.1 percent between 1974 and 1987 (Appendix 3). No state experienced a decline. Between 1977 and 1987, there were increases in 35 of the 46 possible cases, albeit to levels well below those in the HD states (Tables 5.17 and 5.18). The smallest proportion of states had an increase in their independent school and special districts.

Number of Bargaining Units

Accompanying this increase in the propensity of local government employees to be represented by a bargaining unit was a proliferation in the number of bargaining units—an 80 percent increase from about 19,700 in 1974 to over 35,300 in 1987.

Despite the fact that more than one-half of the organized workers are members of three national organizations,[11] local government employee organizations are highly decentralized. This decentralization is one factor that differentiates the American public sector from its private sector counterparts as well as from the public sector in other democratic societies. Since labor laws are set on a state-by-state basis, the landscape is a broad array of organizations, from those with whom employers need not bargain to full-fledged collective bargaining organizations with diverse types of impasse resolution.

In most states with bargaining laws, bargaining unit determination is based on history, a statutory definition, a community of interest, or some combination of these factors (Haskell, 1982, in Coleman, 1990: 91). When based on history, bargaining is superimposed on previously established units. Using statutory criteria is the most common approach (Coleman, 1990: 91); these criteria usually reflect some mix of government authority, avoidance of fragmentation, and community-of-interest standards (Gershenfeld, 1985, in Coleman, 1990: 91). States that have not clarified the community-of-interest criterion depend on the courts or a third-party entity to operationalize this standard (Pynes and Lafferty, 1993: 18).

Local government units generally are either a broad unit that includes most, if not all, employees of an agency or a unit based on occupation. Most public sector employers and many employee organizations prefer larger, more comprehensive bargaining units (Coleman, 1990: 93).

A number of arguments are offered for broad bargaining units. As many policies, such as pensions, hours worked, vacation, and working conditions, are uniform for a large segment of the workforce, negotiation with separate units on these matters makes little sense. It also is thought best to limit the number of groups competing for resources and thereby to avoid inter-union competition

Table 5.17
Number of States Having an Increase in the Percentage of Local Government Employees Represented by a Bargaining Unit, by Type of Government, Selected Time Periods

High Density States

Time Period	All Governments (16 Possible)	Municipalities (16 Possible)	Independent School Districts (12 Possible)	Counties (14 Possible)	Townships (8 Possible)	Special Districts (12 Possible)
1974-1977	15	11	11	13	8	10
1977-1982	12	9	8	11	6	7
1982-1987	9	12	7	7	6	3
1974-1982	15	11	11	13	8	9
1977-1987	11	10	9	12	6	4
1974-1987	14	12	10	11	8	8

Moderate Density States

Time Period	All Governments (13 Possible)	Municipalities (13 Possible)	Independent School Districts (13 Possible)	Counties (11 Possible)	Townships (5 Possible)	Special Districts (6 Possible)
1974-1977	13	12	12	6	5	4
1977-1982	8	9	5	6	5	5
1982-1987	7	6	4	9	4	3
1974-1982	13	12	13	7	5	6
1977-1987	9	10	6	11	5	3
1974-1987	13	11	12	8	5	6

Table 5.18

Change in Percentage of Employees Represented by a Bargaining Unit, 1977–1987, by Group of States, Government Function, and Type of Government, by State

State	By Type of Government		Change in % of Employees Represented by a Bargaining Unit (1977-1987)				
	Number Applicable	Number with an Increase or No Change	Municipality	Independent School Districts	County	Township	Special Districts
High Density States							
Alaska	2	0	D	na	D	na	na
California	4	1	D	I	D	na	D
Connecticut	4	2	D	I	na	D	I
Delaware	3	3	I	I	I	na	na
Hawaii	2	2	I	na	I	na	na
Maryland	3	2	D	na	I	na	D
Massachusetts	5	3	D	I	I	I	D
Michigan	5	1	D	D	I	D	D
Minnesota	4	3	I	I	I	na	D
New Jersey	5	4	I	I	I	I	D
New York	5	4	I	D	I	I	I
Oregon	4	4	I	I	I	I	D
Pennsylvania	5	3	I	D	I	I	D
Rhode Island	2	2	I	na	na	I	na
Washington	4	4	I	I	I	na	I
Wisconsin	5	3	D	I	I	I	D
HD States Total	62	41	10	9	12	6	4
Moderate Density States							
Florida	4	4	I	I	I	na	I
Illinois	5	4	I	D	I	I	I
Iowa	3	2	I	D	I	na	na
Maine	4	3	I	D	na	I	I
Montana	3	3	I	I	I	na	na
Nebraska	4	2	I	D	I	na	D
Nevada	3	3	I	I	I	I	na
New Hampshire	4	4	I	I	I	na	na
North Dakota	3	2	D	I	I	na	na
Ohio	5	2	D	D	I	I	D
South Dakota	3	3	I	I	I	na	na
Utah	4	1	D	D	I	na	D
Vermont	3	2	I	D	na	I	na
MD States Total	46	35	10	6	11	5	3

na = not applicable; D = decline; I = increase or no change.

where unions try for an agreement that either equals (''me-tooism''), or sur-
passes (''leap-frogging'') the gains of another union.

One of a union's major functions is determining a bargaining package that
will be acceptable to the average member. ''Some of the most important bargaining under unionism goes on *inside* the union, where the desires of workers
with disparate interests are weighed in a political process that decides the union's
positions at the bargaining table'' (Freeman and Medoff, 1979: 84). This internal
bargaining can be greatly affected by the composition of a bargaining unit. One
having a broad cross-section of members with diverse agendas can make this
task especially difficult for employee representatives, but may make the bargaining less difficult for management.

The reality, however, is that most local government bargaining involves relatively small, fragmented units. New York City has more than 100 units, although at one time it had over 400. While there likely are many reasons for
fragmentation, one is that most statutes give the initiative for bargaining to the
employees. Employee organizations define whom they wish to represent and it
usually is easier to organize a small, compact group—one occupation or work
site (Coleman, 1990: 93). The vagueness of the community-of-interest criterion
encourages fragmentation since small units pass most tests under that standard
(ibid.: 94).

For the five years between 1977 and 1982,[12] three-quarters of the increase in
the number of bargaining units (2,778 of 3,690) took place in those with fewer
than 25 members; this was true for all types of local governments. By 1982,
over 40 percent (13,872) of the units had fewer than 25 members; more than
three-quarters of the units (25,256) had fewer than 100 members. Jerry Wurf's
goal in 1962 ''to strengthen local autonomy'' (Goulden, 1982: 81) had been
achieved.

Table 5.19 depicts the growth in the number of bargaining units that took
place between 1974 and 1987. As with the other collective voice indicators,
there are wide variations among the groups of states and types of local government.

HD States. Nationally, three-quarters of the 35,300 bargaining units in 1987
were in these sixteen states. The number of units rose from 14,708 in 1974 to
26,317 in 1987, a 79 percent increase. All types of government had large increases, more than doubling in counties, townships, and special districts; municipalities and independent school districts had increases of 62 and 60 percent
respectively. For the eight years ending in 1982, the number of units increased
by almost 9,700.

MD States. The number of bargaining units increased in these states as well—
from 3,430 in 1974 to 6,735 in 1987. While this was almost a doubling in
number, it represented less than 20 percent of the national total, far fewer than
in the HD states.

BC States. About 6 percent of the bargaining units are in these states. Virtually
all of the growth in the number of units occurred between 1974 and 1977. Over

Table 5.19
Number of Local Government Bargaining Units, by Group of States and Type of Government, 1974, 1977, 1982, and 1987

Type of Government	High Density States				Moderate Density States				Low Density States			
	1974	1977	1982	1987	1974	1977	1982	1987	1974	1977	1982	1987
Municipality	4,022	5,574	6,298	6,513	926	1,310	1,581	1,748	471	583	567	578
Independent School	7,017	9,942	10,879	11,220	2,152	3,532	3,608	3,769	971	1,393	1,431	1,328
County	1,493	2,235	2,799	3,382	131	262	356	568	59	95	146	133
Township	1,651	2,725	3,257	3,935	106	187	273	375	1	12	2	4
Special District	525	938	1,165	1,267	115	152	229	275	68	92	106	110
All Governments	14,708	21,414	24,398	26,317	3,430	5,443	6,047	6,735	1,570	2,175	2,252	2,153

60 percent of the bargaining units represent employees of independent school districts, where these states have imposed fewer constraints.

Collective Bargaining or Meet-and-Confer

Additional insights into the employees' pursuit of a collective voice strategy can be garnered by examining whether they moved from a meet-and-confer system to the more formal and rigorous collective bargaining process. Their voice would become stronger as they became equals at the bargaining table. Unfortunately that information is not available, but the Bureau of the Census does provide data for the labor relations policies adopted by the various types of local government, and those changes are explored here.

Governmental Labor Relations Policies

In 1972, a labor relations policy covering either collective bargaining or meet-and-confer had been enacted in 10,636 local governments. By 1987, 14,379 governments had done so; this represented 27 percent of the local governments employing at least one full-time employee (Table 5.20).

HD States. The number of governments adopting a labor relations policy increased 1,081 between 1972 and 1977 and an additional 997 over the subsequent decade, for a 1987 total of 8,741 governments or 44.2 percent of the governments with at least one full-time employee. There was wide variation among the various types of government (20 percent for special districts and over 90 percent for counties).

MD States. By 1987, 3,878 of these local governments had adopted a policy, an increase of 1,361 over the 1972 level. The largest increase (966) occurred between 1972 and 1977; during the subsequent decade the increase was 395. While this group did experience increases, the various proportions are substantially below those of the HD states.

A Shift to Collective Bargaining

While the number of governments with adopted labor relations policies increased, two very different changes were taking place over the 1972–1987 period. Collective bargaining increased, while meet-and-confer declined.

HD States. Between 1972 and 1987 the number of governments engaged in collective bargaining in these sixteen states increased more than 3,000 to 7,993 (Table 5.20). Over this same period, those using meet-and-confer declined more than 2,500 to 3,475 (Table 5.20).

About two-thirds of the shift to collective bargaining occurred between 1972 and 1977; the balance took place over the subsequent decade (collective bargaining increased 956; meet-and-confer declined 713). Again there was great variation among the types of government. The 1987 rankings for the proportion of governments with full-time employees having a collective bargaining policy was (highest to lowest): county, independent school district, municipality, township, and special district.

All types of government experienced declines in adopted meet-and-confer policies and, by 1987, fewer than one-third of each type had such a policy.

MD States. These thirteen states also witnessed a shift to collective bargaining, but to a lesser degree than the HD states. Between 1972 and 1987, 1,929 governments enacted collective bargaining policies, while almost 1,000 left meet-and-confer (Table 5.20). By 1987, however, the proportion of governments engaged in collective bargaining in these states was substantially below that in the HD states for all government types: counties, 31 percent compared to 89 percent; independent school districts, 51 compared to 82 percent; municipalities, 15 compared to 36 percent; and special districts, 6 compared to 15 percent.

State-by-State Differences

The growth in collective bargaining and the accompanying decline in meet-and-confer was not universal within each group of states, but it did happen in a majority of states. As reflected in Table 5.21, a majority of both the HD and MD states experienced increases in collective bargaining policies and decreases in meet-and-confer for each type of local government.

SUMMARY

The analysis presented in this chapter suggests several patterns regarding the propensity of local government employees to organize and bargain collectively.

Regarding the propensity to organize, density, the following patterns emerge.

First, density differences among the various functions of local government lend support to the existence of occupational communities, at least for certain employees, most notably those providing fire protection, instructional education, and police protection.

Second, there are three groups of states with markedly different propensities for their local government employees to organize. Legislative constraints on local collective bargaining have been enacted in one group of 21 BC states, but there are no constraints in either of the other two groups—the sixteen HD states and the thirteen MD states.

The densities in the HD states are substantially higher than in the MD states despite having the same statutory environment for local government collective bargaining. Further, the HD state densities were the highest when compared to other groups of American employees in both the public and private sectors. Densities in the HD states are similar to those in many Atlantic community countries.

To summarize 1987 densities: overall private sector 13.4 percent; local government in the 21 BC states 26.1 percent; public sector 36 percent; full-time state government 39.7 percent; full-time local government 47.5 percent; local

Table 5.20
Labor Relations Policy, by Type of Policy, Group of States, and Type of Government, 1972, 1977, 1982, and 1987

Labor Relations Policy
Number of Governments

Type of Government	High Density				Moderate Density				Low Density			
	1972	1977	1982	1987	1972	1977	1982	1987	1972	1977	1982	1987
Municipality	1,446	1,629	1,787	1,930	332	509	573	666	213	244	242	297
Independent School	3,801	4,195	4,109	4,254	1,970	2,626	2,535	2,594	1,106	1,439	1,193	1,199
County	387	465	495	515	73	138	183	245	74	62	104	131
Township	624	869	1,016	1,209	64	107	147	197	0	5	4	7
Special District	405	586	734	833	78	103	133	176	63	73	85	126
Total	6,663	7,744	8,141	8,741	2,517	3,483	3,571	3,878	1,456	1,823	1,628	1,760

Percent of Governments with Full-Time Employees

Type of Government	High Density				Moderate Density				Low Density			
	1972	1977	1982	1987	1972	1977	1982	1987	1972	1977	1982	1987
Municipality	na	36.1	39.8	41.6	na	13.8	15.3	17.2	na	3.9	3.6	4.4
Independent School	na	81.3	78.7	83.9	na	54.8	54.8	56.8	na	29.4	24.4	24.9
County	na	82.0	87.3	90.8	na	19.6	26.1	34.9	na	3.5	5.9	7.4
Township	na	18.5	23.7	22.7	<	<	<	<	<	<	<	<
Special District	na	17.9	23.5	19.9	na	5.6	9.7	7.4	na	2.2	3.1	2.6
All Governments	na	42.5	46.0	44.2	na	24.9	27.6	26.3	na	10.9	9.9	9.3

Collective Bargaining Policy: Number of Governments

Type of Government	High Density				Moderate Density				Low Density			
	1972	1977	1982	1987	1972	1977	1982	1987	1972	1977	1982	1987
Municipality	2,899	3,975	4,036	4,134	1,155	2,070	2,204	2,336	324	664	762	740
Independent School	923	1,362	1,537	1,649	203	412	496	584	96	156	163	182
County	316	419	481	503	26	109	161	216	24	29	66	81
Township	590	837	983	1,086	61	97	138	148	0	4	2	2
Special District	239	444	576	621	41	79	110	131	20	40	45	55
Total	4,967	7,037	7,613	7,993	1,486	2,767	3,109	3,415	464	893	1,038	1,060
Percent of Governments with Full-Time Employees												
Municipality	na	77.1	77.5	81.6	na	43.2	47.6	51.2	na	13.6	15.6	15.4
Independent School	na	30.2	34.2	35.5	na	11.1	13.2	15.1	na	2.5	2.4	2.7
County	na	73.9	84.8	88.7	na	15.5	23.0	30.7	na	1.6	3.7	4.6
Township	na	17.8	22.3	20.4	<	<	<	<	na	<	<	<
Special District	na	13.5	18.4	14.9	na	4.3	8.0	5.5	na	1.2	1.7	1.1
All Governments	na	38.6	43.0	40.4	na	19.7	24.1	23.1	na	5.3	6.3	5.6

Meet-and-Confer Policy: Number of Governments

Type of Government	High Density				Moderate Density				Low Density			
	1972	1977	1982	1987	1972	1977	1982	1987	1972	1977	1982	1987
Municipality	3,564	2,130	1,538	1,617	1,799	1,474	1,102	852	1,080	1,150	800	747
Independent School	1,159	973	960	801	302	269	298	225	218	169	155	176
County	337	230	273	186	64	83	90	65	76	49	71	84
Township	556	504	519	489	45	50	72	87	0	3	2	5
Special District	403	351	424	382	61	57	64	65	57	42	59	98
Total	6,019	4,188	3,714	3,475	2,271	1,933	1,626	1,294	1,431	1,413	1,087	1,110
Percent of Governments with Full-Time Employees												
Municipality	na	41.3	29.5	31.9	na	30.8	23.8	18.7	na	23.5	16.3	15.5
Independent School	na	21.6	21.4	17.3	na	7.3	7.9	5.8	na	2.7	2.3	2.6
County	na	40.6	48.2	32.8	na	11.8	12.9	9.3	na	2.8	4.0	4.8
Township	na	10.7	12.1	9.2	<	<	<	<	na	<	<	<
Special District	na	10.7	13.6	9.1	na	3.1	4.7	2.7	na	1.3	2.2	2.0
All Governments	na	23.0	21.0	17.6	na	13.8	12.6	8.8	na	8.5	6.6	5.9

na = not available; < = fewer than 10,000 full-time employees.

Data Source: U.S. Department of Commerce, Bureau of the Census (June 1991, May 1985, October 1979, November 1974a).

Table 5.21
Change in Number of Governments with a Labor Relations Policy, by Type of
Policy, Group of States, and Type of Government, by State, 1977–1987

State	Municipality		Independent School		County	
	Collective Bargaining	Meet-and-Confer	Collective Bargaining	Meet-and-Confer	Collective Bargaining	Meet-and-Confer
High Density States						
Alaska	0	(6)	na	na	0	(1)
California	41	(56)	137	(307)	39	(6)
Connecticut	5	(4)	2	(3)	na	na
Delaware	0	2	(7)	(5)	0	(1)
Hawaii	0	0	na	na	1	0
Maryland	3	0	na	na	3	(5)
Massachusetts	1	10	13	1	0	2
Michigan	27	(13)	(52)	(50)	15	(1)
Minnesota	30	(26)	52	39	8	(8)
New Jersey	42	13	14	(56)	0	(7)
New York	30	11	(20)	32	0	11
Oregon	23	(2)	31	(60)	0	(5)
Pennsylvania	18	(66)	(45)	(18)	6	3
Rhode Island	0	4	<	<	na	na
Washington	25	(6)	10	3	1	(12)
Wisconsin	42	133	23	(90)	11	(14)
HD States Total	287	(172)	158	(514)	84	(44)
Number of States with an Increase	(12 of 16)	(5 of 16)	(8 of 12)	(4 of 12)	(8 of 14)	(3 of 14)
Moderate Density States						
Florida	44	5	(3)	(8)	13	3
Illinois	29	(10)	119	(220)	26	(5)
Iowa	22	6	35	(92)	27	0
Maine	2	(9)	9	(18)	<	<
Montana	0	(1)	38	(53)	3	(5)
Nebraska	8	1	43	(118)	8	(3)
Nevada	1	3	3	(3)	1	(4)
New Hampshire	1	(5)	18	(9)	3	2
North Dakota	0	(2)	(2)	7	0	(1)
Ohio	56	(41)	1	(44)	23	(6)
South Dakota	3	0	(3)	(49)	(6)	0
Utah	3	11	2	(8)	1	1
Vermont	3	(2)	6	(7)	<	<
MD States Total	172	(44)	266	(622)	99	(18)
Number of States with an Increase	(11 of 13)	(5 of 13)	(10 of 13)	(1 of 13)	(9 of 11)	(3 of 11)

Table 5.21 (continued)

State	Township Collective Bargaining	Township Meet-and-Confer	Special District Collective Bargaining	Special District Meet-and-Confer	All Governments Collective Bargaining	All Governments Meet-and-Confer
High Density States						
Alaska	na	na	na	na	0	(7)
California	na	na	50	44	267	(325)
Connecticut	10	(20)	9	1	26	(26)
Delaware	na	na	<	<	(7)	(4)
Hawaii	na	na	na	na	1	0
Maryland	na	na	0	(2)	6	(7)
Massachusetts	75	(14)	15	0	104	(1)
Michigan	5	(12)	19	6	14	(70)
Minnesota	<	<	2	1	92	6
New Jersey	36	(2)	7	4	99	(48)
New York	36	1	2	5	48	60
Oregon	na	na	16	(2)	70	(69)
Pennsylvania	81	22	12	(19)	72	(78)
Rhode Island	4	0	<	<	4	4
Washington	na	na	34	(8)	70	(23)
Wisconsin	3	6	6	2	85	(129)
HD States Total	250	(19)	172	32	951	(713)
Number of States with an Increase	(8 of 8)	(3 of 8)	(11 of 12)	(7 of 12)	(14 of 16)	(3 of 16)
Moderate Density States						
Florida	na	na	13	(4)	67	(4)
Illinois	3	12	15	10	192	(213)
Iowa	<	<	<	<	84	(86)
Maine	10	(8)	7	1	28	(34)
Montana	<	<	<	<	42	(59)
Nebraska	<	<	3	(2)	62	(122)
Nevada	<	<	<	<	3	(4)
New Hampshire	10	6	<	<	34	(4)
North Dakota	<	<	<	<	(2)	8
Ohio	26	17	12	(4)	118	(78)
South Dakota	<	<	<	<	(6)	(50)
Utah	na	na	(1)	2	5	6
Vermont	2	9	<	<	11	0
MD States Total	51	36	49	3	638	(640)
Number of States with an Increase	(5 of 5)	(4 of 5)	(5 of 6)	(4 of 6)	(11 of 13)	(2 of 13)

na = not applicable; < = fewer than 1,000 full-time employees statewide.

127

government in the thirteen moderate density MD states 46.6 percent; and local government in the sixteen high density HD states 65.8 percent.

Third, there are consistent density differences among the various types of local government. A general pattern can be observed (highest to lowest): (1) dependent school district, (2) independent school district, (3) municipality, (4) township, (5) special district, and (6) county. These differences maintain the patterns identified for the nine functional categories as well as the three groups of states.

Fourth, over the fifteen year period that began in 1972, densities in the HD and MD states remained relatively stable at about 65 and 45 percent respectively, although the number of organized employees increased in each group. There were no major changes in these groups either by government function or type of local government over this period of time.

Fifth, for the same fifteen year period the overall decline in local government density is accounted for by the BC states in which density declined from 42 to 26 percent. These 21 states had declines in all government types and in virtually all functions.

Regarding the propensity to bargain collectively, the following patterns emerge.

First, ranking the states on the basis of their local bargaining propensities provides virtually the same three groups as those based on density. Only Nevada, not one of the sixteen high density states, was among the highest bargaining states. Excluding independent school district employees, propensities in the HD states were twice those of the MD states.

Second, unlike density, the bargaining propensities increased between 1974 and 1987 in both the HD and MD states as summarized below:

	Density		Bargaining Unit Representation	
	1972	1987	1974	1987
HD States	65.7	65.8	53.9	65.2
MD States	44.1	46.6	29.4	42.1
BC States	42.2	26.1	11.8	11.8
All States	54.1	47.4	35.8	41.8

Third, increases were realized in all types of local government in the HD and MD states between 1974 and 1987. This suggests that the employees moved to a stronger form of collective voice and sought to become equals at the bargaining table.

Fourth, as with density, there were substantial differences in bargaining propensity among the various types of local government. A general, albeit not perfect, pattern can be discerned in the HD states (highest to lowest): municipality, independent school district, county, township, and special district. A similar pattern is evident in the MD states, except that municipalities and independent school districts changed rankings.

Fifth, the number of bargaining units almost doubled between 1974 and 1987 in both the HD and MD states. That growth occurred in units that represented relatively few employees, mainly less than 100. However, more than three-quarters of all bargaining units in 1987 were in the sixteen HD states.

Sixth, there is a pattern of movement to a more intensive use of employee collective voice as local government labor relations policy moved away from meet-and-confer to a more voice-intensive collective bargaining policy in both the HD and MD states.

Regarding the propensities to organize and bargain on a state-by-state basis, the following patterns emerge for the 1972–1987 period.

First, in both the HD and MD states, density changed very little, but the propensity to bargain increased in each by 12 percentage points to 65 and 42 percent respectively.

Second, in the HD states, neither density nor the propensity to bargain declined in a majority of the possible combinations of government function and type of local government. Two-thirds of the relevant combinations (41 of 62) had a constant or increasing bargaining propensity between 1977 and 1987. Over 60 percent of the relevant density combinations (120 of 194) did not decline over that same decade.

Third, in the MD states, there were similar increases in the relevant bargaining and density combinations, but to levels well below those in the HD states. Excluding independent school district employees, the 1987 bargaining propensity of the thirteen MD states was one-half that of the sixteen HD states (65 versus 32 percent).

Finally, a consistent, albeit not perfect, *ranking based on type of local government* emerges for the various indicators of the use of collective voice by the employees. Municipalities and independent school districts are consistently among the highest, while townships and special districts are among the lowest. The 1987 rankings for the HD and MD states are presented in Table 5.22.

What may help explain these differences in density and bargaining unit representation? Occupational communities are important. State imposed bargaining environments also are a factor. But what explains the differences between the HD and MD states, which have the same statutory environments? Further, what explains the differences between the various types of local government within a state? Why are municipality and independent school district rates consistently among the highest? Why are special district rates consistently at such low levels?

Are these varying levels of employee collective voice related to the voice strategy used by the taxpayers? Did the taxpayers' voice, fiscal discontent, intensify the need for local government employees to maintain a level of collective voice in the budgeting process, as hypothesized in this research? There has been only brief mention (for example, Lewin, 1986; Valletta, 1989), but no systematic analysis, of any explicit relationship between these two changes, which have

Table 5.22
Rankings of Employee Collective Voice Indicators, by Type of Government and Group of States, 1987

Type of Government	Density	Represented by a Bargaining Unit	Increase in Number of Bargaining Units (1974-1987)	Percent of Governments with Collective Bargaining
High Density States				
Municipality	1	1	2	3
Independent School	1	2	1	2
County	3	2	4	1
Township	4	4	3	4
Special District	5	5	5	5
Moderate Density States				
Municipality	2	2	2	3
Independent School	1	1	1	1
County	4	3	3	2
Township	<	<	<	<
Special District	3	4	4	4

< = Fewer than 10,000 full-time local government employees.

had major ramifications for many American local governments. This relationship is explored in Chapter 6.

NOTES

1. In October 1987, 39.5 percent of all local government employees were members of an employee organization. For the 7.8 million who worked full-time, the rate was 47.4 percent, compared to 10.5 percent for the 2.2 million part-time employees.

2. The Bureau of the Census classifies employees according to the major function or activity of the agency, office, or other organizational entity in which the individual is employed. The police protection function, for example, includes both the sworn officers and the civilian employees in the agencies that provide that service.

3. These 59,497 governments include 27,324 special districts, 15,446 townships, 13,896 municipalities, 2,730 school districts, and 101 counties.

4. Introducing additional classifications reduces the size of the data elements. This analysis does not consider any category with fewer than 10,000 full-time employees, thereby eliminating about 1.1 percent (90,170) of the 1987 full-time employment. Appendix 2 provides details.

5. The first comprehensive data are available for 1972.

6. In mediation, a neutral third-party participates in the negotiation process and tries to assist the parties in reaching an agreement. In fact-finding, problem issues are placed before a third party, who conducts a hearing and makes non-binding recommendations. In arbitration, a third-party, unaccountable to the voters, makes a decision binding on the parties (Pynes and Lafferty, 1993: 161).

7. A 1988 survey conducted by the International City Management Association found that 91 percent of the 824 cities reporting had a management rights clause in at least one contract with public employee unions or associations (Chandler, 1989: 93). These clauses pertained to the following matters: determining mission, policies, budget, and general operations (87 percent); determining the size and composition of the workforce (85 percent); policies regarding disciplinary action (84 percent); setting levels of service and standards (83 percent); recruitment and promotion procedures (80 percent); job classification (68 percent); and contracting (56 percent).

8. Census data is not reported separately for full-time employees; however, based on the density data and the fact that many bargaining units explicitly exclude part-time employees, a reasonable assumption would be that the rate for full-time employees would not be lower, and could be somewhat higher, than the combined rate.

9. The Bureau of the Census does not report collective bargaining data by function of government.

10. The Bureau of the Census did not report this data until 1974.

11. AFSCME, National Education Association (NEA), and American Federation of Teachers (AFT).

12. These are the only years for which the Bureau of the Census reports this data.

6

When Voices Meet

As described in Chapter 5, there were large differences in the use of collective voice by local government employees among three groups of states. In 1987, 65 percent of the employees in the sixteen HD states were represented by a bargaining unit compared to 42 percent in the thirteen MD states and 12 percent in the 21 BC states. When independent school district employees are excluded, the differences are even larger—65, 32, and 7.5 percent respectively. The average densities were similarly disparate—59, 34, and 12 percent excluding instructional education and fire protection employees. Large variations in both bargaining unit representation and density among the various types of local government within each group of states also were delineated.

The various propensities to organize and bargain in the HD states were markedly higher than those in the MD states despite having the same statutory environments for collective bargaining. Those in the HD states were similar to those in the public sector in Austria, Canada, and Switzerland and above those in West Germany, Italy, the Netherlands, and France (refer to Table 4.1). Further, the propensities for the employees in certain local government functions and types of government were higher than for others.

Why have the Americans who work for the local governments in these states chosen collective voice at rates more akin to those of many of their European and Canadian counterparts than to those of most of the 130 million workers in the American civilian labor force?

What influences might help explain the very different levels of employee collective voice? The previous chapter concluded that occupational communities and state imposed bargaining environments are important. This research hypothesizes that fiscal discontent plays a role as well. Other statewide influences also might be hypothesized, among them: political culture, political ideology, or a state's propensity to innovate and accept change. This chapter examines the fiscal discontent hypothesis in detail, but it begins with a review of these alternative explanations.

ALTERNATIVE HYPOTHESES

The observed differences in the use of employee collective voice may be explained in part by differences in political culture, political ideology, or public innovation. Each is examined using the following: Elazar's groupings (1984) to represent political culture, Piskulich's conservatism index (1992: 69) to represent political ideology, and Walker's innovation scores (1971: 358) to represent the relative speed with which states adopt innovations.

In general, the BC states are traditionalistic, ideologically the most conservative, and among the least innovative states. The HD states are individualistic or moralistic, the least conservative, and among the most innovative. The MD states also are individualistic or moralistic, but they are evenly divided ideologically and run the gamut with regard to innovation.

Political culture. Frequently a region will be used in political science "as a surrogate for a common culture, often attributed to the unique historical, economic, or demographic composition of large areas of the nation" (Erikson, McIver, and Wright, 1987: 797). Political culture is "the particular pattern or orientation to political action in which each political system is imbedded" (Elazar, 1966: 84). It can be "an attractive but elusive way of characterizing differences between states, regions, and localities" (Roeder, 1994: 17). Elazar's mapping "is forthrightly comparative, but it too is largely impressionistic in its assignment of contemporary cultural influences" (Erikson, McIver, and Wright, 1987: 797). However, it "calls attention to differences in public values, attitudes, and beliefs across state boundaries, suggesting the existence of distinct state electorates" (Roeder, 1994: 17).

Regarding a hypothesis that the disparities among the states in the use of collective voice by their local government employees are based upon differences in political culture, there does seem to be an association between a state's political culture and its statutory environment for collective bargaining (Table 6.1). The "traditionalistic dominant" states constrain the bargaining environment. However, no pattern emerges in those states where bargaining is not constrained. Those states that are "moralistic" or "individualistic" dominant have no bargaining constraints, but no association is evident regarding the rate of employee organization or the propensity to be represented by a bargaining unit.

Political ideology. Using Piskulich's conservatism index,[1] the BC states are the most conservative, and the HD states are the least (Table 6.2). However, no pattern is evident for the MD states, which have the same statutory environment for local government bargaining as the HD states. Only West Virginia among the BC states is among the least conservative. Four of the HD states are not

Table 6.1
Employees' Use of Collective Voice, Political Culture, and Fiscal Discontent, by Group of States

Political Culture	High Density	Moderate Density	Low Density
MORALISTIC	California Michigan Minnesota Oregon Washington Wisconsin	Iowa* Maine* New Hampshire* North Dakota* South Dakota* Utah* Vermont* Montana	Colorado Idaho Kansas
INDIVIDUALISTIC	Alaska Delaware Hawaii Maryland Massachusetts New Jersey New York Pennsylvania Rhode Island Connecticut*	Illinois* Nebraska* Ohio* Nevada	Indiana Missouri Wyoming*
TRADITIONALISTIC		Florida*	Georgia* North Carolina* Virginia* West Virginia* Alabama Arizona Arkansas Kentucky Mississippi New Mexico Oklahoma Louisiana South Carolina Tennessee Texas

*Did not experience fiscal discontent.
Source: ''Political Culture'' based on Elazar (1984).

Table 6.2
Employees' Use of Collective Voice Relative to Rankings for Conservatism and Innovation, Number of States, by Group of States

States	High Density	Moderate Density	Bargaining Constrained
Piskulich's Conservatism Index			
Sixteen Least Conservative	12	3	1
Twenty-One Most Conservative	0	5	16
Thirteen "In-Between"	4	5	4
Walker's Composite Innovation Scores			
Fourteen* Most Innovative	11	2	1
Twenty-One Least Innovative	1	6	14
Thirteen "In-Between"	2	5	6

*Excludes Alaska and Hawaii.

among the sixteen least conservative—California, Pennsylvania, Alaska, and Delaware.

Innovation. Using Walker's innovation scores,[2] a similar pattern emerges (Table 6.2)—fourteen of the BC states are among the least innovative, and eleven of fourteen HD states (excluding Alaska and Hawaii) are among the most, but again the MD states run the gamut.

State Government Employees

If statewide variables such as these help explain the differences among the states, one might expect the propensity of state employees to use collective voice to be similar to that of its local government employees. However, there are striking differences between the percentage of state and local employees who are represented by a bargaining unit. The data (Table 6.3) suggest that something is occurring at the local level to differentiate it from the state. In the HD states, the local percentage exceeds that for state employees in ten of the fifteen states where a comparison can be made (Maryland restricts bargaining by state workers); the differences are substantial, ranging between 18 and 143 percent. In contrast, in the MD states the opposite is true. In seven of the ten states that can be compared, the percentage for state workers exceeds that for local workers; in six instances that variation is 25 percent or more.

Private Sector Employees

Regarding a relationship between densities in the private and public sectors, Meltz (1989: 151) concluded that "the relationship appears to be small but

Table 6.3

Employees' Use of Collective Voice: Local Governments, State Governments, and Private Sector, by High Density and Moderate Density States, by State, 1987

State	Percent Represented by A Bargaining Unit			Private Sector Density 1980/1988	Ratio of 1987 Local Government to 1988 Private Sector Density (excluding Instructional Education)
	Local Governments	State Governments	Local/State Ratio		
High Density States					
Washington	67.8	27.9	2.43	17.1/18.7	3.20
Delaware	62.3	30.7	2.03	8.4/10.3	5.51
Wisconsin	53.8	31.6	1.70	17.5/16.3	3.43
Oregon	64.5	40.9	1.58	18.1/14.8	4.17
Minnesota	58.1	39.6	1.47	18.3/14.4	3.78
Hawaii	89.6	63.6	1.41	19.3/21.4	3.73
New Jersey	76.5	54.4	1.41	17.2/17.9	3.25
Rhode Island	76.5	56.8	1.35	15.3/11.9	5.92
Michigan	50.9	40.3	1.26	25.5/21.3	3.16
California	65.5	55.6	1.18	17.5/12.8	4.02
New York	72.4	74.1	0.98	23.0/18.9	5.99
Massachusetts	67.0	74.4	0.90	17.5/11.7	4.47
Alaska	48.2	55.1	0.88	15.6/13.2	3.94
Pennsylvania	60.0	69.5	0.86	20.2/16.7	3.03
Connecticut	62.2	76.4	0.81	12.8/12.9	4.66
Maryland	63.9	Restricted	na	15.0/10.4	5.24
Moderate Density States					
Iowa	38.4	60.0	0.64	12.2/11.6	2.31
Florida	50.9	74.3	0.69	5.5/4.4	7.48
Illinois	39.9	57.0	0.70	18.0/17.4	2.46
New Hampshire	41.9	58.9	0.71	6.2/6.5	5.00
Vermont	31.1	43.5	0.72	6.9/5.2	3.56
Maine	47.5	66.0	0.72	13.2/9.8	3.55
Montana	37.5	38.9	0.96	8.0/11.3	2.61
Ohio	37.8	35.1	1.08	21.5/18.5	1.86
Nebraska	36.7	25.9	1.42	12.5/7.5	4.09
South Dakota	32.6	12.3	2.65	6.6/4.8	3.92
Nevada	68.0	Restricted	na	16.6/15.4	2.70
North Dakota	23.4	Restricted	na	10.2/6.7	3.93
Utah	44.8	Restricted	na	7.9/5.9	6.89

Restricted = State restricts collective bargaining by state employees; na = not applicable.

Data Sources: U.S. Department of Commerce, Bureau of the Census (June 1991); Private sector data in Troy (1994: 219).

positive.'' However, Troy (1994: 42) found that public sector densities are far higher than those in the private sector in virtually every state—two to eight times higher in 43 states in 1988. Further, he notes that the disparity is greatest in those states with the weakest private sector union traditions. Applying Troy's analysis, the ratio of local government density (excluding instructional education) to the private sector in 1988 ranges between 3.0 and 6.0 in the HD states, and between 1.9 and 7.5 in the MD states (Table 6.3). Further, private sector densities declined in the vast majority of the HD and MD states between 1980 and 1988, in contrast to the increases in the local government sector that were documented in the previous chapter.

A FURTHER EXPLANATION: FISCAL DISCONTENT

Cultural, political, and occupational community variables may explain some of the differences in the rates of organization and use of collective bargaining by local government employees among the various states and functions of government. But what can explain the difference in propensities between the HD and MD states? Further, what explains the differences among the types of local government within a state? Why, for example, did police, welfare, and hospital employees who work for municipalities in the HD states organize at higher rates than did their counterparts working for counties (refer to Table 5.7)?

This research hypothesizes that fiscal discontent can help explain some of these differences. As described in Chapter 3, by the early 1980s 33 states had implemented limitations on the discretion of elected officials in the fiscal arena.

THE COLLECTIVE VOICES MEET

Table 6.4 presents a state-by-state tabulation relating the use of employee collective voice to the fiscal discontent voice of the taxpayers.

- Sixteen of the seventeen states (the HD states plus Nevada) in which local government employees had the highest propensities to be represented by a bargaining unit (refer to Table 5.13) experienced fiscal discontent. Only Connecticut did not.
- Eleven of the twelve states with moderate bargaining propensities (the MD states minus Nevada) did not experience fiscal discontent. Only Montana experienced it.
- Sixteen of the 21 BC states with state-imposed constraints on local bargaining experienced fiscal discontent.

A pattern is evident between the existence of fiscal discontent and the propensity to be represented by a bargaining unit in 27 of the 29 states that do not inhibit local government collective bargaining.

Table 6.4
Fiscal Discontent, by Group of States

High Bargaining	Moderate Bargaining	Bargaining Constrained
Fiscal Discontent States		
Alaska	Montana	Alabama
California		Arizona
Delaware		Arkansas
Hawaii		Colorado
Maryland		Idaho
Massachusetts		Indiana
Michigan		Kansas
Minnesota		Kentucky
New Jersey		Louisiana
New York		Mississippi
Oregon		Missouri
Pennsylvania		New Mexico
Rhode Island		Oklahoma
Washington		South Carolina
Wisconsin		Tennessee
		Texas
Nevada		
Non-Fiscal Discontent States		
Connecticut	Florida	Georgia
	Illinois	North Carolina
	Iowa	Virginia
	Maine	West Virginia
	Nebraska	Wyoming
	New Hampshire	
	North Dakota	
	Ohio	
	South Dakota	
	Utah	
	Vermont	

DIFFERING FISCAL STRUCTURES

As discussed elsewhere, the heterogeneity of local government manifests itself in many ways. Three are important for examining the fiscal discontent hypothesis of this research. One is labor intensity, the degree to which a government relies on its own employees to provide services. A second is the share of own-source taxes collected by each type of local government. The third is the degree to which local governments rely on own-source taxes to finance their expenditures. Each is reviewed here.

Labor Intensity

The various types of local government differ in terms of the percentage of their expenditures devoted to salaries, wages, and employee benefits. In 1986–1987 the shares (highest to lowest) were 82 percent for independent school districts, 63 percent for counties, 59 percent for municipalities and townships, and 38 percent for special districts (U.S. Department of Commerce, Bureau of the Census, 1988: Table 29).[3]

Share of Own-Source Taxes

Since fiscal discontent was, at least in part, a revolt against taxes and spending, it is reasonable to assume that its impact will vary based on the share of own-source taxes collected by the various types of local government. In 1987, municipalities and independent school districts collected about two-thirds of all local own-source taxes in each group of states. Counties and townships collected an additional 25 to 33 percent; the remaining 3 to 6 percent went to special districts (Table 6.5).

The growth of own-source taxes differed substantially among the various types of local government for the fifteen years, beginning in 1972. Table 6.6 summarizes the changes for selected time periods. Population change is not accounted for in the analysis. Since the BC states have constrained the collective voice of their local government employees, they are not included in the subsequent analysis.[4]

1972–1977. The growth in own-source taxes in both the HD and MD states was relatively uniform and in line with the 45 percent inflation of this period. However, independent school districts and townships in the MD states lagged other types of government as well as inflation. Special districts surged, albeit from a much lower starting point.

1977–1982. Fiscal discontent took its toll in the HD states, checking the growth in local taxes. Independent school districts lost over 40 percentage points to the 59 percent inflation of this period. Other government types lost 28 to 33 percentage points to inflation.

In contrast, the MD states, which did not experience fiscal discontent, fared

Table 6.5

Own-Source Taxes: Percent Distribution by Group of States and Type of Government, 1972, 1977, 1982, and 1987

Type of Government	High Density States				Moderate Density States				Low Density States			
	1972	1977	1982	1987	1972	1977	1982	1987	1972	1977	1982	1987
Independent School	33.7	32.5	30.7	29.5	51.2	48.6	44.8	42.3	39.8	38.0	35.3	34.0
Municipality	36.7	37.3	38.9	38.6	26.1	27.0	27.6	27.4	32.8	31.5	32.2	30.7
County	19.9	19.9	19.9	20.9	16.0	17.3	18.5	20.8	25.3	28.5	30.3	31.6
Township	8.0	8.2	8.3	8.4	4.0	3.0	3.4	3.5	0.3	0.2	0.2	0.2
Special District	1.7	2.1	2.1	2.7	2.6	4.1	5.7	6.0	1.9	1.8	2.0	3.5
Total	100%	100%	100%	100%	100%	100%	100%	100%	100%	100%	100%	100%

Table 6.6
Percent Increase in Own-Source Taxes, by Group of States and Type of Government, Selected Time Periods

Type of Government	1972 to 1977	1977 to 1982	1982 to 1987	1972 to 1982	1977 to 1987	1972 to 1987
High Density States						
Municipality	51.9	31.2	49.6	99.2	96.3	198.1
Independent School	44.6	18.7	44.6	71.6	71.5	148.0
County	49.8	25.4	58.7	87.9	99.1	198.3
Township	53.4	27.3	51.8	95.4	93.4	196.6
Special District	82.6	30.3	88.2	138.0	145.3	348.0
All Governments	49.6	25.6	50.9	88.0	89.6	183.7
Moderate Density States						
Municipality	47.4	54.7	46.5	128.0	126.6	234.1
Independent School	35.1	39.4	39.6	88.3	94.7	162.9
County	53.9	62.2	65.7	149.6	168.9	313.8
Township	6.9	70.3	51.1	82.1	157.2	175.1
Special District	122.3	108.0	56.6	362.3	225.6	623.9
All Governments	42.5	51.2	47.7	115.5	123.4	218.3
Bargaining Constrained States						
Municipality	49.6	65.3	51.6	147.3	150.6	274.9
Independent School	48.9	50.3	53.3	123.8	130.4	243.0
County	75.9	71.5	66.2	201.6	185.1	401.5
Township	<	<	<	<	<	<
Special District	45.8	83.5	175.3	167.5	405.0	636.3
All Governments	55.8	61.7	59.1	151.9	157.2	300.7
Inflation	45.0	59.2	17.7	130.0	87.5	172.5

< = Fewer than 10,000 full-time employees.

much better—a 51.2 percent overall increase, compared to 25.6 percent in the
HD states. All growth rates were above those in the HD states. Independent
school districts and municipalities lost ground to inflation—20 and 4 percentage
points respectively.

1982–1987. There were large increases across the board during this period,
far greater than the 17.7 percent inflation.

1972–1987. For this entire fifteen year period, while it was a "bumpy road,"
only independent school districts in both the HD and MD states failed to keep
pace with the 172 percent inflation.

Reliance on Own-Source Taxes to Finance the Budget

Equally important for this research, there were differences among the various
types of local government with respect to the degree to which they relied on
own-source taxes to finance their expenditures. Townships relied most heavily
on local taxes, followed, in descending order, by municipalities, independent
school districts, counties, and special districts. The range of difference is quite
large, and special districts were well below the others (see Table 6.7).

The degree to which own-source taxes were used to finance expenditures
changed in differing degrees among the various types of local government between 1972 and 1987.

1972–1977. The reliance on own-source taxes by independent school districts
to finance expenditures fell below 50 percent by 1977 in both the HD and MD
states. In the HD states, the overall decline was relatively small (47.9 to 46.9
percent), with both municipalities and special districts experiencing increases.
In the MD states, which did not experience fiscal discontent, the overall decline
was dramatic (52.3 to 42.9 percent) and was shared by all governments except
special districts.

1977–1982. The decline in the use of own-source taxes to finance expenditures continued in the HD states during this period when fiscal discontent was
reaching a crescendo (46.9 to 40.3 percent). Independent school districts declined 8 additional points to 40.7 percent, counties 6 more points to 34.2 percent,
municipalities 4.5 points to 45.5 percent, and special districts 5.5 points to 14
percent; townships also declined 8 points to 59 percent. The MD states stabi-
lized, not repeating the large declines of the previous five years.

1982–1987. This was a period of relative stability both overall and for the
various types of governments, but at levels well below those of 1972.

A Period of Great Change

The changes in the growth and availability of own-source taxes, especially
over the 1972–1982 decade when fiscal discontent was underway, were an explosive mixture for local governments to contend with. Governments that, in
1972, had relied on their own-source taxes to finance 40 to 50 percent of their

Table 6.7
Own-Source Taxes as a Percentage of Direct General Expenditures, by Group of States and Type of Government, 1972, 1977, 1982, and 1987

Type of Government	High Density States				Moderate Density States				Low Density States			
	1972	1977	1982	1987	1972	1977	1982	1987	1972	1977	1982	1987
Municipality	48.1	50.0	45.5	48.7	52.8	43.5	45.3	46.2	48.9	41.9	40.9	40.5
Independent School	*52.0*	48.7	40.7	39.3	54.0	44.2	42.5	41.4	38.9	36.1	32.1	32.9
County	42.8	40.5	34.2	36.9	49.9	40.8	37.8	38.9	*44.8*	*41.6*	*42.3*	*43.7*
Township	*69.3*	*67.1*	*59.0*	*60.9*	<	<	<	<	<	<	<	<
Special District	17.3	19.5	14.1	16.7	25.5	30.2	29.7	34.9	11.8	11.6	9.5	17.6
All Governments	47.9	46.9	40.3	41.6	52.3	42.9	41.8	42.1	41.3	37.8	35.5	36.8

Italics indicate item is not in descending order by more than one percentage point; < = fewer than 10,000 full-time employees.

expenditures were confronted with real losses in these revenues of enormous proportions. Own-source taxes in the HD states grew 88 percent for the decade, 42 percentage points less than inflation; for independent school districts the differential was 58 points. In the MD states the differential was less, about 15 percentage points. The voice of the taxpayers had an impact!

SUMMARY

The analysis presented in this chapter suggests several patterns as well as several ''non-patterns'' regarding fiscal discontent and its relationship to employee collective voice as hypothesized in this research.

Regarding the influence of political culture or ideology as explanatory variables, the following can be said.

First, over three-quarters of the 21 BC states that constrain collective bargaining for local government employees have similar political cultures and ideology—mainly traditionalistic and conservative. For the 29 HD and MD states that do not constrain collective bargaining, no association is evident.

Second, on a state-by-state basis, the propensity of employees to use collective voice differed between those who work for local governments and those who work either for the state government or the private sector. These differences draw into question a hypothesis based solely on statewide variables such as political culture or ideology.

Third, the 33 states that experienced fiscal discontent are divided almost equally among two groups of polar opposites with regard to political culture and ideology. Sixteen were the most politically conservative BC states, while fifteen were among the least politically conservative HD states. Two states fell within the range of these opposites.

Regarding a relationship between fiscal discontent and the propensity of local government employees to organize and bargain, the following patterns emerge.

First, there is a relationship between fiscal discontent and the propensity of local government employees to use collective voice in 27 of the 29 states that do not inhibit that use of employee voice. Sixteen of the seventeen states with the highest propensities to bargain in 1987 had experienced fiscal discontent. Eleven of the twelve states with the lower propensities to bargain among these 29 states had not experienced discontent.

Second, as presented in Chapter 3, there is little evidence to support a proposition that collective bargaining contributed to fiscal discontent. Furthermore, as presented in this chapter, the 33 states that experienced fiscal discontent are divided equally between those that constrained collective bargaining by their local government employees and those that did not—sixteen and seventeen states respectively. In the other seventeen states that did not experience fiscal discontent, local government employees had full collective bargaining rights in twelve of them.

Third, the overall density experience in the two groups of fiscal discontent

Table 6.8

Rankings of Employee Voice and Fiscal Discontent Indicators, High and Moderate Density States, 1987

Type of Government	Employee Voice Indicators				Fiscal Discontent Indicators		
	Density	Represented by a Bargaining Unit	Increase in Number of Bargaining Units (1974-1987)	Percent of Governments with Collective Bargaining	Share of Own-Source Taxes	Own-Source Taxes as Percent of Expenditures	Percent of Budget for Compensation
High Density States							
Municipality	1	1	2	3	1	2	3
Independent School	1	2	1	2	2	3	1
County	3	2	4	1	3	4	2
Township	4	4	3	4	4	1	3
Special District	5	5	5	5	5	5	5
Moderate Density States							
Municipality	2	2	2	3	2	1	3
Independent School	1	1	1	1	1	2	1
County	4	3	3	2	3	3	2
Township	<	<	<	<	<	<	<
Special District	3	4	4	4	4	4	4

< = Fewer than 10,000 full-time employees.

states is dramatically different—relative stability in the HD states, but large declines in the BC states. In the non-discontent MD states, overall density increased slightly, but to levels well below those of the HD states.

Fourth, the rankings of the various indicators of the use of collective voice by the employees of the various types of local government presented in the previous chapter are similar to the rankings for the three fiscal discontent indicators presented in this chapter: share of own-source taxes collected, own-source taxes as a percent of expenditures, and labor intensity (Table 6.8). This pattern is consistent with the hypothesis of this research.

Fifth, a decline in own-source taxes is associated with an increase in bargaining unit representation. In those types of local government most dependent on own-source taxes to finance their budgets, and thus most adversely affected by fiscal discontent, the employees have moved to the more voice-intensive collective bargaining model. For example, the share of independent school district employees in the HD states that were represented by a bargaining unit increased from about one-half to two-thirds between 1974 and 1987 while the share of their expenditures financed by own-source taxes declined from 52 to 39 percent.

To explore these patterns and interrelationships in greater detail, a case study of one local jurisdiction that experienced fiscal discontent is presented in Chapter 7.

NOTES

1. Piskulich's conservatism index is based on the voting records of each state's congressional delegation, as represented by the mean difference between the annual "scorecard" produced by the Americans for Constitutional Action and that produced by the Americans for Democratic Action for the years 1960 through 1984 (Piskulich, 1992: 68).

2. Walker's innovation scores represent the relative speed with which states adopt innovations. It is based on an analysis of 88 different programs enacted by at least 20 state legislatures in a broad cross-section of twelve program areas, including labor and taxes. Each state received a number corresponding to the percentage of time that elapsed between a program's first adoption and a state's acceptance of the program. A state that has been faster, on average, in responding to new ideas or policies receives a higher innovation score (Walker, 1971: 357).

3. The calculations for counties, municipalities, and townships include dependent school districts.

4. The BC states, on average, fared the best of the three groups of states despite having experienced fiscal discontent.

7

A Case Study:
Montgomery County, Maryland

This chapter presents a case study of local government in Montgomery County, Maryland, a jurisdiction that experienced fiscal discontent within its own borders during the 1970s as well as a second taxpayers' revolt in 1990. This case replicates many of the patterns identified in previous chapters; it also adds important information about the context and timing of events. It provides additional insights about the more subtle aspects of events that can be helpful in testing the hypothesis of this research, that fiscal discontent can help explain why local government employees have chosen collective voice at a rate substantially higher than their private sector counterparts.

The "battle of collective voices" in the county's budgeting process is examined within the general framework described in Chapter 2. The evolution of the collective voice strategy used by the taxpayers to limit the discretion of elected officials in the budgeting process is examined. Fiscal discontent in the county was not an overnight phenomenon. Rather, much like the cases presented in Chapter 3, approving the ballot question was only the culmination of a series of events that occurred over a number of years. These events and their implications for the local government employees in Montgomery County are set forth in this chapter.

The collective voice strategy, as it was used or not used by the employees in the county's five government agencies, is also examined. As with fiscal discontent, the move to collective bargaining by many employees evolved over time as they organized and moved to a meet-and-confer system before gaining equality at the bargaining table. The organizing and bargaining were brought about, and reinforced, by a confluence of events over a period of years. This case study identifies fiscal discontent as one of those events, supporting the hypothesis of this research.

As elsewhere in the United States, not all employees in Montgomery County have exercised their right to bargain collectively. This case study seeks to shed light on the reasons for certain employees choosing not to use their collective voice. The differences among the various types of local government identified in the national data are replicated in the county. Employees in those agencies less dependent on own-source taxes and thus less embroiled in the "battle of collective voices" in the budget process are those who have chosen not to bargain collectively.

CASE STUDY METHODOLOGY

This case study relies on five sources of information—documents, archival records, direct observation, participant observation, and interviews.

The documents and archival records include budgets and annual financial reports, collective bargaining agreements, state and county statutes, governing body resolutions and minutes of meetings, public hearing transcripts, commission reports, staff memoranda, and newspaper articles and editorials. Most documents were available for the entire period under study, but, in some instances those from earlier years were less comprehensive.

These documents and records tell a great deal about the "what," but not as much about the "how" or "why," of events. Observations and interviews have been used to provide information about these important dimensions.

The researcher for this study was both a participant observer and a direct observer of events as a member of the county council staff for nineteen years, long before this research was even a glimmer in his mind. This opportunity has provided access to deliberations as well as an insider's perspective, recognizing the clear potential for bias.

Interviews also were conducted since they can provide "an essential source of case study evidence" (Yin, 1989: 90) as well as a "most comprehensive understanding of the subject of study, based on the intuitive feel for the subject that comes from extended observation and reflection" (Babbie, 1992: 293).

Thirty-six present and former officials were interviewed. A purposive sample was used to select individuals who it was believed would provide unique perspectives and meaningful insights into the events that took place in the county. Those selected come from four broad groups of participants—labor leaders, elected officials, chief executive officers, and senior appointed officials responsible for their agency's budget and labor relations processes. Those interviewed did not object to being identified as a participant in this research, but all required that their views and comments not be attributed.

Open-ended unstructured interviews were conducted between June 1994 and September 1995. Among the lines of questioning were the following: Why do some employees continue to use collective voice? Why have others chosen not to bargain? Do these choices relate to the use of the voice strategy by the taxpayers? Are the employees better off than they otherwise would have been had they not engaged in collective bargaining? What effect do union activities have on the budget process? What role do they play in the political process?

MONTGOMERY COUNTY TODAY

Local government in Maryland consists of 23 counties and the independent City of Baltimore. Each of these general purpose governments has a fiscally dependent public school system. The city and eleven of the counties have home rule powers with broad authority over their affairs. The state also has 223 special districts and 154 municipalities, towns, and "villages."

Montgomery County, one of the eleven home-rule charter counties, is a 500 square mile area located in the Washington, D.C., Metropolitan Statistical Area (MSA).[1] It is the state's most populous jurisdiction, having an estimated 1997 population of 828,000. About one-quarter of its residents are non-white; African-Americans number 110,000; 80,000 are of Asian descent. The estimated 305,000 households average 2.7 persons.

The median age of its residents is 35 years (60,000 are under 5 years of age; 92,000 are in the 65-and-over age group). Over 92 percent of those 18 years old and older are high school graduates; 55 percent of the 25-and-over group have completed four or more years of college.

It is a high income community, comprising about 23 percent of the state's personal income, but 17 percent of its population. Both per capita income ($38,400 in 1996) and average household income ($102,950) rank first in the state and first among major jurisdictions in the Washington MSA; nationally it ranked fourteenth in per capita income among the more than 3,100 counties and independent cities. Despite its overall affluence, many are less well-off; over 5 percent of the residents are below the poverty line, and 22 percent of the children enrolled in the public schools qualify for free or reduced price lunches.

The county is the only major suburban area in the Washington MSA that has a majority of residents working within its own borders—almost 245,000 (59 percent) in 1990. About one-quarter work in Washington, D.C.

It is the MSA's second largest suburban employment center and ranks first in the state. At-place employment was almost 480,000 in 1997, accounting for about 20 percent of the MSA's 2.4 million jobs—390,000 in the private sector, 38,000 for the state and local governments, and 52,000 for the federal government.

It is the home of 24 federal agencies, including the National Institutes of Health, Food and Drug Administration, National Institute of Standards and Technology, and Nuclear Regulatory Commission. It also is the headquarters for the Marriott International and Lockheed Martin corporations. Among the more than 20,000 private employers are a large number of relatively small high-technology and biotechnology firms drawn to the county, in part, by the afore-mentioned federal agencies. Many firms contract with federal agencies, although much of the work is done elsewhere. The value of contracts awarded in 1993 was $2.7 billion, second in the metropolitan area.

There is an agricultural sector as well, with about 30 percent of the land area designated for that purpose. The county is home for 561 farms and 350 horticultural businesses.

LOCAL GOVERNMENT IN MONTGOMERY COUNTY

Five major independent organizations comprise local government in the county—the Montgomery County Government, the Montgomery County Public Schools, Montgomery College, the Maryland–National Capital Park and Planning Commission, and the Washington Suburban Sanitary Commission.[2] Each has a different governance structure: two have elected leaders; three are governed by appointed bodies—one appointed by the governor, one by the county council, and one by the county executive. Two are bi-county commissions shared with Prince George's County, its eastern neighbor.

Montgomery County Government

The county was founded in 1776 and operated under a county commissioner form of government until 1948 when a council-manager home-rule government was approved by the voters. Twenty years later the voters again amended *The Charter of Montgomery County, Maryland*, providing for a separation-of-powers form of government, which was implemented in the general election of 1970.

The legislative branch is the nine-member elected county council; four are elected at-large, and five must reside and are elected by the voters in five councilmanic districts.[3] The charter does not require council members to serve full-time and thus they may hold other employment, although most have not.

The council has all legislative powers that may be exercised by the county under the Constitution and Laws of Maryland. It also has all planning, zoning, and subdivision powers. The council is not empowered to legislate for the 25 municipalities, towns, villages, or special districts on any matter covered by the powers granted to those jurisdictions by the state.[4]

The executive branch is headed by a full-time elected county executive, who has "no legislative power except the power to make rules and regulations expressly delegated by a law enacted by the Council or by the Charter" (Montgomery County, Maryland, December 1996: Section 201).

The executive appoints a chief administrative officer (CAO) subject to the council's confirmation. The CAO is a professionally qualified administrator who supervises all executive branch departments and offices, advises the executive on all administrative matters, and administers the County Government's personnel system. The executive appoints the directors of the 28 departments and principal offices, after receiving the advice of the CAO and subject to confirmation by the council.

The County Government provides the so-called traditional municipal services including police, corrections, transportation, environmental protection, health and human services, libraries, recreation, solid waste, housing, and economic development. An independent Housing Opportunities Commission established by state law is responsible for operating public housing in the county.

Fire and rescue services are provided by nineteen independent volunteer fire and rescue corporations, staffed by 827 uniformed career firefighters and rescue workers augmented by about 900 trained volunteers. In 1987, county legislation transferred the employment of the paid employees from these volunteer corporations to the executive branch Department of Fire and Rescue Services.

The courts and judicial system are operated in conjunction with the elected State's Attorney, Sheriff, Clerk of the Circuit Court, and the fifteen Circuit Court judges. The judges are first appointed by the governor, but stand for election at the general election following their appointment.

Montgomery County Public Schools

The school system provides the pre-kindergarten and K–12 public education program in the county, operating within the framework of state law.[5] The system is independent in all except fiscal matters, for which it is dependent on the county council. Education policies are established by the seven-member elected county board of education. Five members represent the five board of education districts and two members are elected at-large. There also is one student member, who is a county resident regularly enrolled as a junior or senior in a county public high school.

The superintendent is the chief executive officer who administers the system in accordance with state laws, the bylaws of the Maryland Board of Education, and the policies of the local board. The system operates 181 elementary and secondary schools, 24 other facilities, and owns more than 32,000 acres of land.

Student enrollment of 122,500 in the fall of 1996 placed it among the nation's 20 largest school systems. About one-third of the students are non-white, compared to about one-quarter of the general population. About 20 percent of the students are African-American, and 12.5 percent are of Asian descent. An additional 12.5 percent are Hispanic.

Montgomery College

Montgomery College is a comprehensive two-year college, the first in the state, founded in 1946. More than 20,500 students were enrolled on three campuses and numerous satellite locations in the 1996 fall semester.

One of sixteen two-year colleges in the statewide system, it is administered in accordance with state law.[6] Policy is established by the state Board of Higher Education and by an eight-member local board of trustees who are county residents appointed for six-year terms by the governor, subject to confirmation by the state senate. There is an additional student member. The president is the chief executive officer.

Maryland–National Capital Park and Planning Commission

This bi-county commission (shared with Prince George's County) was established by the Maryland General Assembly in 1927 and reorganized in 1959.[7] It is authorized (1) to acquire, develop, maintain, and administer a regional park system; and (2) to prepare and administer a General Plan for land use. The MNCPPC's authority embraces virtually all of both counties except for certain incorporated towns and municipalities (seven in Montgomery County).

There are ten commissioners, five appointed by each county to comprise the counties' respective Planning Boards. No more than three members from each county may be members of the same political party. In Montgomery County, the appointments are made by the council subject to the approval of the county executive. The chair and vice-chair of the commission are rotated annually between the two planning board chairs.

Most of the commission's work is carried out by the two planning boards. Each council establishes priorities for the respective land use planning departments and park systems (28,000 acres of parkland and 336 developed parks in Montgomery County) through budget approvals and the review of work programs.

Washington Suburban Sanitary Commission

The sanitary commission is a second bi-county agency, established by the General Assembly in 1918.[8] It has responsibility for the construction, operation, and maintenance of water supply and sanitary sewerage systems in both counties. It is the nation's seventh largest water and sewer agency.

The WSSC is governed by a six-member commission, with three commissioners appointed by each county executive and confirmed by each county council. Members must reside in the county from which they are appointed. The commission appoints a general manager who is the chief executive officer.

HUMAN RESOURCES MANAGEMENT

Each of the county's five independent agencies is responsible for managing its respective organizations, including human resources. About 80 percent of the full-time employees are covered by a collective bargaining agreement with one of the ten bargaining units. The result is a diverse system with a broad array of human resource policies, practices, and procedures. The following presents an overview of that mosaic.

Montgomery County Government. Human resource policies are established in accordance with the county charter, which states in part,

The merit system shall provide the means to recruit, select, develop, and maintain an effective, non-partisan, and responsive workforce with personnel actions based on demonstrated merit and fitness. Salaries and wages . . . shall be determined pursuant to a uniform salary plan. The Council shall prescribe by law a system of retirement pay. (Section 401)

Employees covered by a collective bargaining agreement "may be excluded from the provisions of the merit system only to the extent that such provisions are subject to collective bargaining" (ibid.). The CAO, under the county executive's direction, is responsible for administering the system. Employees of the Sheriff's Department are members of the county system; those of the State's Attorney's Office and the Circuit Court are state employees.

There are about 7,050 permanent employees, of which about 5,600 are represented by one of four bargaining units. The county executive negotiates with the three unions that represent the employees in these units.

- The Montgomery County Government Employees Organization, United Food and Commercial Workers Union, Local 1994, AFL-CIO, represents about 1,450 employees in the Service, Labor and Trades (SLT) Unit and 2,750 employees in the Office, Professional, and Technical (OPT) Unit.
- The Fraternal Order of Police, Montgomery County Lodge 35, represents over 800 non-supervisory sworn police officers.
- The Montgomery County Career Fire Fighters Association, International Association of Fire Fighters, Local 1664 represents over 600 career, non-supervisory firefighter and emergency rescue employees.

Montgomery County Public Schools. The over 16,000 full- and part-time employees (14,700 full-time equivalents) of the public school system are employed by the board of education, not the County Government. State law provides that "public school employees may form, join, and participate in the activities of employee organizations of their own choice for purposes of being represented on all matters that relate to salaries, wages, hours, and working conditions" (Maryland, 1997: *Education*, Section 6–402[a]).

The employees elect their exclusive representative, but any employee may refuse to join or participate in the activities of the employee organization. Strikes are prohibited.

The elected school board negotiates with representatives of three employee groups, which represent virtually all public school employees.

- The Montgomery County Education Association represents 7,860 teachers.
- The Montgomery County Council of Supporting Services Employees, SEIU Local 500, AFL-CIO, represents more than 7,800 support and maintenance employees.
- The Montgomery County Association of Administrative and Supervisory Personnel represents more than 450 professional and administrative employees.

Montgomery College. Personnel and compensation policies are the responsibility of the appointed board of trustees. Only the 415 full-time faculty, represented by the College Chapter of the American Association of University Professors, engage in collective bargaining. Compensation policies for all other employees, including part-time faculty, are established by the board of trustees.

Maryland–National Capital Park and Planning Commission. The commission's 1900 career employees are members of its bi-county merit system. As such, all policies must be uniformly applied to the employees in both counties and must be approved by the bi-county commission. Only park police officers, represented by the Fraternal Order of Police, Lodge 30, engage in collective bargaining. Salaries, benefits, and working conditions for all other employees are established by the commission, subject to the budget actions of the county councils.

Washington Suburban Sanitary Commission. Another bi-county merit system, all compensation policies must apply uniformly to the commission's 2,030 employees. Policies are established by the commission except for the 550 mainly blue-collar maintenance and trades, hourly wage employees who bargain collectively; this group, represented by Baltimore-based AFSCME Council 67, constitutes less than 30 percent of the commission's workforce.

Salary and Benefit Structures

There are two dozen pay plans among the five agencies, many with very different structures both within and between the agencies (Table 7.1). Some pertain to specific occupations—school teachers, college faculty, non-supervisory police officers, or firefighters. In contrast, others cover a broad array of occupations and, in many instances, six pay schedules may be available. Administrative and office positions, for example, are included in the following: (1) the pay plan for the County Government's OPT unit, (2) the County Government's non-represented schedule, (3) the MCPS supporting services plan, (4) the college staff plan, (5) the MNCPPC salaried employee schedule, or (6) the WSSC general plan.

To cite one example, the minimum salary in 1997 for a Principal Administrative Aide position had a range of 20 percent: $24,600 at the college; $23,700 at the school system; $22,800 at the County Government; $20,600 for the MNCPPC; and $20,500 for the WSSC.[9] The opportunity for "leapfrogging" and "me-tooism" is apparent when comparisons are made among the agencies, let alone when they are made with other public and private sector employers in the region.

There also are numerous combinations of employee benefit packages[10] with an assortment of cost-sharing arrangements.[11] With certain exceptions in the pension arena, benefits are locally financed and most are subject to bargaining. However, in the school system only the cost-sharing arrangements are subject to bargaining; a joint union-management committee periodically reviews the

Table 7.1
Fiscal Year 1997 Pay Structures, Local Government Agencies, Montgomery County, Maryland

Agency	Pay Plan	Number of Pay Grades	Fixed/Variable Steps Within Pay Grades	"Normal" Annual Step Increase
County Government	Service, Labor, and Trades Unit	22	Variable	3.5%
	Office, Professional, and Technical Unit	22	Variable	3.5%
	Police Bargaining Unit	4	Fixed (15)	3.5%
	Fire Fighters Bargaining Unit	4	Fixed (15)	3.5%
	Non-Represented Employees	36	Variable	3.5%
	Police Management	5	Variable	3.5%
	Seasonal & Temporary	6	Variable	na
Public Schools	Teachers	Degree (4)	Fixed (10 @ BA; 19 others)	1.0 to 5.6%
	Supporting Services	30	Fixed (10)	1.9 to 5.5 %
	Administrative and Supervisory	5	Fixed (10)	3.0%
	Other Professionals (12 month)	1	Fixed (19)	2.0 to 5.2%
College	Full-Time Faculty	Rank	Variable	5.0%
	Administrators	7	Variable	4.5%
	Support Staff	14	Variable	2.0%
	Part-Time Faculty	na	na	na
Park & Planning Commission	Salaried Employees	24	Variable	3.5%
	Police Management	3	Variable	3.5%
	Park Police Bargaining Unit	5	Fixed (15+2)	3.5%/2.5%
	Police Dispatchers	4	Variable	3.5%
	Seasonal and Temporary	15	Variable	3.5%
Sanitary Commission	Hourly Employees Bargaining Unit	13	Variable	3.5%
	General Employees	24	Variable	3.5%
	Executives	6	Variable	3.5%
	Special Rate Scale	7	Variable	3.5%

Employee Benefit Plan and makes recommendations to the school board regarding benefit levels.

Regarding pensions, all public school teachers, certain school administrators, and the full-time college faculty are members of the state teachers' retirement and pension systems, and the employers' contribution to the plan is paid by the state; this benefit is not a subject for bargaining. Locally financed pension plans are provided for the other eligible employees of the school system and college. There also is a locally financed retirement supplement for the teachers.

Each of the bi-county agencies has its own contributory defined benefit plan, which all its employees must join. The County Government's retirement system was created in 1965, when the county left the state plan. It has separate plans for police officers, firefighters, other public safety employees, and all non–public safety employees; each is a contributory plan with rates and benefit structures that vary according to the employee's "hire-date"—before July 1, 1978; July 1, 1978 through September 30, 1994; or after September 30, 1994. The latter is a defined contribution plan; the two earlier plans are defined benefit.

BUDGET OVERVIEW

The combined operating budgets total almost $2 billion for fiscal year 1997[12] exclusive of the $437 million for the bi-county Washington Suburban Sanitary Commission.[13] The public school system is the largest; the subsidy for regional transit service is the smallest (Table 7.2). About two-thirds of the expenditures ($1.33 billion) are dedicated to compensation for the 24,200 employee work-years.

The budget is financed primarily by own-source taxes (71 percent of revenue); the property tax makes up more than one-half of those taxes. Intergovernmental revenues constitute about 18 percent of the resources (Table 7.2). Among all state and local governments in the United States, the county ranks sixtieth based on total 1994 general revenue collections.

BUDGET PROCESSES

The county council makes the final fiscal decisions based upon the proposals and recommendations of the county executive and the respective governing bodies of the four agencies. The council has broad fiscal powers as spelled out in Section 305 of the charter: "The Council may add to, delete from, increase or decrease any appropriation item in the operating or capital budget. The Council shall approve each budget, as amended, and appropriate the funds therefore. . . . The Council shall make tax levies deemed necessary to finance the budgets."

The budget process for the County Government is delineated in Article 3 of the county charter. State law governs the procedures for the other agencies and specifies the powers and responsibilities of the various actors. All have extensive

Table 7.2
Montgomery County, Maryland: Fiscal Year 1997 Operating Budget Profile

Agency	Operating Budget (Millions $$)	Share of Total Budget (Percent)	Employee Compensation (Millions $$)	% of Agency Budget	Workyears
County Public Schools	$915.1	46.9	$794.2	86.6	14,704
Montgomery College	$84.7	4.3	$73.9	87.2	1,186
County Government	$699.3	35.8	$414.5	59.3	7,340
Park and Planing Commission	$64.3	3.3	$49.2	71.1	867
Regional Transit Subsidy	$45.9	2.4	na	na	na
Debt Service (All Agencies)	$143.7	7.3	na	na	na
Total Operating Budget	$1,953.0	100.0	$1,332.5	67.8	24,197
Sanitary Commission	$220.0	na	$120.8	55.0	2,037
WSSC Debt Service	$217.0	na	na	na	na

Operating Revenues (excluding WSSC)		
Source	Millions $$	Percent of Total
Property Taxes	$773.1	39.6
Income Tax	$528.4	27.0
Other Taxes	$100.0	5.1
Total Taxes	$1,401.5	71.7
Intergovernmental Assistance	$355.1	18.2
All Other	$196.4	10.1
Total Operating Revenues	$1,953.0	100.0

public hearing requirements. Each operating budget must be balanced each year.[14]

Montgomery County Government. The executive prepares and submits to the council an annual operating budget for the departments and offices of the County Government. The council must hold public hearings on these proposals, approve a budget, and levy the taxes necessary to balance it. The executive may veto any item in the budget approved by the council; six votes are required to override any veto.

All compensation matters, including those in any collective bargaining agreement negotiated by the executive, are subject to approval by the council.

Montgomery County Public Schools. The superintendent proposes a budget to the board of education, including the moneys to implement all collective bargaining agreements. One of the superintendent's enumerated responsibilities is to "seek in every way to secure adequate funds from local authorities for the support and development of public schools in the county."[15]

The board, after public hearing, submits its recommended budget to the county executive, who specifies any items that are "denied" (i.e., not approved) and the reasons for any denial and forwards the budget as amended to the council. After conducting its public hearing, the council may "restore" items "denied" by the executive as well as make any further "denials" it deems appropriate; the council may not increase the budget above the board's request. The budget is then returned to the board; the executive has no subsequent veto authority. As the school system is fiscally dependent, the council must levy the local taxes necessary to finance the budget.

The council must approve the school budget according to fourteen broad expenditure categories; for example, Administration, Special Education, Student Transportation, Operation of Plant and Equipment, and Instructional Salaries. The categories vary greatly in terms of their dollar amounts—Instructional Salaries were $408 million in fiscal year 1997; Operation of Plant and Equipment was $57 million; Community Services was $600,000. The funds necessary to implement the various collective bargaining agreements will be distributed in various amounts among the fourteen categories.

If the council does not appropriate sufficient funds to implement a collective bargaining agreement signed by the board, "the ball is back in the board's court." The board may reallocate funds within the fourteen expenditure categories, but it may not transfer between them. Thus, it may choose to reprogram within each category to "find" the funds necessary to implement its negotiated agreements. If it does not reprogram, the board must reopen negotiations with the employees' representatives in an effort to reach a new agreement within the bounds established by the council's budget actions.

Montgomery College. The board of trustees prepares a recommended operating budget after receiving the president's proposal. The budget, including the funds necessary to implement any negotiated agreement as well as other changes in the compensation package, is submitted to the county executive, who in turn transmits it along with recommendations (not "denials") to the council. The council, after holding its public hearing, approves a budget and levies the local taxes necessary to finance the county's contribution, which constitutes about 45 percent of the funding; the balance comes from the state and the students. The budget as approved by the council is subject to an executive veto, which may be overriden by six votes.

As with the school system, moneys are appropriated to state-specified expenditure categories, and the board of trustees may reprogram within those categories if the council chooses not to fund fully a collective bargaining agreement or provide sufficient funds to implement compensation changes for other college employees. If the funds necessary to implement a negotiated agreement are not provided, state law provides that either party may reopen it.[16]

Maryland-National Capital Park and Planning Commission. As spelled out in state law,[17] the bi-county commission submits to each county executive proposed operating budgets for the respective planning and parks departments as well as for the bi-county administrative offices (finance, law, human resources). The commission's proposals must include all funding for employee compensation including any negotiated agreements. The executive submits recommendations to the council, which, after public hearing, approves a budget and levies the local property taxes necessary to balance it. The bi-county administrative budget requires joint approval of the two county councils. The county-only portion of the budget is subject to executive veto.

Funding for any collective bargaining agreement as well as all other compensation matters requires joint approval of the county councils; failure to agree constitutes disapproval. If full funding is not provided, either the commission or the employees' representative may reopen it within 20 days of final budget action.

Washington Suburban Sanitary Commission. The commissioners recommend a budget to the two counties based on the general manager's recommendations. The entire bi-county budget is submitted to each county executive, who in turn forwards it with recommendations to the respective council.[18] Funding for all compensation items, including those negotiated with the hourly employees, must be included in the budget. The final budget requires joint approval of the county councils; if they fail to agree to changes, the commission's proposal stands. There is no executive veto authority. The commissioners, not the counties, establish the necessary water and sewer rates, connection and front-foot-benefit charges, and permit fees based on the recommendations of the two county councils.

A HISTORICAL PROFILE

Demographics

A quarter of a century ago Montgomery County was largely a community of residential subdivisions clustered close to the Washington, D.C. core where many of its 545,000 residents worked. In 1972, there were 168,100 households, 126,200 public school students, and about 200,000 jobs located in the county. Since that time the community has undergone great changes. In summary, between 1972 and 1997:

- Population grew to 828,000, a 52 percent increase.

- The number of households increased 82 percent to 305,000; average household size declined from 3.24 to 2.71 by 1982 and has remained at about that level for fifteen years.

- Public school enrollment peaked in the fall of 1973 at 126,300 students; by 1984 it had declined 28 percent to about 91,000, increasing gradually since that time. The fall 1996 enrollment of 122,500 was within 3 percent of the 1973 peak. However, as a percentage of the population, enrollment declined from 22.5 percent in 1972 to 13.2 percent in 1990; it increased slightly to 14.8 percent by 1997. Fewer than one-quarter of the households have children enrolled in the public schools.

- The proportion of the population in the 65-and-over group more than doubled, from about 5 percent to almost 12 percent.

- At-place employment increased 142 percent, from about 200,000 to 485,000.

Expenditures

Budgeted expenditures for 1997 totaled $1.953 billion, or $2,359 per capita.[19] On a real per capita basis, expenditures have been relatively stable since 1978. Expenditures in 1997 were 10 percent higher than 25 years earlier, but about 3 percent above their 1978 level, the year of the county's first expression of fiscal discontent.[20] Expenditures in fiscal year 1997 were just below 6 percent of personal income, compared to 7.3 percent in 1978.

Education receives about one-half of the budget pie, $1 billion. The public school system receives the lion's share ($915 million); an additional $85 million provides higher education at the college. County tax dollars finance 81 and 41 percent of these budgets respectively ($741 million and $35 million).

The $700 million County Government budget, which provides the full range of municipal services, comprises about 36 percent of the total. Debt service requirements are centrally budgeted for all agencies (except WSSC) and constitute 7.3 percent of expenditures. The MNCPPC and the regional transit subsidy are allocated 3.3 and 2.4 percent of the budget respectively.

While public school expenditures have remained relatively stable on a real per capita basis, when measured on a real per student basis a different trend emerges. Real per pupil spending increased steadily between 1972 and 1990 ($4,757 to $8,028), a period when enrollments declined and cost reductions did not keep pace despite the closure of 45 schools. Beginning in 1991, per pupil costs began to decline somewhat reaching $7,470 in 1997. The county share per pupil in real 1997 dollars increased as well—$3,504 in 1972, $6,840 at its 1991 peak, and $6,050 in 1997.

Two important trends are highlighted here.

1. *Intergovernmental assistance for education* has declined over the years, thereby shifting more of the burden to local taxes. In the early 1970s less than three-quarters of the public school system's budget was locally financed; by 1991 that share had risen to 85.6 percent, and in 1997 it was 81 percent ($780 million).

The share of the college budget financed by the state has declined as well—36 percent in 1972, 15 percent in 1992, and 17 percent in 1997. Over the same period, the county share has ranged between one-third and one-half; the balance is paid by the students (45 percent in 1997).

In 1994, the state ceased paying the employer's share of the Social Security and Medicare payroll taxes for all public school teachers and college faculty, which increased the local budget for these items by $29 million. In 1978, the federal government greatly reduced its Impact Aid program for local school districts as well, an action that reduced county revenues $6 million when it was fully implemented.

Accompanying these reductions was the federal PL94–142 mandate that all youngsters are entitled to free and equal public education in the least restrictive educational environment. These special education programs were begun in the county in fiscal year 1978 at a cost of about $20 million; by 1997 their budget was $102 million.

2. *Mass transit services* have expanded greatly in the region over the 25-year period, as have their costs for the county—the $3.6 million in 1972 grew ten-fold to $37.5 million by 1982 and 25-fold to $90 million by 1992. The $100 million budgeted for public transit in fiscal year 1997 is equivalent to $120 per capita.

In 1968 the national capital region adopted a plan to build a new 101-mile rapid rail system (later increased to 103 miles), substantially more ambitious than the 33-mile system that had been considered a decade earlier. In the early 1970s, when the privately operated bus systems in the metropolitan area went out of business, the regional agency stepped in and began providing regional bus service as well. By the middle of the decade the costs of these actions had become part of the fiscal landscape for the local jurisdictions, even though a large share of the initial capital cost was borne by the state and federal governments. The county has a special area property tax rate earmarked for mass transit, which increased from 8 cents in 1972 to 21 cents by fiscal year 1979, the year of the county's first taxpayers' revolt.

Employment and Compensation

The public school system is the county's largest agency, employing 60 percent (14,700 workyears) of its 24,200 workyears. It is followed by the County Government, which has 30 percent (7,340 workyears), the college (5 percent), and the planning commission (4 percent). The bi-county workforce at the sanitary commission consists of 2,037 workyears.

Each agency, except WSSC, is a labor intensive organization. Employee compensation costs consume 86 percent ($795 million) and 80 percent ($74 million) of the school system and college budgets respectively.[21] Sixty percent of the County Government budget and 71 percent of the planning commission budget are earmarked for employee compensation.

Relative to population the number of workyears peaked in fiscal year 1980 at about 345 per 10,000 population. By fiscal year 1987 that ratio had declined to 292 per 10,000, where it essentially has remained for a decade.

Revenues

The property tax (40 percent), the local individual "piggyback" income tax (27 percent), and intergovernmental assistance (18 percent) comprise about 85 percent of the county's operating revenue.[22] Table 7.3 summarizes the history of revenue collections since the early 1970s.

Property taxes for fiscal year 1997 were budgeted to be $773 million, or $934 per capita. On a real per capita basis, property tax revenue has had a roller-coaster ride since 1973. It peaked on two occasions—in 1978 and again in 1990—the years when the county taxpayers finally revolted, the fiscal discontent discussed in the next section.

As a percentage of personal income, the property tax has remained relatively stable since the early 1980s (a range of 2.4 to 2.6 percent), well below the 3.27 percent of 1978, the year when fiscal discontent first emerged.

The local individual income tax was budgeted to be $528 million for fiscal year 1997, or $638 per capita.[23] On a real per capita basis, this source of funds has increased steadily over the last 25 years. Its growth in fiscal years 1993 and 1994 reflects an increase in the piggyback rates authorized by the General Assembly in 1992. As a percentage of personal income, this source has gradually increased since the late 1980s to stand at 1.6 percent in 1997.

Intergovernmental assistance for fiscal year 1997 was budgeted to be $355 million, about $430 per capita. On a real per capita basis, assistance peaked in 1977 and has declined since that time, reaching a low point in 1993. As a percentage of operating expenditures it has declined since 1979, although a second decline began in 1986 with the end of federal general revenue sharing and the national government's efforts to reduce the federal budget deficit with its enactment of the Gramm-Rudman-Hollings legislation.[24]

PROPERTY TAXES VERSUS EMPLOYEE COMPENSATION

By 1974 the synergy between property taxes and the compensation levels for local government employees had begun to manifest itself. Changes in property

Table 7.3
Montgomery County, Maryland: Real Per Capita Revenues (1997 dollars), Selected Years

Fiscal Year	Property Taxes		Income Tax		Intergovernmental Revenue	
	1997 $$	Index (1978=100)	1997 $$	Index (1978=100)	1997 $$	Index (1978=100)
1973	$869	84.7	$360	93.8	$434	88.0
1978	$1,025	100.0	$384	100.0	$493	100.0
1983	$858	83.7	$427	111.3	$428	86.9
1988	$991	96.7	$534	139.0	$367	74.5
1990	$1,031	100.5	$589	153.4	$372	75.4
1993	$972	94.8	$561	146.0	$294	59.7
1997	$934	91.1	$638	166.2	$430	87.0

Percent of Personal Income

Fiscal Year	Property Taxes	Income Tax	Other Taxes	Total Own-Source Taxes
1973	2.94%	1.22%	0.20%	4.36%
1978	3.27	1.22	0.47	4.96
1983	2.56	1.27	0.50	4.33
1988	2.46	1.32	0.48	4.26
1990	2.58	1.47	0.40	4.46
1993	2.53	1.46	0.51	4.51
1997	2.35	1.61	0.30	4.26

assessment practices imposed by the state reduced the real property taxable base; to maintain revenue levels, tax rates were increased. Further rate adjustments were required to meet the service level demands of a growing jurisdiction and the double-digit inflation rates of that time. The tradeoff between homeowners and employees became the focus of debate about competing equities.

In the spring of 1974, the political campaigns for the November elections, the second under the new form of government, were well underway. Two members of the council were candidates in the Democratic primary for the nomination to challenge the incumbent Republican executive; a third council member was seeking to unseat the popular Republican incumbent in Congress; the four remaining members of the council were seeking reelection. It was in this political environment that the fiscal year 1975 budget and tax rates were debated and decided.

Projected property tax revenues had been reduced $30 million when the governor reduced the assessment level for real property from 60 to 50 percent of market value, a 16 percent reduction. The Republican executive recommended a seventeen-cent increase (about 5 percent) in the property tax rate to offset some of the loss, as well as to deal with an 11.8 percent rate of inflation and the newly emerging energy crisis. A 5.5 percent average cost-of-living adjustment (3 percent plus $300) was proposed for all agency employees.

The council agenda was to "improve upon" the executive's proposals, which meant to increase service levels and provide a salary increase for the employees, but hold the increase in the property tax rate below seventeen cents. In its final actions, the council approved the average 5.5 percent cost-of-living adjustment as recommended and approved expenditure levels $10 million above those recommended.

The council was able to limit the increase in the politically sensitive property tax rate to 5 cents, or 12 cents less than the increase proposed by the executive. To accomplish this, the council approved several "funding gimmicks," which relied heavily on "one-time" revenue to finance continuing expenditures.[25] Per capita property taxes increased 1.3 percent when inflation was running at an annual rate of just under 12 percent. Virtually everyone recognized that these actions were "digging a huge hole" for fiscal year 1976, but the political goal was to capture the office of the executive and retain control of the council in the upcoming election.

In November, the Republican county executive was reelected in the heavily Democratic county.[26] The seven-member Democratic Party slate for county council was also elected, and the four incumbents were reelected.

Three months after the election, on February 1, 1975, the *County Executive's Recommended Fiscal Year 1976 Operating Budget* included a 24-cent property tax rate increase ($3.42 to $3.66 per $100 of assessed valuation), but no cost-of-living adjustment (COLA) for the employees of the County Government or any of the agencies. The school board had negotiated a 10.1 percent adjustment with its two unions as part of a 17 percent overall budget increase ($210 to $245 million). The executive's message said in part,

> The budget contains no cost-of-living increase which, by test of equity, our employees are entitled to in view of severe inflation. . . . I do not believe it would be responsible to make such a recommendation considering the tax burden facing the property owner and perhaps no growth salary situation or unemployment. In addition, by foregoing a cost-of-living increase . . . we should be able to avoid layoffs—a situation now affecting over 5% of the County's workforce—with all the human tragedy which unemployment entails. . . . The no COLA decision is not an easy one to make. It was made in recognition of the factors of current unemployment, inflation, availability of revenues, and the needs of our citizens.

In May the council's approved budget did not reflect the executive's proposals. The council provided funding for paying $750 per full-time-equivalent employee as an across-the-board cost-of-living adjustment.[27] To pay for this action, the council approved a property tax rate of $3.75 per $100, 35 cents above the previous year's rate and eleven cents more than the executive had recommended. The actions of the prior year had taken their toll. Real per capita property taxes were increased 18 percent ($797 to $937) from the artificially low levels of fiscal year 1975. Other taxes also were increased—the telephone and fuel-energy tax rates were increased 20 percent; the admissions and amusement tax went from 4.5 to 7 percent. As will be discussed in the next section, it was these tax increases in the spring of 1975 that led directly to the fiscal discontent of the taxpayers and to the charter limit that was petitioned to the ballot three years later in 1978.

One year later, in February 1976, the executive's budget proposal maintained property tax rates at $3.75, but again included no COLA for the employees of any agency.

> [W]ith the concurrence of many Council members, I pledged that the FY77 budget would not contain a property tax rate increase. I have honored this pledge. . . . Regrettably, we must forego a cost-of-living increase for employees if another property tax increase is to be avoided. . . . However, on the positive side for employees, I am recommending no massive layoffs . . . the workforce can be slightly reduced through attrition, which is certainly more palatable than the alternative of cost-of-living increases and large scale firings. To provide a 3% cost-of-living would cost the county approximately $9,000,000 and would necessitate a tax increase of over 16 cents or a possible layoff of 700 to 900 employees. I do not believe this is acceptable to our taxpayers. Neither alternative, in good conscience, is acceptable to me.

His message closed by stating that despite the budget difficulties, "In this bicentennial year, all of us have much to be thankful for in Montgomery County." Not all of the employee groups shared that view. A page-one headline in the March 11, 1976, edition of the local *Montgomery Journal* newspaper read, "Teachers, Police Consider Strikes."

The council, in its approved budget, provided funding for a 3 percent COLA and reduced the property tax rate 6 cents to $3.69. The school board had negotiated a 3 percent COLA with its unions but, in an exercise of its management rights, reduced all twelve-month teacher contracts to ten-month contracts, resulting in a substantial reduction in annual salary for many.

In both 1975 and 1976 the council was confronted with a difficult set of choices—how much to restrain the escalating property tax bills of homeowners, how to provide for the economic well-being of the employees in a time of high inflation, and how to continue to provide a high level of public services in an affluent and growing community. Adding to the financial strain, it was during this period that the region's new rapid rail system was beginning to operate, and the financial resources that had been committed to operate it a decade or more earlier were beginning to come due.

Many council members had viewed the executive's proposals as extreme and sought to find a middle ground. These Democrats also were displeased with the political dilemma the Republican executive's recommendations confronted them with—the homeowners versus the unions versus the service recipients. The executive seemed to be "getting the best of all worlds" politically.

THE VOICES OF THOSE REQUESTING SERVICES

As described in Chapter 2, those requesting government services employ the collective voice strategy to make their views known to the elected decision makers. The process can become one of "street fighting pluralism" (Yates, 1977: 34). Various tactics are employed; meetings and rallies, call-in and letter-writing campaigns, and public hearing appearances are among the most frequently used. And, of course, there is always the threat of retaliating on election day.

Montgomery County was not immune to these tactics. Thousands of letters and phone calls were received and hundreds of meetings were held during each "budget season." Thousands attended the public hearings to hear the hundreds of speakers. Unfortunately, good information is available regarding only the hearings, but it provides an excellent indicator of the use of collective voice by those requesting services.

The data presented in Table 7.4 illustrate several points. First, the dominance of collective voice in the public hearing process is clear. Individuals consumed less than 15 percent of the allotted time. Countywide groups (for example, the League of Women Voters, the Human Relations Commission, the Commission for Children and Youth) and local organizations (for example, a civic association, PTA, or local chamber of commerce) dominate. These groups present their views to the elected officials frequently before a standing-room-only (SRO) audience of more than 300 voters and, in later years, those watching the local

Table 7.4
Montgomery County Council Public Hearings, Annual Operating Budget, Speakers Profile, Selected Years

	FY 1973	FY 1976	FY 1977	FY 1988	FY 1997
TOTAL SPEAKERS	90	115	148	144	114
SPEAKERS REPRESENTING (number and allotted time)					
Countywide Groups	30 (3 Hours)	29 (3 Hours)	33 (3.25 Hours)	57 (4.75 Hours)	55 (4.75 Hours)
Local Groups	36 (2.5 Hours)	52 (3.75 Hours)	50 (3.5 Hours)	58 (4.75 Hours)	31 (2.5 Hours)
Employee Groups	4 (20 Minutes)	4 (20 Minutes)	6 (30 Minutes)	9 (1 Hour)	8 (45 Minutes)
Individuals	20 (1 Hour)	30 (1.5 Hours)	39 (2 Hours)	20 (1 Hour)	20 (1 Hour)
TIME ALLOTTED TO SPEAKERS	7 Hours	8.5 Hours	9.5 Hours	12 Hours	9 Hours
TOTAL HEARING TIME	10 Hours	12 Hours	14 Hours	15 Hours	12 Hours
HEARING SESSIONS	5	6	6	5	4

cable channel (and maybe taping it to play back when it is to their advantage). Elected officials find it difficult to ignore these voices!

Not only did the number of groups using the collective strategy increase from 66 in 1972 to 115 in 1987 but, of equal significance, the interests represented by those groups were far more diverse and included more than the civic associations, PTAs, and chambers of commerce.[28]

Second, the data reflect the relatively little time used by employees at the hearings in the 1970s. In both fiscal years 1976 and 1977, when the county executive was recommending no cost-of-living adjustment for the employees, only 20 to 30 minutes of public hearing time was allotted for their collective voice. Only the four organizations then in existence testified. By the late 1980s and in the 1990s their public hearing time allotment had increased; more important, the public hearing forum provided an opportunity for the employees to stage mass rallies and "pack" the hearing chamber with their members.

THE VOICE OF THE TAXPAYERS

Maryland in the 1970s

The citizens of Maryland may not sponsor petitions to place referenda issues on the state ballot, although, as will be discussed, some local governments do allow citizen initiatives on the local ballot. Nonetheless, during the 1970s Maryland homeowners were expressing their displeasure with ever-increasing property tax bills, and that issue rose to the top of the agendas of both the governor and the General Assembly. In Maryland, the assessment of real and personal property is a state responsibility, and beginning in 1974 a series of actions were taken to offset the effects of rapidly rising real property market values in the hope of restraining the burdens on homeowners; this meant that the property tax collections of local governments were reduced.

In 1974, the governor issued an executive order that rolled back the real property assessable base from 60 to 50 percent of full market value. In 1977, the General Assembly enacted a tax credit for owner-occupied residential properties, which exempted from taxation any assessment increase greater than 15 percent of the prior year's taxable assessment. One year later, the General Assembly again rolled back the assessable base, this time from 50 to 45 percent of full-market value. In the following year, the Assembly further reduced the taxable base, establishing a triennial assessment system. Beginning in fiscal year 1981, any increase in the market value of the one-third of the properties reassessed each year would be phased in by equal installments over the ensuing three year period; declines, however, would be effective in the first year. A statewide "growth limit" also was imposed on the overall increase in the assessable base. The effect of these changes was a further roll-back in the taxable base to 40 percent of full-market value.[29]

In 1977, a "full disclosure" requirement was enacted. Known as the constant-yield-tax-rate process, it required local governments that intended to levy a tax rate that would produce additional property tax revenue in the budget year to advertise that fact in a quarter-page advertisement in a general circulation newspaper, hold a public hearing, and present the reasons for the proposed increase. No allowance was made for inflation or population growth in calculating the constant-yield rate; these factors could be stated as reasons for any increase. Local officials were not required to levy the constant-yield rate, only to follow the process.

In other actions, the General Assembly expanded the state-financed "circuit-breaker" program in 1978 to include all homeowners under the age of 60, although the maximum credit was established at a lower level ($450 versus $900). The state also provided some relief for local property tax burdens by assuming responsibility for several programs, most notably in the criminal justice arena. It also undertook to assist localities in financing large capital-intensive construction projects: public schools, community colleges, corrections facilities, and water and sewer facilities.

With regard to controlling the growth of the state budget, the General Assembly established a Joint Committee on State Taxing and Spending Limitations. Annual budget increases were limited to the growth in the income of state residents.

Montgomery County in the 1970s

The issue of increasing property taxes also was on the 1970s political agenda in Montgomery County, brought to the fore by the 35-cent property tax rate increase to finance the fiscal year 1976 operating budget and culminating in the local elections of 1978. County homeowners had become increasingly agitated by their tax bill increases despite the actions taken by the governor and the General Assembly to restrain that growth.

The debate in the spring of 1975 that led to the 35-cent increase for fiscal year 1976 was acrimonious. As part of that debate, the council held a public hearing to elicit citizen views on options to fund the budget beyond the county executive's proposal for a 24-cent increase and no employee COLAs. Options presented included the following: (1) provide a 10.1 percent COLA for all employees as the board of education had negotiated with its employees and raise the property tax rate 87 cents; (2) some combination of property tax increases and increases in an array of local excise taxes on fuel-energy, telephone use, admissions and amusements, and hotel rooms; (3) an increase in solid waste tipping fees; and (4) a new real property recapture tax to collect taxes on under-assessed property when its ownership transferred.

Two evenings of hearings were held at which 208 people spoke, again before SRO crowds. Not surprisingly, all but two speakers, who were representing teachers and librarians, opposed any tax increase. Individual taxpayers, 174 of the 208 speakers, dominated the hearing. There was no taxpayers' collective voice, a condition that changed virtually overnight with the incorporation of the Montgomery County Taxpayers' League that spring. The seeds of fiscal discontent had been sown, more than three years before the question ever appeared on the ballot.

Three years later, in a petition drive initiated and led by the County's Taxpayers' League, the so-called TRIM amendment (Tax Relief In Montgomery) was placed on the 1978 ballot as Question E. It proposed to amend the county charter to limit the real property tax rate to $2.25 for each $100 of assessed valuation and to prohibit the levy of any new taxes. These restrictions could be waived only if six of the seven council members declared that an emergency existed, after conducting a public hearing on that declaration.

In an effort to offer the voters a more moderate alternative, the council unanimously endorsed placing a second question on the ballot (Question D) that proposed limiting annual operating budget increases to the rate of inflation unless five of the seven Council members voted to exceed that amount.

In the November 7, 1978, general election, Question D was approved (68,532 to 55,583), while the more restrictive TRIM amendment was narrowly defeated (78,862 to 74,003). This was a gubernatorial election year, and 93 percent of those who voted for governor also cast a vote regarding TRIM. The approved amendment to Section 305 of the charter reads as follows:

The aggregate operating budget, excluding the WSSC, the bi-county portion of the M-NCPPC and the WSTC, which exceeds the budget for the preceding year by a percentage increase greater than that of the Consumer Price Index for all urban consumers for the Washington metropolitan area for the preceding calendar year, shall be approved by the affirmative vote of five Council members.

In a related matter before the voters in 1978, a charter amendment limiting the authority of elected officials to approve capital improvement projects was also adopted. It requires that certain projects must be individually authorized by local law, thereby providing voters an opportunity to petition those projects to referendum if they are able to collect the requisite signatures of 5 percent of the county's registered voters (about 10,000). The implementing statute established the threshold for this requirement at projects costing $4 million,[30] as well including any project that is determined to "possess unusual characteristics or be of sufficient public importance."

Montgomery County was not alone in the Washington, D.C., area in having the fiscal powers of its elected officials limited by the voters in 1978. In Prince George's County even stricter limits were imposed by placing an absolute dollar cap on property tax revenues with no ability to exceed that cap without a charter amendment (the 1978 limit was $145 million).

The TRIM Debate

The tax limitation measures were only two of the eighteen questions (12 state and 6 county) placed before the voters on the 1978 ballot. But the community focused on the tax limitation debate. The *Washington Post* and the local newspapers editorialized in opposition to both TRIM and Question D.

TRIM is a bad idea . . . also known as the Son of Proposition 13 . . . [it] is widely regarded as a right-wing attack on schools and services. . . . The trouble with these arbitrary and rigid limits is that they strip local governments of the discretionary authority that they need to meet unexpected challenges. But if the solution is a bad one, it also has to be said that the distress is real. Sudden increases in real estate assessments impose unpredictable and inescapable burdens on families . . . Jumps in assessment increase the segregation of suburban neighborhoods by age and income. . . . If the TRIM amendment passes . . . [the county] will have to turn to the state more often. (*Washington Post*, October 30, 1978, editorial page)

The incumbent Republican county executive as well as the Republican candidate for executive opposed TRIM, as did both party slates running for county council. Many candidates supported Question D, although several opposed both measures. In contrast, the county Republican Central Committee supported TRIM, as did the countywide Chamber of Commerce. Many local chambers, including those in Rockville and Bethesda–Chevy Chase, opposed it. A "Fair Share Coalition" of seventeen civil rights, education, labor, and civic organizations was established to oppose TRIM. Both sides held forums, meetings, and rallies to publicize their positions. Paul Gann of California Proposition 13 fame appeared at an August 10 Taxpayers' League forum to rally support for TRIM.

The debate regarding the TRIM question focused on four issues. One concerned the desirability of having tax rate limits enshrined in the county's constitution. The League of Women Voters undertook an "action campaign" in opposition to TRIM, arguing that "rates should not be set by referendum and that the county government should have the exclusive right to change tax rates."

A second issue argued that businesses that had large property holdings would derive large reductions in their property tax bills at the expense of services for homeowners and public education. Examples cited included a $900,000 savings for the Potomac Electric Power Company; $500,000 for the C&P Telephone Company; $200,000 for the Washington Gas Company.

A third debate concerned the impact that placing a tax limit in the charter would have on the county's coveted triple-A bond rating. The county had received that rating in 1974 and was one of only eleven counties in the nation rated AAA both by Moody's and by Standard and Poor's.

A fourth matter, while on its face highly technical, was important in that it involved the legal interpretation of the amendment. There was great uncertainty about the interpretation of the $2.25 tax rate limit explicitly stated in the TRIM question. The county has ten real property tax rates—a county-wide General Fund rate plus nine special tax area rates.[31] Some are applied countywide, but others have limited geographic boundaries. The General Fund tax rate in fiscal year 1978 was $2.60 per $100 of assessed valuation, and the Taxpayers' League was very clear in the debates that their intent was for the $2.25 limit to apply only to that rate. Their stated intent was to achieve a 35-cent tax rate reduction, equal to the 35-cent increase that had been levied three years earlier to finance the fiscal year 1976 operating budget. They did not intend to reduce the special area rates, which totaled an additional 98 cents per $100 of assessed valuation. The Taxpayers' League retained legal counsel, which issued an opinion in support of its position. The County Attorney and other legal and fiscal experts, on the other hand, were not prepared to issue an opinion supporting that interpretation. Their view was that the TRIM proposal amended the charter section under which seven of the ten county property tax rates were levied and thus the $2.25 limit could apply to these special taxing areas as well. The differing interpretations had very different fiscal implications—a 35-cent reduction equivalent to $25 million versus an 80-cent reduction equivalent to $55 million. As total property tax collections in fiscal year 1979 were $236 million, the reduction would be either 11 or 25 percent.

In a related legal issue, the matter of placing a fixed tax rate limit in the charter at a time when the governor and General Assembly were reducing the taxable assessable base was also a matter of concern. As described, by 1978 the taxable base had been reduced from 60 to 45 percent of market value and there was no certainty that it would stop there; and it did not, going to 40 percent in fiscal year 1981.[32] The issue for the TRIM debate was whether a charter limit of $2.25 would be adjusted automatically if the assessment rate were changed by the state. Again there was some disagreement, but most agreed that the stated rate could not be adjusted automatically unless the charter language explicitly provided for it, and as drafted it did not.

Despite these many uncertainties and ambiguities, 48.5 percent of the more than 150,000 who cast a vote on TRIM supported it. The more moderate Question D alternative proposed by the county council was approved by 55 percent of the voters. The message to the elected leadership was very clear—reduce the burden of the property tax. Fiscal discontent was alive and well in the county!

Montgomery County in the 1990s

A dozen years later, as the 1990 local election year began, county homeowners again were unhappy with the level of their property tax bills, and in another citizen-led petition drive a charter amendment was placed on the ballot as Question F. It was approved by 56 percent of those who voted on the question at the November 6 general election (105,086 to 83,057); of those who cast a vote for governor in that election, 91 percent also voted on Question F. The amendment, called Fairness In Taxation (FIT), did two things: (1) it limited the ability of the council to increase property tax revenues, and (2) it created a macro-budgeting prepreparation budget process, as described in Chapter 2. The following language was added to Section 305 of the charter.

Unless approved by an affirmative vote of seven Councilmembers, the Council shall not levy an ad valorem tax on real property to finance the budgets that will produce total revenue that exceeds the total revenue produced by the tax on real property in the preceding fiscal year plus a percentage of the previous year's real property tax revenues that equals any increase in the Consumer Price Index as computed under this section. This limit does not apply to revenue from (1) newly constructed property, (2) newly rezoned property, (3) property that, because of a change in state law, is assessed differently than it was assessed in the previous tax year, (4) property that has undergone a change in use, and (5) any development district tax used to fund capital improvement projects.

The Council, sitting as a spending affordability committee, shall annually adopt spending affordability guidelines for the capital and operating budgets, including guidelines for the aggregate capital and aggregate operating budgets. The Council shall by law establish the process and criteria for adopting spending affordability guidelines. Any aggregate capital budget or aggregate operating budget that exceeds the guidelines then in effect requires the affirmative vote of seven Councilmembers for approval.

By 1994 the taxpayers were agitating again about tax burdens. Maryland is one of eleven states that authorizes local governments to levy an income tax,[33] but in Maryland, unlike the other states, it is mandatory, not permissive. The 24 local subdivisions must levy a local "piggyback" income tax of at least 20 percent, but not more than 60 percent, of the state rate on individual income only. The maximum "piggyback" rate was increased from 50 to 60 percent by the General Assembly in 1992 and became effective for the fiscal year 1993 budget. Montgomery County chose to use the higher rate, phasing in the increase over two fiscal years—55 percent in calendar year 1992 and 60 percent the following year. Many taxpayers felt that using the higher income tax rate should have been offset by a comparable reduction in property taxes, which was not done. A petition drive was mounted by Robin Ficker, a well-known anti-tax activist in the county, to place the issue before the voters. The amendment would have required "the rollback of the property tax to offset the amount received in the prior fiscal year from the income tax if the rate were 52 percent of the state income tax." To override the requirement would have required a unanimous vote of council members. The amendment was narrowly defeated (114,728 to 111,966). The fact that 49.3 percent of those who cast a vote supported this further limitation sent another strong message to the elected leadership.

THE VOICE OF THE EMPLOYEES: AN OVERVIEW

The road to securing collective bargaining rights by the employees began in the late 1960s and continued for twenty years, involving different processes and approaches for the various employee groups. The County Government employees had first to persuade the voters to amend the charter and then to persuade the council and executive to enact the implementing legislation. For the employees in the other agencies, legislative approval from the General Assembly and governor was needed. The history of each is summarized here.

Public School Teachers. County teachers have been organized for more than 125 years. The *1870 Annual Report of the Maryland State Department of Education* included the following regarding Montgomery County (Jewell, 1973: 63): "A Teachers' Association was organized last winter in the Third Election District under the auspices of the District School Commissioners. . . . [A]ll matters pertaining to education are discussed. The efficiency of these associations as an auxiliary to the development of our school system is well attested."

County board of education minutes for March 9, 1937, included the following economic agenda: "A study should be made in cooperation with the teachers' association of the county . . . for the employment of expert authority in connection with the study of salaries" (ibid.: 342).

Five years later, in March 1942, the board's minutes reflected the following regarding non-economic matters (ibid.).

The teachers appreciate the opportunity they have had to share in the formation of policies and to participate in the development of our county program of public education. This close working relationship between teachers and the Board of Education has resulted in the unification of the program throughout the county and in making each teacher feel that this keen interest in current problems contributes to the success of the program.

The teachers secured collective bargaining rights about 100 years after they organized. They were the first county employees to do so, with the passage of state legislation in 1968. It is the view of most that an illegal teachers' strike in February 1968, which closed the schools for seven days during the 90-day session of the General Assembly, succeeded in gaining these rights for the county's teachers. While the Montgomery County Education Association (MCEA) had engaged in a meet-and-confer process with the board and superintendent, many teachers were unhappy about a range of non-economic "professional issues"—class size, curriculum, teaching load—as well as their low level of pay when compared to that of other college graduates. Concerns also were expressed about the system's rapid growth, the increase in the number of larger and more impersonal schools, and an uncertainty associated with school assignments.

Other Public School Employees. The Montgomery County Council of Supporting Services Employees (MCCSSE) had been organized in 1973 to provide some level of collective voice for the school system's non-teaching, non-supervisory employees—blue, pink, and white collar alike. It probably is the most diverse of the employee groups in the county—many members have an eighth grade education (building service workers, cafeteria employees), while others have a master's degree (accountants, teacher aides). While organized, they too did not have bargaining rights until the General Assembly enacted the necessary legislation in 1974. Many believe that granting collective bargaining to the teachers had set the precedent for these employees.

The Montgomery County Association of Administrative and Supervisory Personnel (MCAASP) was formed in 1982 and began bargaining that year as well.

Montgomery College. In 1978, the General Assembly established collective bargaining rights for the employees of Montgomery College, but not for those at any of the state's fifteen other two-year colleges. The legislation excluded only those "involved directly in the determination of policy; supervisory or confidential employees; and student assistants."[34] However, only the 415 full-time faculty, defined in state law as equivalent to those teaching 12 credit hours per semester, engage in collective bargaining regarding salaries, benefits, and working conditions. They are represented by the College Chapter of the American Association of University Professors (AAUP).

The AAUP succeeded in having state legislation introduced by state senator and soon-to-be county executive, Charles Gilchrist. The motivating force, as described by those interviewed for this research, was an "environment of general distrust" that existed between the faculty and the then-college board and president. "A singular lack of quality leadership" resulting in a perception that they were being "mistreated" regarding a broad range of non-economic issues—abolishing tenure, revising the system of professorial ranks, and a lack of consultation on a range of matters including curriculum and plans for expansion. Economic issues seem to have been of secondary importance.

The initial battle was for the 250 full-time faculty members to choose an employee representative. The election has been described as "bitter and divisive," with the AAUP narrowly defeating the local teachers union, MCEA. Today, about two-thirds of the full-time faculty are AAUP members.

Bargaining the first agreement was "mainly a battle about governance;" it took two years to negotiate the management rights provisions. The first agreement on economic matters was included in the fiscal year 1980 budget.

The administrative and support staff employees have chosen not to exercise their right to bargain collectively. AFSCME and the Montgomery County Government Employees Organization (MCGEO) have tried at different times, but each has failed to collect sufficient signatures to call an election to select a representative.

Park and Planning Commission. The General Assembly enacted legislation in 1986 granting collective bargaining rights to the bi-county park police officers in the rank of sergeant and below.[35] They sought bargaining largely as a way to improve their salaries and benefits, which lagged well behind the levels in both Montgomery and Prince George's counties. The first contract was negotiated for fiscal year 1988.

A 1993 state law[36] authorized four additional bargaining units—professional/technical, service/labor, office, and trades (those with special manual skills). The legislation excludes attorneys, confidential employees, supervisors, those in pay grades 20 and above, and probationary employees. As of fiscal year 1996 none of these employee groups had chosen to bargain collectively.[37] MCGEO failed in a 1992 effort to organize the park system's service/labor and trades employees.

Sanitary Commission. There are no state or local statutes applicable to collective bargaining rights for commission employees. The policy is that they may organize and bargain if they so choose; however, only the maintenance and trade blue-collar workers have done so. Many believe that this was brought about by the commission's action to change the practices at its 24-hour-a-day operations from scheduled overtime to scheduled shift-work at a shift differential substantially less than the time-and-one-half overtime rate. There is no agency shop, but the commission does provide dues check-off for the approximately 150 (of 550 employees) who pay dues.

In the mid-1970s, there was a white collar group, represented by AFSCME, which organized when the commission threatened to eliminate its longevity pay policy. The group did not last long and ultimately was decertified. Several years later the Communication Workers of America attempted an organizing campaign, but an election was never held.

COUNTY GOVERNMENT EMPLOYEES ORGANIZE A COLLECTIVE VOICE

The road leading to full collective bargaining rights for County Government employees begins in 1975 and ends a dozen years later with the enactment of local legislation. Its evolution is presented here.

The debates surrounding cost-of-living adjustments during the fiscal year 1976 and 1977 budget deliberations, as described earlier, focused on limiting employee compensation increases. While upsetting to the employees, these debates were "low-key" compared to the furor generated by legislative proposals introduced in May 1975 (six months after the general election), which threatened to reduce pay and retirement benefits, not merely to limit their growth. It was these proposals that led directly to the organizing, for the first time, by County Government employees.

Proposals to Reduce Employee Compensation: The 1975 Model

Within days after the public hearing at which over 200 citizens spoke in opposition to tax increases to fund the fiscal year 1976 budget, one member of the council sponsored emergency legislation,[38] which would have: (1) given the council the authority to initiate amendments to the County Government's pay structure and retirement system, an authority that resided with an independent Personnel Board; (2) amended the structure of the County pay plan, changing the "normal annual step increase" from 5 percent to 2.5 percent after the third step and eliminating the 5-percent "longevity pay increase" after the tenth, fourteenth, and eighteenth years of service. This change in the "normal annual step" meant that it would take an employee eleven, rather than seven, years to move from the minimum to the maximum salary for a given pay grade; and (3) amended the retirement plan to change the formula for calculating the defined-benefit pension from the high twelve-month to the high 36-month salary. As drafted, the change applied to all employees, both present and future; an amendment to make its application prospective only was introduced. Since these were emergency bills designed to take effect immediately,[39] their enactment would require approval of five of the seven council members.

The reaction by County Government employees was virtually immediate. As described in the *Montgomery Journal* newspaper (May 15, 1975: A-1), "several employees have assumed leadership roles in an effort to organize a movement" to launch a "full scale battle" against the legislation. An Employee Defense Fund (EDF), comprised of employees from virtually every department including public safety, was "hastily established."

At a May 21 "mass meeting" on the roof of the County parking garage, more than 1,000 County employees heard the leader of the EDF, Frances Abrams, enumerate two issues on the new organization's agenda: "how to defend ourselves against the legislature and whether to establish a permanent organization" (*Montgomery Journal*, May 29, 1975). A representative from AFSCME spoke as well, "You may overcome this one, but tomorrow there will be another problem" (ibid.).

More than 600 employees registered to speak at the legislative public hearing, far more than could be accommodated on the two afternoons and evenings reserved. The 1,200-seat auditorium was filled to capacity at each session mainly by government workers, their families, and friends; large crowds remained outside as well. Virtually all of the testimony opposed the legislation, including that by the Republican county executive, who said these were "extreme proposals representing a step backward for the County's progressive merit system." One citizen noted that they were "forcing County employees into the arms of a labor union . . . a pattern too common in other jurisdictions." The employees' rhetoric included vignettes such as "cheap attempts . . . to subsidize the operation of County Government at the expense of County employees" and "the any Tuesday pay bill," referring to the fact that the council regularly meets on Tuesdays. Many employees, especially those closest to retirement, raised questions with regard to the deleterious effects the changes would have on their individual financial plans.

At its first legislative session after the public hearing, the legislation's sponsor made the motion to defeat the bills, which was adopted unanimously. In his remarks, the sponsor praised the employees saying, "their testimony has been interesting, stimulating, amusing at times, enlightening and thought provoking. In short . . . typical for Montgomery County." However, he cautioned that "some changes must be made, but in doing so we must develop a consensus as to the need and desirability of the changes."

Having successfully defeated the legislation, the County Government employees pursued the second item on their agenda—organizing themselves. As the EDF leader, Frances Abrams stated, "Such action is long overdue. Employees have come to recognize (because of these bills) just how defenseless they are" (*Montgomery Journal*, June 12, 1975: A-12). At a June 16 meeting the employees formed the Montgomery County Government Employees Organization (MCGEO) as an independent, permanent employee organization. Today it has become Local 1994, United Food and Commercial Workers, AFL-CIO.

Proposals to Reduce Employee Compensation: The 1978 Model

Almost three years later, in February 1978, the County Council, under the leadership of newly appointed Council Member William G. Colman,[40] a former president of the county school board and former executive director of the Advisory Commission on Intergovernmental Relations, made a second attempt to amend the County Government's retirement plan[41] and pay structure. These legislative amendments were enacted by the council in May of the local election year and were signed by the lame-duck executive; in many ways they were more severe than those defeated in 1975.

The new pay structure eliminated the "fixed step increase" and specified only a minimum and a maximum salary for each pay grade. The "normal annual increase" was reduced from 5 percent to 2 percent, but managers were given discretion to grant larger increases. For employees who received a "normal" 2 percent increase, it could take as long as 23 years to move from the minimum to maximum salary, well beyond the then-existing plan and twice as long as the defeated 1975 proposal.

The new retirement plan became effective July 1, 1978, but it covered only those hired on or after that date. Employees hired previously were given an option to join the new plan, which did the following:

- Reduced the employee contribution for non–public safety employees from 6 percent to 3 percent of salary up to the Social Security wage base; the contribution remained at 6 percent above that salary level. For public safety employees, the respective rates were 7.5 and 3.75 percent.
- Changed the formula for calculating the pension benefit from the high twelve-month to the high 36-month salary (the same as defeated in 1975).
- Integrated the pension benefit with the Social Security benefit, reducing the local pension when the retiree reached age 65.
- Capped the full-inflation cost-of-living protection for the pension benefit at 5 percent in any year, below the unlimited protection in the pre-1978 plan.

The atmosphere surrounding the debate on these bills was quite different from that of 1975. While the employees were organized, the environment had changed—the taxpayer revolt had begun, the fiscal landscape had changed, and the retirement plan changes applied only to "new hires."

To soften the impact that these changes would have on employees, as well as deal with the political dilemma they had confronted in their fiscal year 1976 and 1977 budget deliberations, the council introduced legislation[42] in July requiring the executive to include funding for a cost-of-living adjustment in the recommended budget. It was enacted by the lame-duck council (four of the seven members were leaving) on November 17, ten days after the general election. Its legislative intent was "to provide for and ensure in an orderly, uniform manner as part of its budgetary process, guaranteed annual wage adjustments to merit system employees of the County Government to compensate them for increases in areawide consumer prices and other cost-of-living factors."

The executive was required to include sufficient funds in the proposed operating budget to fund fully a COLA equal to 75 percent of the change in the Washington, D.C., consumer price index. It further provided that

The Council shall accord one of the highest priorities to the full funding of the . . . adjustment unless reasons are given for not doing so, and shall make a finding in the budget resolution as to the extent to which full funding is achieved. Unless otherwise provided for . . . that implementation of the full amount of the adjustment would necessitate substantial layoffs of personnel or result in other widespread hardship to County Government employees.

The chief administrative officer was authorized to provide a higher adjustment if "funds are available and approved by the County Council for such purposes." These provisions remained in effect through fiscal year 1987, when collective bargaining appeared on the landscape.

Meet-and-Confer

The County Government's first "Employer-Employee Relations Act" was introduced by the council in April 1976 and enacted in December of that year.[43] The legislation permitted "the election and certification of employee organizations for the purposes of meeting with county officials concerning conditions of employment and the resolution of grievances." The legislative intent stated that

government should take the initiative in providing a vehicle whereby government employee representation can emerge and evolve in a fashion consistent with both the needs of the employee and those of the government. . . . that this can best be accomplished by enacting local legislation which provides for the voluntary representation of government employees by their duly designated and elected employee organizations. . . . that the efficient administration of the County Government is enhanced by providing employees an opportunity to participate in the formulation and implementation of policies and practices affecting the conditions of their employment.

The legislation did the following:

1. Entitled a recognized employee organization "to meet at reasonable times with county representatives to discuss" permitted subjects. However, it did "not obligate either the county or an employee organization to agree to any proposal or to make any concession with respect to any matter discussed by the parties at such a meeting. Any decision made at any such meeting is in no way binding upon the parties." In the final analysis the chief administrative officer decided all matters.

2. Prohibited any employee organization to "Call or engage in a strike, work stoppage or slowdown, picket the County in connection with a strike, work stoppage or slowdown in a County-employee dispute, or condone any such activity by failing to take affirmative action to prevent or stop it."

3. Established employee units on the basis of "a clear and identifiable community-of-interest. Such factors as . . . sharing common skills, working conditions, physical locations, organizational structures, and integrated work processes should be considered." The units were to be as large as possible consistent with maintaining a community of interest. A limit of seven units was imposed.

4. Made "any County merit system employee working on a continuous full-time, career or part-time, career basis" eligible to be a unit member, but there was a long list of exceptions: (a) employees who reported directly to, or whose immediate supervisor reported directly to, an elected official; (b) all directors, deputy or assistant directors of principal departments and offices as defined in the charter and any employees providing direct staff or administrative support to these directors, including division, office, or section directors; (c) all employees of the legislative branch, the Office of County Attorney, the Office of Management and Budget, the Personnel Office, and the Office of Employee Relations; and (d) for the uniformed services, eligibility was limited to those in the rank of corporal and below.

5. Made membership in a recognized employee organization a voluntary decision on the part of each employee. The legislation did not supersede any merit system laws or regulations. For example, employees were permitted to "pursue an individual grievance through established administrative procedures."

6. Established a procedure for certifying representative employee organizations. An election was required if at least 30 percent of the employees in a unit signed a petition requesting that a unit be formed. The ballot had to include the name of any organization that presented written evidence by at least 10 percent of the eligible employees as well as an option for "no representation." A valid election required participation by at least 60 percent of the employees *eligible* to participate. To be certified, an organization had to receive a majority of the votes cast; a runoff was required if necessary.

Almost immediately after the legislation became effective in March 1977, the CAO established a unit for non-supervisory police officers; and in June 1977 the Fraternal Order of Police, Montgomery County Lodge 35, was certified as the employee representative. Six months later, in January 1978, the CAO established a General Government unit for all other eligible employees, and in the election that followed, MCGEO was the only organization on the ballot. It received 1,882 votes; 142 voted for "no representation;" however, 2,024 votes did not constitute 60 percent of the 3,804 eligible voters, and thus MCGEO was not certified.

The November 1978 general election brought substantial change in the elected leadership of the County Government. The Republican county executive was succeeded by a Democrat and former state senator. Four new members were elected to the all-Democratic seven-member council.

Employee representatives undertook a major lobbying effort to amend the meet-and-confer statute to ease the requirement for certifying an employee organization. After much debate, in October 1979 the requirement was changed from 60 percent of those eligible to vote to 50 percent of the valid votes cast in an election.

In March 1981, the next CAO established three units rather than the one General Government unit—a Service, Labor, and Trades unit (SLT); an Office, Professional, and Technical unit (OPT); and a Supervisory unit.

An SLT unit election was held in September 1981 with four organizations plus "no representation" on the ballot; no organization was certified even after an October runoff election. Of the 1,231 employees eligible to vote, 715 voted for "no representation," 249 voted for AFSCME, and 267 did not vote.

An OPT election was conducted in December 1981, and after a runoff election in January 1982, MCGEO was certified, receiving 477 votes compared to 405 votes for the runner-up, the county teachers' union (MCEA). Of the 2,400 eligible voters, 882 participated and 477 chose the winner.

At the time many expressed surprise that the white and pink collar employees had selected a group representative while the largely blue collar SLT employees had not. But a major issue in the county, as it was across the nation in the late 1970s and early 1980s, was pay equity. The County Government had enacted legislation in 1979, "[to] ensure all occupational classes, except those on the minimum wage/seasonal salary schedule . . . involving comparable duties, experience, responsibilities, and authority are paid comparable salaries that reflect the relative value of the services performed." (Montgomery County, Maryland, 1996: Section 33–11[b][5])

Many employees in the OPT unit worked in female-dominated jobs—public health nurses, human services workers, librarians, clerical workers—and MCGEO had aligned itself with a number of organizations[44] in actively representing these employees during the controversy that surrounded the implementation of a Quantified Job Evaluation System (QES) to carry out the provisions of the pay equity statute. At one public hearing[45] MCGEO testified, "Pay equity is the single most important economic issue for working women today. . . . Nurses, librarians, and secretaries are essential to their employers, yet the QES system makes them less valuable than traffic signal technicians or landfill supervisors."

Collective Bargaining

While County Government employees had succeeded in having the meet-and-confer legislation enacted in December 1976, that had not been their first choice. In the fall of 1975, about four months after its formation, MCGEO proposed state legislation that would have authorized collective bargaining for County Government employees. However, the county's senators and delegates in Annapolis did not support the bill during the 1976 session of the General Assembly; similar legislation failed in the 1977 and 1978 sessions as well.

The County Attorney issued an opinion (#78006) that enactment of a public local law by the state legislature was not necessary since the county had the authority, under its home-rule powers, to submit a charter amendment on this matter to the voters if it chose to do so; it was the county attorney's view that enactment of state legislation would be unconstitutional.

In 1978, a member of the council did propose a charter amendment to authorize collective bargaining, but there was not sufficient support on the council to place the matter on the November ballot. The various tax limitation measures (TRIM and Question D) would be before the voters at that time, and a council majority believed that the timing was not appropriate for a second major issue.

The county has a bipartisan Charter Review Commission,[46] which studied the collective bargaining issue during its 1979–1980 term, and in its May 1980 report recommended against amending the charter to authorize the council to enact collective bargaining legislation. A majority of commissioners expressed concerns about fragmenting the merit system. One of the many examples cited was the charter requirement for a uniform salary plan, which would not be possible if multiple bargaining units were established. It did recommend, however, strengthening the meet-and-confer process by establishing an impasse resolution procedure. There was a further recommendation to establish a task force of citizens and employees to review "what charter and legislative changes would need to be made in order to initiate collective bargaining" (Montgomery County, Maryland, May 1980: 30).

But the employee groups, most notably the Fraternal Order of Police, were not standing still. In a signature campaign spearheaded by police officers, a proposed charter amendment was petitioned to the ballot in the November 1980 general election. Question F was adopted by a vote of more than 2 to 1 (141,099 to 69,482). In this presidential election year, 80 percent of those who cast a vote for president voted on Question F, which added a new Section 510 to the charter: "The Montgomery County Council shall provide by law for collective bargaining with binding arbitration with an authorized representative of the Montgomery County police officers. Any law so enacted shall prohibit strikes or work stoppages by police officers."

The debate over the amendment was polarized. One police officer commented that "Meet-and-confer is nothing more than an employee suggestion box with the anonymity removed." At a September 30, 1980, public hearing conducted by the Charter Review Commission, the FOP representative stated, "The desire of employees to have a voice in discussing the working conditions which affect our whole lives . . . [the] need of police officers to have a meaningful dialogue with management . . . and the need for the formal procedures to insure that the dialogue does not break down . . . [a] need for a method to resolve impasse."

The Democratic county executive opposed the amendment.[47] The tax limits approved by the voters two years earlier were being implemented, and he placed his argument four-square on the fiscal aspects in testimony at the same September 30 hearing. "The principal reason for this position is my consistent opposition to compulsory arbitration of fiscal issues. In my view elected officials must be accountable for such issues as part of the budget process. Compulsory arbitration interferes with the responsibility of those elected officials to the electorate by transferring fiscal decisions to outside parties."

The *Washington Post* in a November 3 editorial also opposed the amendment: "The County Executive and others urging a vote AGAINST argue—correctly, in our view—that the procedures would diminish the accountability of elected officials for financial matters."

The legislation to implement bargaining for all sworn officers in the rank of corporal and below was enacted on April 6, 1982. The statute maintains the council's role as the final fiscal authority.[48] Specifically, any provision of an agreement negotiated between the executive and the representative of the police officers that requires an appropriation must receive the explicit approval of the council. A failure of the council to provide the necessary funding negates that provision of the agreement.

The Fraternal Order of Police was elected as the police officers' bargaining representative, and the first contract was agreed to on April 12, 1983, to be effective for fiscal year 1984. Among its many provisions was one for an agency shop.

By 1984 the pressure was increasing to extend collective bargaining rights to other County Government employees. The Charter Review Commission (Montgomery County, Maryland, May 1984) unanimously recommended adding a new section to the charter to permit, not require, the council to enact collective bargaining legislation for the remaining employees of the County Government.[49] The proposal appeared as Question B on the November 1984 ballot and was approved by the voters by more than 2 to 1 (162,921 to 70,070). In this presidential election, 80 percent of those who cast a vote for president voted on Question B. A new Section 511 was added to the charter: "The Montgomery County Council may provide by law for collective bargaining, with arbitration or other impasse procedures. . . . Any law so enacted shall prohibit strikes or work stoppages for such officers and employees."

The charter also was amended to permit exclusions from the merit system "only to the extent that such provisions are subject to collective bargaining."

In presenting the employees' perspective Gino Renne, the president of

MCGEO, stated the following at the October 17, 1983, Charter Review Commission public hearing:

County employees have suffered reduced benefits, and reduced cost-of-living adjustments and yearly increments. RIF's are becoming more common. . . . [T]hings do not look promising for public employees. . . . Under meet-and-confer reality is that we request and they decide. What they decide is what goes . . . what we have is paternalism. . . . Collective bargaining would not make public workers fiscally irresponsible . . . we are taxpayers. . . . We accept the fact that the teachers and the police have won collective bargaining as an effective tool to solve problems. To deny other county employees the same consideration would be unjust. . . . Collective bargaining provides a natural funnel for employee ideas and suggestions to be more forcefully brought to management's attention.

Legislation[50] to implement charter section 511 was not introduced until March 25, 1986, more than sixteen months after the voters had authorized it; it was enacted in late June by the lame-duck Council (three of seven members were leaving) and signed by the lame-duck executive,[51] and it was effective for bargaining for the fiscal year 1988 budget.

The legislative policy stated,

It is the public policy of Montgomery County to promote a harmonious, peaceful, and cooperative relationship between the County Government and its employees and to protect the public by assuring, at all times, the responsive, orderly, and efficient operation of County government and services. . . . [It] is in the public interest that employees have the opportunity to bargain collectively . . . It is also in the public interest that the County government and a representative of County employees bargain collectively in good faith without interference with the orderly process of government. (Montgomery County, Maryland, 1996: Section 33–101)

The legislation included a strong employer rights provision enumerating nineteen specific rights covering a broad range of matters. There was a strong antistrike provision as well. To resolve an impasse there were procedures for factfinding and mediation. The binding arbitration that the charter mandated for police officers was not enacted for other employees. Agency shop was not mandated, but it was a permitted subject for bargaining.

The council retained its authority regarding any matters that required funding. "Any agreement shall provide for automatic reduction or elimination of wage and/or benefit adjustments if: (1) the Council does not take action necessary to implement the agreement, or a part of it; (2) funds are not appropriated; or (3) lesser amounts than those stated in the agreement are appropriated" (ibid.: Section 33–108[j]).

Many of the other provisions remained the same as those in the meet-and-confer statute. There were notable exceptions: all supervisory positions were excluded from bargaining as were all positions in pay grades 27 through 40; bargaining was permitted only for non-supervisory employees in pay grades 5 through 26. Also excluded were any positions jointly financed by the state, which affected many in the health and human services functions. The legislation limited bargaining to two units—OPT and SLT—similar to those established under meet-and-confer. When the firefighters and emergency rescue workers became county employees in 1987, a third unit was established for those non-supervisory employees.

In 1994 the career firefighters petitioned a charter amendment to the November ballot that was a virtual carbon copy of the charter provision for police officers described earlier. Section 510A mandates collective bargaining and requires the use of binding arbitration for career firefighters. Question C was adopted by the voters 77–23 percent. It was a gubernatorial election year, and 86 percent of those who cast a vote for governor voted on this issue.

Virtually all employees in the various agencies now have the statutory authority to bargain collectively. Why have some chosen to use it? Why not others? These matters are addressed in the next section.

THE EMPLOYEES USE COLLECTIVE VOICE IN THE MID-1990s

Why have some employees chosen collective voice? Why not others? Is fiscal discontent an important consideration? Is the political dimension important? Have the employees benefited from using their collective voice? Has management benefited? What is today's employee agenda? Has it changed over time?

In an effort to address these questions, interviews were conducted with a cross-section of county leaders representing broad groups of participants in the public sector labor-management relations arena—elected officials, senior appointed officials, and labor leaders. The general methodology has been discussed earlier. When the themes elicited from the interviews can be summed up by one individual's comments, those are quoted.

Why Have Some Chosen to Bargain Collectively?

Two themes emerged in the interviews with the elected and appointed officials as well as the labor leaders regarding the reasons for choosing collective voice. First, it is "a voice that will be heard"; and second, it provides "access to the process and the decision makers." Labor leaders added such vignettes as "power in numbers" and "clout in unity."

Employees were asking, "Who is standing up for my interests?" And as one appointed official put it, "Voicing concerns is much more difficult without an organization." One elected official added, "You bet the leadership of a group that represents several hundred or even thousands of citizens will get on my calendar to present their agenda and views. . . . That's true for the PTA's, the chambers [of commerce], or the unions. . . . I doubt some anonymous individual would get one-on-one time."

An individual "only has a limited arsenal to influence outcomes. . . . An organization can represent the little guy by providing a voice and some measure of protection." As one appointed official noted, "A formal agenda for access is established. It puts them as equals at the table." And as one labor leader said, "Resolving disputes, which is what the bargaining process is all about, requires a level table. There must be an adult relationship, not another parent-child relationship."

Special interest politics also was mentioned by many. As one elected official said, "Given the importance of special interests in the political process, there is no alternative to organizing if one wants to foster a position and be heard." As an appointed official noted, "Special interest politics have become so very important during difficult budget times. Bargaining enables employees to have their views heard without being unilaterally imposed by management."

Most agreed that there are additional dimensions for certain employee groups, especially public safety. They "have a community of interest," not found in other more diverse employee groups. "They are accustomed to teamwork . . . their lives depend on each other." Firefighters, for example, "live and sleep under one roof." There also is a certain fraternal dimension ("billiards and beer"), as well as the employees' perception of their "unique situation and needs." A final point, which several made, is that public safety employee organizations "are built from within and are not organized by outside influences or groups. . . . This enhances solidarity."

Does Fiscal Discontent Play a Role?

The prevailing view is that fiscal discontent played a significant role in motivating the employees to bargain collectively.

The virtually unanimous view of the labor leaders was summed up by one in the following way: "The budget process is critical to achieving our economic agenda and is important for achieving our non-economic objectives as well. [The 1990 Fairness In Taxation revolt] just made it much more difficult." The pre-preparation Spending Affordability Guidelines process enacted in 1990 "requires all of the participants to engage earlier and fight longer to get their share of the shrinking pie." It "created a zero sum game." Another added, "FIT introduced a 'cap' not unlike a salary cap in sports. Within that cap a union must address the community's priorities as well as its own." An elected official agreed, noting that "everyone, the agencies, the employees, and the decision-makers were forced to prioritize their objectives."

"TRIM [in 1978] began a public debate, but after a few years the public fell asleep. Since FIT everyone is awake." And as one elected official said, "FIT eliminated the tax option for the foreseeable future. The tradeoff now is public services versus compensation and employment levels." Another official noted, "The limits imposed by the taxpayers changed the negotiating dynamic for the less-visible employee groups. . . . Funding for supporting services activities in the schools is harder to achieve when they come up against direct classroom instruction.''

''Before the revolts we didn't need to look at the budget. All we had to do was present our position to the elected officials,'' is how one labor leader put it. Labor leaders agree that they now must analyze all aspects of the budget. ''FIT in combination with the recession of the early Nineties forced us to look at issues which previously we had absolutely no interest in, and to educate ourselves about budget and economic matters—bond ratings, enterprise funds, unappropriated surplus, and the like.'' ''Why do we need a triple-A bond rating? Maybe a double or a single-A is just fine.'' The local unions rely heavily on assistance from the international unions and the Montgomery County Public Employees Council for research, coordination, and disseminating information to the membership. They now also hire outside experts and consultants, which increases their expenses and has led many to increase their dues; for example, MCGEO's bi-weekly dues increased in 1994 from $9.50 to $12.50.

Several elected and appointed officials perceive communication problems between the union leaders and their members and wonder if the leaders reflect the views of the membership. Labor leaders emphasized the importance of communicating with their members about the union's agenda as well as ''the big picture regarding economic realities.'' ''The members frequently do not understand the complexities surrounding many bargaining issues. They want more than access. They want their position adopted 100 percent of the time.'' ''The members expect their leaders to 'bring home the bacon.' We must educate the members that we will not always succeed, but we will be successful frequently enough to make a difference.'' Another added, ''We have to change their expectations regarding the outcomes at the bargaining table.'' As one of the leaders of a group that has binding arbitration said, ''I must constantly remind the members that an arbitrator will not always accept our position, and when the arbitrator rules I am legally bound to support that decision.''

Why Have Some Chosen Not to Bargain Collectively?

The experience in Montgomery County follows closely one of the patterns that emerged in the national data presented in Chapter 5—lower density and less use of collective bargaining by the employees of special districts and those governments that rely to a lesser degree on tax revenues to support their operations. Several distinct groups of county employees have chosen not to bargain collectively even though they are authorized to do so—four of the groups at the planning commission, the white and pink collar employees at the sanitary commission, and all of the non-faculty employees at the college. Why have they not pursued the same avenue as their counterparts in the County Government and school system? Is there something in the water? When those interviewed for this research were asked about these differences, various reasons emerged, some generic, others specific to the organization. They can be summarized as follows:

- The employees do not perceive "severe" fiscal restraint. Their fiscal environment does not rely as heavily on local taxes to finance the budget. Rather, user fees are used extensively—water and sewer charges, student tuition, enterprise funding. Further, the council does not have detailed line-item control over the budget.

- "The county is not part of their world." They do not see the government as their employer and thus do not perceive an important role for the elected executive or council member or school board. There is a strong identity with the agency for which they work: they are in the utility business, they operate the golf course, they provide higher education.

- "The political dimension is much less apparent." The appointed governing bodies matter. "There is a layer of insulation between the elected officials and the employees."

- Employees feel they have a voice, that they are listened to, and that management will respond. They have access to their *appointed* governing bodies, and there is a high level of employee involvement and participation on matters that affect them. "A recipe for unionization is to unilaterally approve take-aways." Management does not act unilaterally, thereby minimizing conflict. For example, at the college there is a Staff Assistant to the President for Staff Concerns; a "Staff Senate" similar to the "Faculty Senate" meets regularly with the president and the human resources director. At the sanitary commission, "those who demonstrate strong labor-management relations skills" are placed in management positions. There is a "foundation of trust." "The employees perceive that they are treated fairly."

- Their agency "is a good place to work." There has been "no disruptive issue" and "no driving force to organize." The compensation package is competitive, the working conditions are good, and there is general job security. These employees have experienced few, if any, layoffs or furloughs. If there were no COLAs, employees continued to receive within-grade step increases. But when "a compelling reason is perceived" the employees will seek bargaining—park police were paid less than officers in both counties; the loss of scheduled overtime by WSSC employees; governance issues for college faculty.

- For the bi-county agencies, organizing employees is somewhat more difficult because of their geographic dispersion (1,000 square miles) as well as the cultural differences and identities between the counties. With a widely dispersed workforce over several jurisdictions, they do not possess much "political clout."

The Political Dimension

Although all of the county's employee organizations do not actively participate in political activities (notably MCAASP and the AAUP), the majority do. Participation in the local political process by employee groups and their members is an important voice dimension of the local bargaining process. The view of one labor leader was echoed by many of them. "The political process is the name of the game. We cannot achieve what we want without participating in it. Supporting the winner will get us in the door to talk whenever we need to."

Another added that the membership "expects officials to deliver and we do not hesitate to punish" those who do not.

But is that rhetoric or reality? As one elected official said, "One is never quite sure where the locus of power is in a given election." Another noted that "The reality may be different from the perception, but the perception of many elected officials is that employee groups have political power" and if "elected officials think the unions have political clout it gives them political leverage." Many cited the teacher, police, and firefighter organizations as powerful special interests, equal to those of business and civic groups. "The teachers' union has great political clout. It is more important in a board of education election than the countywide PTA." As evidence to support this view, many cited the action taken by the school board in fiscal year 1996 when, "with no demand for a give back from the unions," it raised average class size by one student to fund, within the council adopted budget categories, a 2.7 percent cost-of-living adjustment for its three unions, rather than the 2 percent funded by the council.

One elected official put it this way: "When the unions think strategically they can be a powerful political force. But they may not be fully aware of their power and may not use it as well as they could." The potential impact that a job action by MCCSSE could have on the school system was one frequently cited example. If boiler operators, janitors, bus drivers, cafeteria workers, teacher aides, and similar workers were to "revolt," they would "close the schools." But it is that diversity of membership that makes it difficult to develop a unified position.

Many members of the various groups "do not accept a union mind-set and are unwilling to participate in any overt actions such as protests or working to the rule." In Montgomery County, it was noted by many, employees must be careful not to generate a public relations backlash as happened when many teachers "broke a bond of trust" when they refused to write recommendation letters for students applying for college. Such actions created a rift between the union and the PTAs, which came to view the union as "solely self interested. Then the elected officials had to choose a side."

There was general consensus that the efforts of an employee organization can make a difference in the outcome of a close election, especially a Democratic party primary for a single-member district office. When the county changed to a system of electing five members of both the county council and the board of education by district rather than at-large, it likely enhanced the influence of the various employee groups, especially the teachers and public safety employees. In certain districts the employees represent a relatively large proportion of the electorate, which can be important in the primary. For example, about 12,000 to 16,000 votes are cast in the Democratic primary for a district seat on the council; for the non-partisan school board election the numbers are somewhat higher. The 1990 Democratic primary election for county executive was won by Neal Potter when he defeated the incumbent, Sidney Kramer, by less than 3,700 votes out of more than 83,000 cast (52 to 48 percent). Potter had been supported by the teachers union, which "worked tirelessly" in support of his candidacy, which he felt "made the difference" in his narrow victory.

One view shared by many of those who have run for elective office is the importance of employee groups in providing "people power" for a campaign. "They can be the eyes, ears, legs, and arms of a campaign." Their role in "getting out the vote" on election day was frequently cited as an important function, as well as staffing a headquarters office, operating phone banks, distributing literature, and working the polls. But, as one labor leader noted, it has become increasingly difficult to mobilize participation. "Our active members are aging and it is difficult to energize many of the younger members"—two-worker households, the need to hold two jobs, and family commitments compete for their free time. Increasingly, union activities are expanding beyond the normal venues to trying to influence neighbors, church communities, parents of children in the neighborhood, grandparents and their senior citizen colleagues, and the like.

Most elected officials indicated that, on balance, they try to avoid politically antagonizing the employee groups. In an election "it is better that they be neutral and silent rather than in vocal opposition." If they are against you they may seek a candidate to oppose you in the primary, or you may have to focus your entire campaign on overcoming their opposition.

Several noted that the county's unions in recent times have not been as politically skillful as in the past. Union leaders acknowledge that and attribute it to resource limitations; only a small percentage of members contribute to their political action committees. The unions have begun to prioritize issues and candidates, either for support or defeat, and no longer try to address every issue and candidate. They have begun to target their resources, "especially in the primaries, to defeat those who walk on the big issues and support those who are with us."

One vehicle used by the employee groups, especially for Democratic party primary candidates, is the questionnaire to elicit positions on matters of interest to them. Responses are often used to "hold their feet to the fire" if elected, and they "are read back to you when a particular matter is debated." It may be difficult to avoid a "flip-flop." As one elected official noted, if the union actively supports a successful candidate, "they expect 150 percent support in return on matters of interest to them during your term of office."

If the union can get "their candidate" elected, it can make a proportionally greater difference at the local level. "It's like a basketball team where one player can have a major impact. Supporting a winning executive or supporting one or two members of a 7-member body makes a big difference."

Does Collective Voice Provide Benefits for the Employees?

The prevailing view shared by all groups is that with collective bargaining the employees are better off than they otherwise would have been, but one official noted, ''The net benefit is unlikely to be as great as the union leadership claims since the dues can be burdensome.'' The views of two appointed officials are noteworthy.

By joining together employee issues appeared on the radar screen for decision makers. . . . Funding for compensation was no longer a budgetary residual. Management could no longer just allocate an amount for COLAs and benefits based on a political judgment *after* allocation decisions had been made about service levels and tax burdens.

If the employees were not organized and bargaining, they would be shafted by management even in a place as paternalistic as Montgomery County.

A distinction was drawn by many between bargaining about economic and non-economic issues. On the economic front, the prevailing view is that despite difficult fiscal and economic times, the employees have been very adept at ''protecting their past economic gains.'' In certain instances, they have been able to achieve further gains. Had they not been organized, most believe employee benefits would have been reduced substantially, even for current workers. Salaries are somewhat higher than they would have been, although they did not keep pace with inflation. Job security was likely enhanced, with fewer layoffs and less privatization than would have otherwise occurred. ''MCGEO employees accepted mandatory furlough days to protect jobs.'' As the issue of job security increased in priority for the MCGEO employees, the bargaining agreements included provisions to provide a modicum of voice for them—a 90-day notification requirement, if management chooses to privatize.

But it is in the arena of non-economic and governance issues that most believe the employee groups have made their greatest strides. ''They have made major gains in work rules and governance which were agreed to in lieu of changes in the economic package.'' ''They were able to reduce management prerogatives and thereby attain many of their governance objectives.'' ''The unions were pampered. . . . The bargaining was too collegial. . . . The elected officials made concessions and gave away many management rights with no quid pro quo. . . . The unions now have too much of a policy role.'' ''Management rights have been eroded a little bit in each contract. How far will it go?'' Few were able to provide a response.

What Has Management Gained?

One appointed official summed it up this way: ''I cannot overstate the importance of a negotiated agreement in managing an organization. We negotiate the what, but even more so the how.'' ''Management flexibility is reduced'' was the major negative cited by the appointed officials who manage these large organizations. But the prevailing view is that they also benefit in certain ways from collective bargaining. It ''describes a relationship that simplifies matters.

... Management gains a centralized process that is helpful.'' Human resources management is made easier when "managers only have to deal with the union rep and not each individual employee.'' "The biggest help is that it reduces grievances and centralizes the process.''

A second frequently cited benefit is that "the union can serve as an excellent communication network to reach the general membership.'' They can be "very helpful in explaining a given situation to their membership'' and, if the leadership is convinced about a situation, "can help to bring about the wholesale changes that may be necessary.'' Two examples cited were the County Government's negotiated agreements to change from a defined benefit to a defined contribution pension in 1994 and to eliminate its indemnity health plan in 1995.

A third benefit frequently mentioned is that "organizing keeps management on its toes.'' It can "increase accountability and thereby force managers to do a better job.'' "The unions can bring expertise, creativity, and a national perspective to an organization. . . . We need to foster that.'' As one elected official added, "It forces elected officials and appointed managers to articulate their positions on issues raised. This is a benefit for all concerned, especially the taxpayers.''

Several appointed officials noted that various forms of group work are at the foundation of contemporary strategies in the public management arena, including total quality management (TQM), quality of worklife, and employee participation programs. Organizing for purposes of collective bargaining has many of the same objectives—empowerment, participation, recognition, and respect. One labor leader noted that an employee organization can help management plan and implement changes to improve efficiency and effectiveness, the very goals of these management strategies.

One appointed official noted the importance of management's ability and experience in being able to work effectively with unions. Said one official, "Agreements can inhibit communication between managers and their employees. . . . Their legalistic and adversarial structure may stifle partnerships and participation.'' But another added, "We need to develop partnerships and overcome distrust. . . . Keep the stewards informed and let them help.''

Employee Concerns and Agendas

"Protection'' was an almost universal response to sum up the employee agenda in the mid-1990s—their job, their benefits, their pay. The major concern is "to keep what we fought so hard to gain.''

The prevailing view is that job security is the primary concern for the vast majority of the non–public safety employee organizations. "Protecting benefits'' ranks second for all employee groups, but is "a major priority for single parents, older workers, and part-timers.'' "Wages, a top priority a decade ago, no longer are for most groups,'' although many blue collar and public safety employees "remain focused on the pocketbook.'' Working conditions are no longer a major issue, although there are certain arenas where they are important—school safety and public safety are examples. An employee's age is an important factor regarding priorities—"younger workers want cash in their pocket while older workers focus on benefits."

Privatization and the loss of employment is "labor's major concern and issue du jour" noted one elected official. A labor leader added, "Downsizing and privatizing are both on the management agenda. Employees are boxed between both. Incumbents are now beginning to lose their jobs." The increased use of part-time, non-career employees also is of concern to many labor leaders.

"Job security versus dollars is the number one tradeoff" for most of the non–public safety employees in the mid-1990s. In many instances the employees have accepted the former in lieu of the latter. To avoid layoffs, County Government employees accepted an agreement with no cost-of-living adjustment for three consecutive fiscal years (1992, 1993, 1994) as well as five furlough days in 1993. But, as one appointed official said, "In the not too distant future, management will have to confront these matters which are 'strike issues' for many unions."

Beyond job security and protecting benefits, other concerns expressed by those interviewed mainly pertain to selected groups of employees; among them were empowerment, greater participation in policy development and decision making, to be treated with respect and be recognized as professionals, salary comparability, and the need to update and enhance skills (technology, management, handling hazardous materials, etc.).

SUMMARY

The case study replicates many of the patterns that were identified in earlier chapters regarding both fiscal discontent and its relationship to the use of a collective voice strategy by local government employees.

First, fiscal discontent began in the county well before the first tax limitation measure appeared on the ballot, similar to the experience in California and Massachusetts. The voices of hundreds of individual taxpayers erupted in opposition to large increases in the property and other less significant local taxes at a public hearing in the spring of 1975. Within weeks, the County Taxpayers' League was formed creating the collective voice that led the petition drive to place a tax limitation measure on the ballot in November 1978.

Second, the county's budget process emphasizes the use of voice by the participants. Each agency budget is the subject of at least two public hearings before it is finally approved. The budget actors have relied heavily on a collective voice strategy at these hearings as well as in other forums where the budget is debated. Individual voice in this context is relatively weak. As those interviewed emphasized, collective voice provides the access and opportunity to put forward a group's position on an issue, even if it is not ultimately adopted.

Third, the collective voice of those requesting services has been relatively strong at least since the early 1970s and has become even stronger over recent decades.

Fourth, employees of the various agencies have different propensities to organize and bargain collectively. County Government and school system employees as well as college faculty have chosen to bargain with their respective employers. Most of the other employees have chosen not to use their collective voices.

Fifth, certain employee groups organized themselves well before the emergence of fiscal discontent—teachers in the nineteenth century, firefighters in 1966, and county police officers in 1969. These groups are the occupational communities described in Chapter 5.

Sixth, the more than 7,000 full-time employees of the County Government organized their collective voice in 1975 in response to legislative proposals to reduce their compensation package. That legislation had been put forward in response to growing budget pressures and the aforementioned uprising by the taxpayers in the spring of that year—the early years of fiscal discontent in the county. The initial organizing by the employees to protect their economic interests led directly to the creation of the Montgomery County Government Employees' Organization (MCGEO) in the summer of 1975 and ultimately to their securing collective bargaining rights a decade later. This series of events is consistent with the hypothesis of this research.

The prevailing view among those interviewed is that fiscal discontent plays a significant role in motivating the employees to bargain collectively today. Fiscal discontent eliminated the option to increase taxes, and the battle for a share of a fixed or shrinking budget pie between those requesting services and the employees became a zero sum game. Group and special interest politics became enmeshed in the budget debate.

Seventh, the employees of those agencies least dependent on discretionary own-source taxes have the lowest propensities to organize their collective voices despite having the right to bargain collectively. Employees of the Maryland–National Capital Park and Planning Commission and the Washington Suburban Sanitary Commission as well as the administrative and support staff at Montgomery College follow the pattern delineated in Chapter 6.

Those interviewed offered the opinion that these employees do not perceive the same competition for fiscal resources as those in the school system and County Government. Further, many believe that the employees do not perceive the local elected officials as being "part of their world." These data and opinions again are consistent with the hypothesis of this research.

Eighth, the collective voice of the employees strengthened over a period of years as they gained equal status at the bargaining table. A full century passed between the time the teachers organized and the time they achieved collective bargaining rights. County Government employees accomplished it in about a decade—organized in 1975, gained a meet-and-confer process in 1977, and attained collective bargaining in 1986. This evolution to full bargaining follows a pattern at least suggested by the data presented in Chapter 5.

Ninth, those interviewed agree that the participation by employee groups in the local political process is an important voice dimension of the local collective bargaining process. Elected officials at least perceive that employee groups have political power, especially when they target a candidate in a close race in a Democratic primary election for a single member district office. Employee organizations also provide important human and financial resources for the conduct of an election campaign.

Virtually all of the employees in the two agencies governed by *elected* officials bargain collectively. In contrast, in the three agencies governed by *appointed* officials virtually none of the employees are organized, let alone bargain collectively; only the full-time college faculty, the park police, and blue collar employees at the sanitary commission have chosen to use their collective voices.

Tenth, both economic and non-economic issues have been important for the employees. In the mid-1990s, however, the non-economic agenda seems to be paramount, led by protecting both jobs and past economic gains. Several groups also are seeking greater participation and voice in the operations and long-term direction of their agencies.

NOTES

1. The data for this section have been excerpted from Montgomery County, Maryland, 1997.

2. Two regional agencies also provide services to the county, but because they are metropolitan-wide entities they are not included in this study. The Washington Metropolitan Area Transit Authority is a regional agency responsible for the construction and operation of the 103-mile Metrorail system and the operation of a regional bus system. Thirteen of the system's stations and about nineteen of its miles are located in the county. The Authority is governed by a regional Board of Directors of which two members appointed by the county executive and confirmed by the county council represent the county. Among the Authority's numerous funding sources are the subsidy payments from its participating jurisdictions.

The Metropolitan Washington Council of Governments also has a role in certain arenas. Comprised of eighteen local governments in the national capital area, it facilitates and coordinates regional responses on matters of mutual interest—transportation, environment, public safety, and a cooperative purchasing program are examples. Member governments make annual payments to help support its operations.

3. Prior to 1990 there were seven members, all elected at large, but five were required to reside in each of the five councilmanic districts.

4. Both the incorporated municipalities (Rockville and Gaithersburg are the largest) and the "villages" (for example, Friendship Heights and Chevy Chase Village) have separate governing bodies, all with limited powers—street and sidewalk maintenance, trash collection, recreation, land use regulation, and code enforcement are examples.

5. Maryland, 1997, *Education*.

6. Ibid.

7. Maryland, 1997, Volume 3, Article 28.

8. Ibid., Volume 3, Article 29.

9. Local Government Personnel Association, 1997.

10. In addition to Social Security, Medicare, unemployment insurance, and worker's compensation, virtually all agencies include in varying ways the following: pension plan, life insurance, medical and dental insurance, long-term disability coverage, time off with pay, and insurance coverage for retirees.

11. These differences in both pay plans and benefit structures among the agencies have been the subject of much study and debate over the years. After studying the issues for two years, a seven-member blue-ribbon citizens' advisory panel, the Compensation Task Force, was unable to recommend any feasible way to achieve uniformity, given the greatly differing statutory frameworks and collective bargaining arrangements (Mont-gomery County, Maryland, June 1985). The Task Force was chaired by Coleman Raph-ael, then-President and CEO of Atlantic Research Corporation and later Dean of the Business School at George Mason University. Members included Robert Fredlund, the former Executive Director of the President's Panel on Federal Compensation (1975–1976); Robert J. Myers, a former Deputy Commissioner of the Social Security Admin-istration and its Chief Actuary (1947–1970); and Winn Newman, a former General Counsel for AFSCME and the IUE, AFL-CIO.

12. Unless otherwise stated, the fiscal data presented in this chapter are for fiscal year 1997. The data in this section are excerpted from the *County Executive's Recommended Budget and Public Services Program, Fiscal Year 1997.*

13. The Washington Suburban Sanitary Commission budget cannot be allocated to each of the counties it serves, as the operation of this water and sewer utility is truly a bi-county enterprise.

14. Each agency also prepares a capital budget and six-year capital improvements program. The charter (Section 312) permits the county to incur debt to finance these expenditures.

15. Maryland, 1997, *Education.* Section 4–205[k][2].

16. Ibid., Section 16–412[g][6].

17. Ibid., Volume 3, Article 28.

18. Ibid., Volume 3, Article 29.

19. Excludes the $437 million for the bi-county Washington Suburban Sanitary Com-mission.

20. Real per capita expenditures for all agencies except the WSSC (expressed in fiscal year 1997 dollars) were $2,138 in 1978, $2,201 in 1983, $2,230 in 1988 and 1993, and $2,359 in 1997.

21. This excludes the $95 million paid by the state as the employer's contribution to the state teachers' retirement system.

22. Excludes the Washington Suburban Sanitary Commission.

23. There is no local corporate income tax.

24. In January 1986, the county council appointed a fourteen-member citizen group, the Economic and Budget Strategy Committee, to provide advice on the possible impacts on the county budget of these federal initiatives. The committee was chaired by Stuart E. Eizenstat, former President Jimmy Carter's domestic policy advisor, and included Barry P. Bosworth of the Brookings Institution and Bernard Aronson of the State De-partment. Its April 1986 report identified three areas of concern—the loss of general

revenue sharing and Community Development Block Grants and likely future reductions in state assistance resulting from its loss of federal resources.

25. Examples include (1) changed accounting practices regarding the manner in which revenues and expenses were accrued, resulting in a one-time windfall; (2) used all surplus funds to finance the budget, leaving none for unanticipated needs or future budgets; (3) changed the policy for using federal general revenue sharing and impact aid for school funds from a conservative policy of using the monies in the year after they were received to a policy of using them in the year they were received, thereby using two years of revenue to finance the fiscal year 1975 budget.

26. In August 1997, there were 425,660 registered voters: 53.3 percent Democrat, 30 percent Republican, 16.5 percent Declines, and 0.2 percent Other.

27. The board of education, operating within its discretion, renegotiated a 5.46 percent COLA with its unions, well below the 10.1 percent agreed to earlier.

28. The operating budget public hearing conducted by the county council in the spring of 1987 included representatives of numerous groups that had not appeared at the hearing in the spring of 1975, including Advisory Committees on Education of the Gifted and Talented, on Guidance and Counseling, on Special and Alternative Education, on Children and Youth, on Head Start, on Child Care, on Aging, on Handicapped Individuals, on Libraries, on Literacy, on the Arts, on Recreation, on Alcoholism, and on Drug Abuse. There were representatives from the National Organization for Women, the Gray Panthers, the Hispanic Coalition, The United Way, the Alliance for the Mentally Ill, and the County Youth Orchestra.

29. In July 1991, a permanent ''growth factor'' of 40 percent of phased-in full cash value was implemented.

30. This amount is adjusted annually to reflect the change in a construction cost index. In fiscal year 1997, the threshold was $8 million.

31. The special tax areas are the countywide mass transit facilities fund, the recreation district, the suburban district, the sanitary district, four fire tax districts, three parking districts, the Washington Metropolitan District, the Washington Regional District, and a county-wide district for funding advance land acquisition. The latter three are mandated, in part, by state law to finance the MNCPPC budget.

32. The estimated sales/assessment ratio for residential properties in the county declined one-third from 45.7 percent in fiscal year 1981 to 30.5 percent two years later.

33. Excluding 2,830 governments in Pennsylvania, 615 cities and school districts in Ohio, and 379 school districts in Iowa, there are 287 local governments that use this own-source tax (ACIR, 1992b: 73).

34. Maryland, 1997, *Education*, Section 16–412[a][14]. In 1990, similar legislation was enacted for Baltimore City.

35. Ibid., Volume 3, Article 28, Section 5–114.1.

36. Ibid., Section 2–112.1.

37. There had been an Employee Advisory Council, which served as a voice mechanism until it was disbanded in 1991 after an unfair labor practice was filed and the legal advice was to abolish the council.

38. Legislative Bills 21, 22, and 23–75.

39. Non-emergency bills required approval of four of the seven council members, took effect 91 days after enactment, and were subject to veto by the county executive.

40. Colman was appointed to fill the unexpired term of Norman L. Christeller, who

resigned to accept an appointment in the federal government. Christeller had been the sponsor of the 1975 legislation to amend the retirement plan and pay structure.

41. Emergency Bill 13–78.

42. Legislative Bill 37–78.

43. Legislative Bill 11–76 codified as Article IV, Chapter 33, Montgomery County, Maryland, 1996.

44. The Commission for Women, Women for Equality, Women in Nursing, and Library Staff Association.

45. Public Hearing of the Compensation Task Force, June 26, 1984.

46. This is an eleven-member standing commission required by Section 509 of the county charter. The commission is appointed every four years. Six members are appointed by the council, five by the executive. No more than six members may be of the same political party.

47. Two years earlier, in the midst of his successful campaign for county executive, then-state senator Charles Gilchrist had been the primary sponsor of the state bill to grant full collective bargaining rights for the employees of Montgomery College.

48. Montgomery County, Maryland, 1996, Section 33–80[g].

49. While unanimous, five of the eleven commissioners did not believe the proposed amendment went far enough. They issued a minority report urging (1) that the language be mandatory, as for police officers, rather than permissive and (2) that strikes not be prohibited.

50. Legislative Bill 19–86.

51. After serving two terms as executive, Charles Gilchrist left politics to become an Episcopal priest.

8

Conclusions and Future Research

This study has sought to gain additional insights regarding why those who are employed by American local governments have a higher propensity to use collective voice than those who work in its private sector. The financial and political constraints imposed on local budget choice making by the collective voice of fiscal discontent during the 1970s and early 1980s are hypothesized to have influenced the employees to pursue a collective voice strategy as well. This chapter summarizes the evidence, which, taken in its totality, supports this hypothesis. Fiscal discontent has not been the sole influence, but it has been an important one that should be added to the list of those identified in previous research.

THE THEORETICAL FRAMEWORK

This study of employee collective voice uses a local budgeting model as its theoretical framework. Various dimensions of that model are important, but the focus here is on the use of collective voice by various groups of budget actors as they seek to achieve their respective goals.

One theme of this research is that, for many actors, exit is not a viable option, at least in the short run; thus, collective voice is relied upon by those seeking to make their views known to decision makers. A "battle of collective voices" ensues among those requesting, paying for, and providing local government services.

This "battle" gained momentum during the decade of the 1960s. Mandates for local governments to conduct public hearings on their use of federal moneys evolved into a process whereby those requesting services rely on collective voice strategies to influence local decision makers. As presented in previous studies and supported by the case study for this research, these collective voices of citizen participation frequently dominate the local budgetary process.

During the 1970s and early 1980s, the taxpayers in 33 states succeeded in limiting the budget discretion of their elected decision makers. Fiscal discontent emerged over a period of years, frequently culminating in highly publicized election day ballot questions to limit revenues and/or government spending. This era of fiscal discontent was characterized by the taxpayers' use of a collective voice strategy. There were numerous impacts, but the most important for this study was to create greater competition for more limited budget resources.

FINDINGS AND CONCLUSIONS

The heterogeneity of American local government has been another theme of this research. One of its manifestations is the degree to which its employees have chosen to use collective voice. Those working for some local governments have not even organized a group, while in others virtually all are organized and bargaining collectively. As we have seen, these propensities can vary based on an employee's occupation, as well as the state and type of local government for which he or she works. For certain fields of endeavor—teaching and public safety, for example—occupational community influences whether the employees are organized. For other occupations, this community dimension is less important.

The conclusion of this research, as summarized hereafter, is that fiscal discontent provides a further explanation for the variations in the use of collective voice by local government employees. Fiscal discontent has influenced many of them to pursue a collective voice strategy as they compete for a share of the budget pie.

Differences among the states. The use of employee collective voice varies widely among the 29 states that do not constrain collective bargaining by their local government employees. By 1987, of the seventeen states with the highest rates of employee collective bargaining, all but one (Connecticut) had experienced fiscal discontent. Of the remaining twelve states with lower bargaining propensities, eleven had not experienced fiscal discontent (only Montana had).

Density in the sixteen fiscal discontent states remained relatively stable between 1972 and 1987, but over that same period, more and more employees sought a stronger collective voice. Bargaining unit membership increased from 54 percent to 65 percent of the employees over that fifteen year period; the number represented by a bargaining unit increased about 700,000 to almost 3 million. These increases were dramatically different from the declines registered in the private sector, as were the very high rates for the use of collective voice. The propensity to be represented by a bargaining unit for this segment of the local government workforce was similar to that of government employees in several countries of the Atlantic Community, notably Austria, Canada, Switzerland, and West Germany.

Employees transitioned to the more voice-intensive collective bargaining model both during and after the years of fiscal discontent. Being organized was not sufficient; nor was the less voice-intensive meet-and-confer process, which declined in popularity as collective bargaining became more widely used. Both the number of governments adopting a collective bargaining policy and the number of bargaining units (many with fewer than 25 members) increased between 1972 and 1987. Much of this growth occurred in those types of local government most dependent on own-source taxes.

This dynamic was illustrated in the Montgomery County case study. Employees in the tax-supported agencies organized and gained the right to meet-and-confer with management, before ultimately gaining a more voice-intensive right to bargain as equals about their wages, benefits, and working conditions.

But were these increases in the use of a stronger collective voice associated with the taxpayers' discontent of that era? The national data show that bargaining unit representation increased as the growth in own-source taxes failed to keep pace with inflation and population growth and as the share of local government expenditures financed by own-source taxes declined.

However, since fiscal discontent evolved over a period of years, establishing an association based solely on the aggregate data is troublesome. The analysis presented in the case study of Montgomery County documents that association—the successful use of collective voice by the taxpayers led many employees, albeit not all, to pursue a similar strategy. A direct link is established between a large local tax increase, the subsequent formation of a collective voice by the taxpayers and the onset of fiscal discontent, which induced elected officials to propose reducing employee compensation, which in turn led to the formation of an employee organization that ultimately gained and exercised its collective bargaining rights a decade later.

Those interviewed for the case study were virtually unanimous in the view that fiscal discontent played a role in motivating the employees to create a collective voice. By eliminating the option to increase local taxes, fiscal discontent created a fierce competition for resources between public services and employee compensation. To compete effectively in an environment of special interest politics, the employees were compelled to organize a collective voice to gain the access necessary to have their views heard, if not always adopted.

This collective voice of the employees has a significant political component. Their willingness to engage in the tactics of multilateral bargaining and their lobbying activities in the local budget process have been documented in the research literature. So has their role in local electoral politics. As those elected officials interviewed for the case study noted, employee organizations can provide important resources, both financial and human, for conducting a political campaign. Many seeking elective office would like to have their support, but they also want to avoid their wrath by not being targeted for defeat, especially in a Democratic primary for a single member district office.

The prevailing view is that with collective bargaining the employees have accomplished more of their agenda than they otherwise would have been able to achieve. While they may not have achieved large economic gains, they have been able to protect those of previous times. In addition, they have made advances in the non-economic arena gaining a greater voice in matters of governance, and in so doing, reducing the scope of management's prerogatives.

Differences among the types of local government. Beyond differences among the states, wide variations have been presented in the use of collective voice among the employees of the various types of local government within a state. Differences in the degree to which these governments rely on own-source taxes to finance their budgets and the share of those budgets devoted to compensation costs have been documented. Supporting the hypothesis of this research, those types of local government that rely most heavily on own-source taxes and have the highest labor intensity have the highest use of employee collective voice. The ranking of the various indicators for fiscal discontent and employee collective voice are similar, adding further evidence to support the hypothesis of this research.

The Montgomery County case study documents these differences among government types as well. Virtually all of the employees are organized and bargaining collectively in those agencies most reliant on own-source taxes to finance their budgets. In contrast, a majority of the employees of those agencies that rely least on local taxes have chosen not to use a collective voice strategy, despite having the statutory authority to do so. As those interviewed stated, these employees do not perceive severe fiscal restraint, and they have access to the management of their respective organizations.

On a state-by-state basis, for the 1977–1987 decade, the use of collective voice increased in a majority of circumstances in the fiscal discontent states, a trend very different from the decline common in the private sector. There was no decline in the proportion of employees represented by a bargaining unit in more than 70 percent of those local governments that experienced fiscal discontent in which the full-time employees have a right to bargain collectively. More than 60 percent of these same governments experienced no decline in density over that same decade.

FISCAL DISCONTENT: AN ADDED DIMENSION

Previous research has offered numerous explanations to help explain why local government employees seek to organize or bargain collectively. Some employees began organizing as long ago as the nineteenth and early twentieth century. The big surge, however, began in the 1960s and early 1970s after the courts ruled that public employees had the right to organize and many state legislatures began to enact the statutes necessary to authorize local government collective bargaining.

Earlier research has documented the numerous agendas, both economic and non-economic, of local government employees during the 1960s and 1970s.

Public school teachers, for example, were concerned not only about their compensation but also about a broad range of governance and policy issues—class size, curriculum, safety, adequate facilities, and the like. Employees also were concerned with improving their professional status in the eyes of others. The leader of the successful effort to organize hospital workers in New York City, most of whom were black females, cited human dignity as the main issue. In that regard, many employee groups aligned themselves with the civil rights and protest movements of those earlier times.

During the 1980s, new issues, notably pay equity and privatization, appeared on the employee agenda, reinforcing the need for a collective voice strategy to express their views regarding these matters as well.

Previous research generally supports a conclusion that, on balance, collective voice enabled the employees to make progress in advancing these various agendas. Wages and benefits increased for members of bargaining units, as did employment in the organizations for which they worked; comparable worth systems were implemented; the probability of contracting with the private sector was reduced in governments that engaged in collective bargaining. The Montgomery County case study and the interviews conducted in conjunction with it support these research conclusions.

During the 1970s and early 1980s, the taxpayers also emerged to express their views regarding state and local budgets and levels of taxation. These collective voice expressions of fiscal discontent were added to the mix, and this research presents evidence that these events also have played a role in influencing employees to remain organized and pursue a stronger collective voice through collective bargaining. Again, fiscal discontent is not the sole reason, but it is an important influence, which remains with us in the mid-1990s.

THE BROADER CONTEXT AND FUTURE RESEARCH

Developing a General Model of Employee Voice

This study of local government employee collective voice and its relationship to fiscal discontent in the context of the local budgeting process has touched upon an array of questions and ideas relative to the more general topic of the use of voice by this segment of the American labor force. Developing a general model regarding public employee voice is a prime candidate for further exploration.

This research has concluded that fiscal discontent is one explanatory variable; occupational community is another. But one can hypothesize a long list of additional variables, both economic and non-economic, collective and individual. Many have been alluded to here, and future research should examine their relative importance—job security in an era of privatization and downsizing; protecting and/or improving upon past economic gains; gender related issues, including pay equity; having a voice in the vast array of matters affecting one's work life; having a political voice; a community's characteristics (its political culture or ideology, population size, demography, location); an organization's profile (its mission, size, form of government, elective or appointed leadership); and the socioeconomic and demographic characteristics of the employees.

Ask the Employees

Having the employees' perspective regarding their use of voice, both as individuals and collectively, would provide valuable insights. The design for this research included interviews with the leadership of the employee organizations in one jurisdiction, but the views of rank-and-file employees were not sought. The resources to do so were not available.

Employee views regarding a range of matters could be elicited,[1] including their current agenda and priorities in an environment of concessions and give-backs, the relative importance of the various items on their economic and non-economic agendas, their perceptions regarding the collective voice strategy, why they have or have not chosen to organize and/or exercise their collective bargaining rights, their views regarding the respective roles of individual and collective voice, their perceptions about fiscal discontent and the local budget process, their role in the local political process, and their satisfaction with their employee organization.

Additional Candidates for Further Research

Less globally, additional matters in the policy and administrative arena are worthy of future exploration and research. Four are highlighted here: (1) models of employee voice, (2) budget choice making techniques, (3) intergovernmental fiscal relationships, and (4) other matters raised in the course of this research.

Models of Employee Voice

One of the goals for the twenty-first century workplace offered by the Commission on the Future of Worker-Management Relations (1994) is to "expand the coverage of employee participation and labor-management partnerships to more workers and more workplaces and to a broader array of decisions." What policies should local governments pursue if they wish to realize this goal? Many of today's legalistic and rule driven collective bargaining systems enshrine an adversarial proceeding and do little more than regulate conflict. There is a need to give employees, both as individuals and as members of a group, more cooperative, goal oriented avenues to express themselves about the full range of matters affecting their work life. Models of employee voice that foster cooperation, creativity, and teamwork need to be developed and implemented.

Budget Choice Making Techniques

In this era of super-budgeting (Caiden, 1988) and continued fiscal discontent, there is a need for a reasoned debate among those involved in the local budgeting process as they make value judgments about priorities from an infinite array of choices.

Yankelovich (1991: 246) highlights the need to implement techniques for doing choicework in the public policy arena. In the local budgeting context, choices need to be presented in ways that enable their consequences to be understood. Macro allocation choices are being made at a very early stage in the process in many local governments, and those representing the broad array of interests need to be engaged in a constructive way at the earliest stages.

Yankelovich (1991: 249) suggests that the techniques for "advanc[ing] two-way communication and dialogue" are available.[2] "The experience of various organizations . . . demonstrates that there are practical means to engage citizens in choicework, that techniques exist for doing so, that these techniques work in practice, and that select leadership organizations are prepared to move ahead with the task of developing public judgment" (ibid.).

The institutional arrangements and public processes for doing this choice work in the "sunshine" of public debate need to be developed to lessen the "shrieking" that occurs in today's "battle of collective voices." Presenting opposing views to decision makers needs to be done in ways that are helpful, not merely forceful.

At a more technical level, the calendars for negotiating contracts and approving budgets should be synchronized to facilitate choice making. In many governments, budgets must be approved before bargaining has been completed, requiring a lump sum set-aside for future agreements. The observation made 25 years ago still pertains in many places: "One result of collective bargaining . . . has been to turn budgeting into a kind of roulette game with about the same odds against winning" (Hayes, 1972: 96).

Intergovernmental Fiscal Relationships

The federal government and many states have been debating the merits of financing, at least in part, certain services, but devolving to local governments the responsibility for the design and delivery of those services. The consequence of placing these federal or state dollars in the local "battle of collective voices" with the potential for very different service outcomes should be considered by those governments providing the resources. As we have seen, there is great diversity among local governments in the manner used to establish personnel policies and compensation levels. The federal and state governments need to consider establishing performance goals and measures for their resources to ensure that they are not merely used, directly or indirectly, to finance negotiated agreements for the members of the 35,000 local bargaining units across the country.

Other Matters Raised by This Research

Several differences in the propensities of various local employee groups to use collective voice have been touched upon, but not analyzed, in this study. Among the questions raised are the following:

1. Why did local government density decline in the 21 Bargaining Constrained (BC) states from 42 percent in 1972 to 26 percent in 1987? This decline occurred even though sixteen of these states experienced fiscal discontent. One hypothesis would be that since many of these employees do not have the right to bargain collectively, they see little value in joining an organization and paying dues.

2. Why do these BC states restrict the right of their local government employees to bargain collectively? Is there more at work than political culture or ideology? Do the employees want bargaining? Are they working for it?

3. In addition to fiscal discontent, are there influences that help explain (a) the relatively low levels of employee organization and collective bargaining in the thirteen Moderate Density (MD) states that do not constrain local government bargaining, (b) the low levels of organization and bargaining by special district employees, and (c) the differences in the use of collective voice between those employed by the state and local governments within a state? This study concludes that political culture and ideology do not explain these differences.

4. What is the extent and nature of the participation by local government employee organizations in the local political process?

5. Has fiscal discontent impacted employee related economic matters (wages, pensions and benefits, employment levels) differently in organizations where collective bargaining is used and those where it is not?

NOTES

1. The *1977 Quality of Employment Survey* (Quinn and Staines, 1979) conducted by the U.S. Department of Labor and the Survey Research Center at the University of Michigan could be adapted for this purpose.

2. He cites the Charles F. Kettering Foundation of Dayton, Ohio, as among those who have developed these techniques.

Appendix 1
Number of Local Governments, by Group of States and Type of Government, 1972, 1977, 1982, and 1987

Type of Government	High Density States				Moderate Density States			
	1972	1977	1982	1987	1972	1977	1982	1987
Number of Governments								
Independent School District	5,205	5,207	5,311	5,112	5,479	4,995	4,850	4,770
Municipality	5,222	5,276	5,295	5,320	5,200	5,212	5,238	5,233
County	567	567	567	568	706	706	704	704
Special District	8,507	9,127	9,891	10,204	5,942	6,682	7,057	7,283
Township	7,560	7,510	7,529	7,526	6,563	6,529	6,511	6,465
Total	27,061	27,687	28,593	28,730	23,890	24,124	24,360	24,455
Governments with Full-Time Employees								
Independent School District	na	5,159	5,219	5,069	na	4,789	4,630	4,566
Municipality	na	4,514	4,495	4,645	na	3,694	3,751	3,873
County	na	567	567	567	na	705	700	703
Special District	na	3,280	3,125	4,182	na	1,843	1,370	2,375
Township	na	4,699	4,285	5,332	na	2,984	2,470	3,239
Total	na	18,219	17,691	19,795	na	14,015	12,921	14,756
Governments with 25 or More Full-Time Equivalent Employees								
Independent School District	na	4,478	4,568	4,506	na	3,092	3,123	3,135
Municipality	na	1,826	1,791	1,872	na	1,116	1,140	1,183
County	na	560	562	564	na	655	645	656
Special District	na	628	676	774	na	321	352	424
Township	na	893	906	970	na	182	205	259
Total	na	8,385	8,503	8,686	na	5,366	5,465	5,657

Appendix 1 (continued)

Type of Government	Bargaining Constrained				All States			
	1972	1977	1982	1987	1972	1977	1982	1987
Number of Governments								
Independent School District	5,097	4,921	4,921	4,828	15,781	15,123	15,082	14,710
Municipality	8,094	8,373	8,555	8,673	18,516	18,861	19,088	19,226
County	1,771	1,769	1,770	1,770	3,044	3,042	3,041	3,042
Special District	9,434	10,200	11,998	11,782	23,883	26,009	28,946	29,269
Township	2,868	2,783	2,724	2,694	16,991	16,822	16,764	16,685
Total	27,264	28,046	29,968	29,747	78,215	79,857	82,921	82,932
Governments with Full-Time Employees								
Independent School District	na	4,895	4,900	4,810	na	14,843	14,749	14,445
Municipality	na	6,229	6,780	6,795	na	14,437	15,026	15,313
County	na	1,768	1,769	1,766	na	3,040	3,036	3,036
Special District	na	3,352	2,714	4,912	na	8,475	7,209	11,469
Township	na	466	275	647	na	8,149	7,030	9,218
Total	na	16,710	16,438	18,930	na	48,944	47,050	53,481
Governments with 25 or More Full-Time Equivalent Employees								
Independent School District	na	4,098	4,231	4,339	na	11,668	11,922	11,980
Municipality	na	2,068	2,236	2,275	na	5,010	5,167	5,330
County	na	1,696	1,726	1,721	na	2,911	2,933	2,941
Special District	na	622	700	747	na	1,571	1,728	1,945
Township	na	5	7	10	na	1,080	1,118	1,239
Total	na	8,489	8,900	9,092	na	22,240	22,868	23,435

na = Bureau of the Census did not report this data.

Appendix 2
Number of Full-Time Local Government Employees, 1987, by Group of States, Type of Government, and Government Function

Function	High Density States				Moderate Density States			
	Municipal	County	Township	Special Dist.	Municipal	County	Township	Special Dist.
Fire Protection	82,119	11,412	8,070	5,739	35,614	5,405	1,365	1,652
Sanitation	34,261	2,573	3,967	488	14,427	2,489	235	275
Police Protection	166,526	57,512	26,680	0	71,852	32,150	2,746	0
Highways	51,818	39,357	21,161	4,889	22,656	23,534	3,761	19
Other Functions	404,660	299,780	51,560	125,808	132,116	140,243	9,046	62,212
Welfare	34,097	100,273	1,481	0	3,206	31,553	490	0
Hospitals	71,214	67,271	611	33,631	6,920	38,622	0	25,580
Education	215,197	106,197	86,427	0	10,012	0	6,617	0
All Functions*	1,059,892	684,375	199,957	170,555	296,803	273,996	24,260	89,738

Function	Bargaining Constrained States				All States			
	Municipal	County	Township	Special Dist.	Municipal	County	Township	Special Dist.
Fire Protection	70,268	6,202	395	2,274	188,001	23,019	9,830	9,665
Sanitation	33,734	5,640	0	563	82,422	10,702	4,202	1,326
Police Protection	120,328	51,062	0	0	358,706	140,724	29,426	0
Highways	43,530	46,038	136	930	118,004	108,929	25,058	5,838
Other Functions	300,805	215,415	517	70,193	837,581	655,438	61,123	258,213
Welfare	7,403	23,223	441	68	44,706	155,049	2,412	68
Hospitals	32,604	95,092	0	70,080	110,738	200,985	611	129,291
Education	65,557	240,404	0	0	290,766	346,601	93,044	0
All Functions*	674,229	683,076	1,489	144,108	2,030,924	1,641,447	225,706	404,401

*Excludes 3,496,967 independent school district employees: 1,333,011 in HD states, 768,121 in MD states, 1,395,835 in BC states.

Appendix 3

Percentage of Full- and Part-Time Local Government Employees Represented by a Bargaining Unit, by Type of Government, Group of States, and State, 1974, 1977, 1982, and 1987

State	Municipalities				Independent School Districts				Counties			
	1974	1977	1982	1987	1974	1977	1982	1987	1974	1977	1982	1987
High Density States												
Alaska	42.6	81.9	62.8	55.1	na	na	na	na	62.6	92.3	51.8	35.3
California	61.4	73.7	74.9	71.4	35.9	54.4	64.8	65.7	73.3	77.3	75.9	69.3
Connecticut	57.9	71.3	66.1	67.4	80.4	50.7	42.9	52.1	na	na	na	na
Delaware	60.3	53.9	53.4	54.6	52.0	57.1	63.1	65.7	49.5	51.1	58.6	61.1
Hawaii	83.0	62.5	81.4	93.7	na	na	na	na	81.0	61.5	83.3	80.0
Maryland	83.5	72.8	74.6	83.1	na	na	na	na	45.5	57.8	60.4	59.2
Massachusetts	61.8	76.4	75.4	65.5	52.7	55.6	62.4	60.4	5.3	22.0	49.7	42.6
Michigan	52.1	62.6	55.8	60.6	59.1	61.4	65.1	51.3	44.4	50.7	51.7	52.4
Minnesota	36.1	38.0	36.4	38.3	54.2	58.3	77.6	81.6	26.5	42.0	48.3	47.4
New Jersey	45.9	59.7	63.3	82.7	47.8	57.2	76.4	71.7	56.8	61.5	68.4	93.2
New York	75.0	78.9	90.4	79.8	59.0	73.0	72.7	65.7	68.4	74.3	72.9	73.7
Oregon	49.7	48.2	48.5	48.7	52.6	71.2	67.2	71.8	41.0	47.2	50.9	54.3
Pennsylvania	61.8	61.5	63.8	64.4	54.9	67.6	65.7	66.5	26.4	31.6	39.5	37.9
Rhode Island	75.7	79.3	84.1	85.9	v	v	v	v	na	na	na	na
Washington	49.1	54.4	58.3	60.6	59.2	76.0	86.7	83.8	39.6	41.9	47.7	52.0
Wisconsin	48.3	63.7	44.4	46.9	42.0	54.7	56.9	58.4	51.7	52.4	56.4	62.6
Average	64.0	70.7	74.4	71.6	49.1	61.4	67.9	65.6	57.0	62.7	64.8	65.0
Moderate Density States												
Florida	32.1	35.6	43.6	46.2	31.2	59.0	52.4	65.0	15.8	20.8	37.9	33.2
Illinois	9.7	11.5	25.3	39.7	40.3	50.5	46.0	44.0	18.1	14.9	10.8	38.6
Iowa	13.4	24.0	29.9	29.8	26.0	55.4	51.3	45.7	2.4	15.9	20.8	22.1
Maine	46.2	40.5	62.1	62.0	38.9	54.6	56.3	51.9	v	v	v	v
Montana	22.2	40.9	40.7	51.5	31.9	30.1	45.7	42.0	8.0	9.5	16.0	19.5
Nebraska	23.0	27.8	35.1	34.2	34.6	52.1	50.6	45.9	14.4	5.4	13.0	13.3
Nevada	58.5	71.6	73.6	71.9	47.1	72.6	81.0	75.5	36.5	47.3	36.6	60.8
New Hampshire	42.6	53.7	55.3	58.9	23.9	43.1	47.5	49.9	0	17.4	25.3	34.3
North Dakota	8.3	12.4	8.3	5.9	24.0	36.4	39.5	49.6	0	0.9	0.6	2.7
Ohio	33.6	43.6	41.5	42.3	48.9	61.0	55.0	46.5	7.7	12.6	9.7	13.2
South Dakota	8.6	14.1	22.8	22.5	39.2	44.8	40.3	48.6	5.7	6.8	6.8	8.7
Utah	16.9	18.4	16.9	16.3	47.7	61.3	59.6	58.4	0.9	0.6	22.4	19.4
Vermont	18.2	24.5	28.0	28.3	24.4	44.4	43.7	38.7	v	v	v	v
Average	24.4	29.5	36.1	41.1	38.5	54.8	51.3	51.1	12.1	15.9	20.9	26.8

212

State	Townships				Special Districts				All Governments			
	1974	1977	1982	1987	1974	1977	1982	1987	1974	1977	1982	1987
High Density States												
Alaska	na	na	na	na	na	na	na	na	53.8	84.7	59.5	48.2
California	na	na	na	na	45.8	46.0	52.3	38.8	49.3	62.3	68.1	65.5
Connecticut	49.0	66.1	58.7	59.5	23.2	39.2	56.4	53.5	52.4	67.2	61.2	62.2
Delaware	na	na	na	na	<	<	<	<	53.0	54.8	59.3	62.3
Hawaii	na	na	na	na	na	na	na	na	82.5	62.2	81.9	89.6
Maryland	na	na	na	na	0.1	30.3	30.0	29.3	55.8	61.3	63.5	63.9
Massachusetts	45.4	55.0	56.0	70.9	72.5	72.2	65.7	65.9	53.0	64.1	65.0	67.0
Michigan	5.7	11.6	13.1	8.6	31.1	42.4	40.8	41.8	52.5	57.9	58.3	50.9
Minnesota	<	<	<	<	54.9	48.7	41.6	47.8	44.8	48.6	56.2	58.1
New Jersey	23.5	37.1	50.6	61.0	28.7	39.9	46.2	33.2	46.2	56.8	68.0	76.5
New York	26.8	34.0	36.3	36.5	38.2	43.1	50.3	47.7	67.3	73.9	80.0	72.4
Oregon	na	na	na	na	31.1	48.8	56.8	50.5	48.9	62.8	61.3	64.5
Pennsylvania	11.4	21.1	27.5	27.8	55.4	60.4	62.3	58.5	51.0	59.0	60.1	60.0
Rhode Island	53.8	61.4	71.7	68.4	<	<	<	<	65.7	71.1	78.1	76.5
Washington	na	na	na	na	33.0	40.8	47.3	44.0	51.4	61.9	68.6	67.8
Wisconsin	0.4	2.1	1.3	2.7	59.7	62.6	44.9	33.5	36.8	55.2	50.5	53.8
Average	33.6	45.5	45.0	50.6	43.4	48.2	51.6	44.4	53.9	62.8	66.9	65.2
Moderate Density States												
Florida	na	na	na	na	0.3	2.2	5.3	5.8	26.8	42.4	44.1	50.9
Illinois	0.1	0.2	0.3	0.4	32.5	30.3	43.5	33.5	29.3	34.3	36.0	39.9
Iowa	<	<	<	<	<	<	<	<	19.1	41.6	40.8	38.4
Maine	25.6	28.6	29.9	36.2	16.3	19.1	23.1	23.2	34.6	38.1	45.8	47.5
Montana	<	<	<	<	<	<	<	<	25.4	27.8	38.1	37.5
Nebraska	<	<	<	<	30.5	32.7	36.6	30.6	28.2	36.8	39.7	36.7
Nevada	<	<	<	<	<	<	<	<	44.6	62.3	61.9	68.0
New Hampshire	0.4	0.5	6.8	7.7	<	<	<	<	19.9	36.2	38.8	41.9
North Dakota	<	<	<	<	<	<	<	<	11.8	20.6	21.0	23.4
Ohio	0.6	2.0	3.0	5.7	12.8	32.8	35.4	32.0	36.2	46.1	41.2	37.8
South Dakota	<	<	<	<	<	<	<	<	26.0	29.8	29.4	32.6
Utah	na	na	na	na	15.9	35.7	31.5	31.7	34.1	42.7	45.7	44.8
Vermont	1.0	3.6	4.4	4.1	<	<	<	<	16.8	34.7	34.2	31.1
Average	5.5	9.0	9.9	11.0	19.8	23.5	29.5	25.6	29.4	40.0	40.4	42.1

na = not applicable; < = fewer than 1,000 full-time employees in the state.

Bibliography

Aaron, Benjamin. 1988. "The Future of Collective Bargaining in the Public Sector." In *Public Sector Bargaining*, 2nd ed., edited by Benjamin Aaron, Joyce M. Najita, and James L. Stern. Washington, D.C.: The Bureau of National Affairs, 314–326.

Aaron, Henry J. 1975. *Who Pays the Property Tax? A New View*. Washington, D.C.: The Brookings Institution.

———, and Cameron M. Lougy. 1986. *The Comparable Worth Controversy*. Washington, D.C.: The Brookings Institution.

Advisory Commission on Intergovernmental Relations (ACIR). March 1993. *State Laws Governing Local Government Structure and Administration*. Washington, D.C.

———. 1992a. *Changing Public Attitudes on Governments and Taxes: 1991*. Washington, D.C.

———. 1992b. *Significant Features of Fiscal Federalism: Budget Processes and Tax Systems, Vol. 1*. Washington, D.C.

———. 1992c. *Significant Features of Fiscal Federalism: Revenues and Expenditures, Vol. 2*. Washington, D.C.

———. 1990. *1988 State Fiscal Capacity and Effort*. Washington, D.C.

———. 1988. *Devolution of Federal Aid Highway Programs: Cases in State-Local Relations and Issues in State Law*. Washington, D.C.

———. 1985. *The Question of State Government Capability*. Washington, D.C.

———. February 1977. *State Limitations on Local Taxes & Expenditures*. Washington, D.C.

———, and Indiana University Center for Urban Policy and the Environment. 1995. *Tax and Expenditure Limits on Local Governments*. Washington, D.C.

AFL-CIO, Public Employee Department. 1994. *Public Employees Bargain for Excellence: A Compendium of State Public Sector Labor Relations Laws*.

Allen, Steven G. 1988. "Unions and Job Security in the Public Sector." In *When Public Sector Workers Unionize*, edited by Richard B. Freeman and Casey Ichniowski. Chicago: University of Chicago Press.

American Nurses' Association. 1986. *Pay Equity: What It Means and How It Affects Nurses.* Kansas City, Mo.: American Nurses' Association.

Anderson, Arvid. 1972. "The Structure of Public Sector Bargaining." In *Public Workers and Public Unions,* edited by Sam Zagoria. Englewood Cliffs, N.J.: Prentice-Hall.

Ashenfelter, Orley. January 1971. "The Effect of Unionization on Wages in the Public Sector: The Case of Firefighters." *Industrial and Labor Relations Review* 24 (2), 191–202.

Avault, John, Alex Ganz, and Daniel M. Holland. 1979. "Tax Relief and Reform in Massachusetts." *National Tax Journal* 32, 289–304.

Babbie, Earl. 1992. *The Practice of Social Research,* 6th ed. Belmont, Calif.: Wadsworth.

Baden, Naomi. 1986. "Developing an Agenda: Expanding the Role of Women in Unions." *Labor Studies Journal* 10 (3), 229–249.

Baer, Jon A. 1981. "Municipal Debt and Tax Limits: Constraints on Home Rule." *National Civic Review* 70, 204–210.

Bahl, Roy. 1979. "Fiscal Retrenchment in a Declining State: The New York Case." *National Tax Journal* 32, 277–287.

Bailey, Robert W. 1984. *The Crisis Regime: The MAC, The EFCB, and the Political Impact of the New York City Financial Crisis.* Albany: State University of New York Press.

Bakke, E. Wight. July 1970. "Reflections on the Future of Bargaining in the Public Sector." *Monthly Labor Review* 93, 21–25.

Bartel, Ann, and David Lewin. 1981. "Wages and Unionism in the Public Sector: The Case of Police." *Review of Economics and Statistics* 63, 53–59.

Bell, Deborah E. 1985. "Unionized Women in State and Local Government." In *Women, Work, and Protest: A Century of U.S. Women's Labor History,* edited by Ruth Milkman. Boston: Routledge and Kegan Paul, 280–299.

Benecki, S. 1978. "Municipal Expenditure Levels and Collective Bargaining." *Industrial Relations* 17, 216–230.

Bennett, James T. 1984. "Introductory Remarks: Symposium on Unions and Politics." *Journal of Labor Research* 5 (3), 263–264.

———, and Thomas J. Di Lorenzo. 1983. "Public Employee Unions and the Privatization of 'Public' Services." *Journal of Labor Research* 4 (1), 33–45.

Blais, Andre, Donald E. Blake, and Stephane Dion. 1991. "The Voting Behavior of Bureaucrats." In *The Budget-Maximizing Bureaucrat,* edited by Andre Blais and Stephane Dion. Pittsburgh: University of Pittsburgh Press, 205–230.

Boehm, Randolph H., and Dan C. Heldman. 1982. *Public Employees, Unions, and the Erosion of Civic Trust: A Study of San Francisco in the 1970s.* Frederick, Md.: Aletheia Books.

Bok, Derek C., and John T. Dunlop. 1970. *Labor and the American Community.* New York: Simon and Schuster.

Boskin, Michael J. 1979. "Some Neglected Economic Factors Behind Recent Tax and Spending Limitation Movements." *National Tax Journal* 32, 37–42.

Botner, Stanley B. 1989. "Trends and Developments in Budgeting and Financial Management in Large Cities of the United States." *Public Budgeting and Finance* 9 (3), 37–42.

Bowman, John H. 1981. "Urban Revenue Structure: An Overview of Patterns, Trends, and Issues." *Public Administration Review* 41, 131–143.

Bradbury, Katherine L., and Helen F. Ladd. January 1982. "Proposition 2½: Initial Impacts, Part I." *New England Economic Review*, 13–24.

———. March 1982. "Proposition 2½: Initial Impacts, Part II." *New England Economic Review*, 48–62.

Brazer, Harvey E. 1981. "On Tax Limitation." In *Financing State and Local Governments in the 1980s*, edited by Norman Walzer and David L. Chicoine. Cambridge, Mass.: Oelgeschlager, Gunn and Hain, Publishers, 19–34.

Break, George F. 1979. "Interpreting Proposition 13: A Comment." *National Tax Journal* 32, 43–46.

Brecher, Charles, and Raymond D. Horton. 1988. "Community Power and Municipal Budgets." In *New Directions in Budget Theory*, edited by Irene S. Rubin. Albany: State University of New York Press, 148–164.

Brennan, Geoffrey, and James Buchanan. 1979. "The Logic of Tax Limits: Alternative Constitutional Constraints on the Power to Tax." *National Tax Journal* 32, 11–22.

Brownlee, W. Elliott. 1979. "The Transformation of the Tax System and the Experts, 1870–1930." *National Tax Journal* 32, 47–54.

Burton, John F., and Terry Thomason. 1988. "The Extent of Collective Bargaining in the Public Sector." In *Public Sector Bargaining*, 2nd ed., edited by Benjamin Aaron, Joyce M. Najita, and James L. Stern. Washington, D.C.: The Bureau of National Affairs, 1–51.

Caiden, Naomi. 1988. "Shaping Things to Come: Super-Budgeters as Heroes in the Late-Twentieth Century." In *New Directions in Budget Theory*, edited by Irene S. Rubin. Albany: State University of New York Press, 43–58.

Castles, Francis G. 1989. "Introduction: Puzzles of Political Economy." In *The Comparative History of Public Policy*, edited by Francis G. Castles. New York: Oxford University Press.

Chambers, Jay G. 1977. "The Impact of Collective Bargaining for Teachers on Resource Allocation in Public School Districts." *Journal of Urban Economics* 4, 324–339.

Chandler, Timothy David. 1989. "Labor-Management Relations in Local Government." In *The Municipal Year Book: 1989*. Washington, D.C.: International City Management Association, 85–96.

———, and Peter Feuille. January 1991. "Municipal Unions and Privatization." *Public Administration Review* 51, 15–22.

Chicoine, David L., and Norman Walzer. 1985. *Government Structure and Local Public Finance*. Boston: Oelgeschlager, Gunn and Hain, Publishers.

Cigler, Allan J., and Elaine B. Sharp. 1985. "The Impact of Television Coverage of City Council." *Journal of Urban Affairs* 7, 65–73.

Citrin, Jack. 1984. "Introduction: The Legacy of Proposition 13." In *California and the American Tax Revolt: Proposition 13 Five Years Later*, edited by Terry Schwadron and Paul Richter. Berkeley: University of California Press, 1–69.

———. 1979. "Do People Want Something for Nothing: Public Opinion on Taxes and Government Spending." *National Tax Journal* 32, 113–129.

———, and Donald Philip Green. 1985. "Policy and Opinion in California after Proposition 13." *National Tax Journal* 38 (1), 15–35.

———, and Frank Levy. 1981. "From 13 to 4 and Beyond: The Political Meaning of the Ongoing Tax Revolt in California." In *The Property Tax Revolt: The Case of Proposition 13*, edited by George G. Kaufman and Kenneth T. Rosen. Cambridge, Mass.: Ballinger Publishing, 1–26.

Clark, Terry Nichols. 1981. "Urban Fiscal Strain: Trends and Policy Options." In *Financing State and Local Governments in the 1980s*, edited by Norman Walzer and David L. Chicoine. Cambridge, Mass.: Oelgeschlager, Gunn and Hain, Publishers, 3–18.

———, and Lorna Crowley Ferguson. 1983. *City Money: Political Processes, Fiscal Strain, and Retrenchment*. New York: Columbia University Press.

Cohany, Harry P., and Lucretia M. Dewey. July 1970. "Union Membership among Government Employees." *Monthly Labor Review* 93, 15–20.

Cole, Stephen. 1969. *The Unionization of Teachers: A Case Study of the UFT*. New York: Praeger Publishers.

Coleman, Charles J. 1990. *Managing Labor Relations in the Public Sector*. San Francisco: Jossey-Bass Publishers.

Commission on the Future of Worker-Management Relations. 1994. *Report and Recommendations*. Washington, D.C.: United States Departments of Commerce and Labor.

Congressional Budget Office. 1979. "Proposition 13: Its Impact on the Nation's Economy, Federal Revenues, and Federal Expenditures." In *The Economics of the Tax Revolt: A Reader*, edited by Arthur B. Laffer and Jan P. Seymour. New York: Harcourt Brace Jovanovich, 110–117.

Conlan, Timothy J. Summer 1991. "And the Beat Goes On: Intergovernmental Mandates and Preemption in an Era of Deregulation." *Publius: The Journal of Federalism* 21, 43–57.

Courant, Paul N., Edward M. Gramlich, and Daniel Rubinfeld. 1980. "Why Voters Support Tax Limitation Amendments: The Michigan Case." *National Tax Journal* 33 (1), 1–20.

———. 1979. "Public Employee Market Power and the Level of Government Spending." *American Economic Review* 69, 806–818.

Cousineau, Jean-Michel, and Anne-Marie Girard. 1991. "Public Sector Unions, Government Expenditures, and the Bureaucratic Model." In *The Budget-Maximizing Bureaucrat*, edited by Andre Blais and Stephane Dion. Pittsburgh: University of Pittsburgh Press, 275–301.

Dahl, Robert. 1961. *Who Governs?* New Haven, CT: Yale University Press.

———. 1956. *A Preface to Democratic Theory*. Chicago: University of Chicago Press.

Dalton, Amy H. Spring 1982. "A Theory of the Organization of State and Local Government Employees." *Journal of Labor Research* 3, 163–177.

Danzinger, James N. Spring 1979. "Rebellion on Fiscal Policy: Assessing the Effects of California's Proposition 13." *Urban Interest* 1, 59–67.

Davenport, John A. 1979. "Voting for Capitalism." In *The Economics of the Tax Revolt: A Reader*, edited by Arthur B. Laffer and Jan P. Seymour. New York: Harcourt Brace Jovanovich, 134–138.

DeCanio, Stephen J. 1979. "Proposition 13 and the Failure of Economic Politics." *National Tax Journal* 32, 55–65.

Deiter, Ronald H. 1985. *The Story of Metro: Transportation and Politics in the Nation's Capital*. Glendale, Calif.: Interurban Press.

Delaney, John Thomas, Jack Fiorito, and Marick F. Masters. 1988. "The Effects of Union

Organizational and Environmental Characteristics on Union Political Action.''
American Journal of Political Science 32 (3), 616–642.

Derber, Milton, Ken Jennings, Ian McAndrew, and Martin Wagner. October 1973. ''Bargaining and Budget Making in Illinois Public Institutions.'' *Industrial and Labor Relations Review* 27, 49–62.

Dickens, William T., and Jonathan S. Leonard. April 1985. ''Accounting for the Decline in Union Membership 1950–1980.'' *Industrial and Labor Relations Review* 38, 323–334.

Dresang, Dennis L. 1991. *Public Personnel Management and Public Policy*, 2nd ed. New York: Longman Publishing.

Dworak, Robert J. 1980. *Taxpayers, Taxes, and Government Spending: Perspectives on the Taxpayer Revolt*. New York: Praeger Publishers.

Dye, Thomas E. 1990. *American Federalism: Competition among Governments*. Lexington, Mass.: Lexington Books.

———. 1977. *Politics in States and Communities*, 3rd ed. Englewood Cliffs, N.J.: Prentice-Hall.

Edwards, Linda N., and Franklin Edwards. July 1982. ''Public Unions, Local Government Structure and the Compensation of Municipal Sanitation Workers.'' *Economic Inquiry* 20, 405–425.

Ehrenberg, Ronald G. October 1973. ''Wages of Fire Fighters.'' *Industrial and Labor Relations Review* 27, 36–48.

Elazar, Daniel J. 1984. *American Federalism: A View from the States*, 3rd ed. New York: Harper and Row Publishers.

———. 1966. *American Federalism: A View from the States*. New York: Thomas Y. Crowell.

Eribes, Richard A., and John Hall. 1981. ''Revolt of the Affluent: Fiscal Controls in Three States.'' *Public Administration Review* 41, 107–121.

Erikson, Robert S., John P. McIver, and Gerald C. Wright, Jr. 1987. ''State Political Culture and Public Opinion.'' *American Political Science Review* 81 (3), 797–813.

Faith, Roger L., and Joseph D. Reid, Jr. 1987. ''An Agency Theory of Unionism.'' *Journal of Economic Behavior and Organization* 8, 39–60.

Farber, Henry S. 1988. ''The Evolution of Public Sector Bargaining Laws.'' In *When Public Sector Workers Unionize*, edited by Richard B. Freeman and Casey Ichniowski. Chicago: University of Chicago Press.

Feuille, Peter, John Thomas Delaney, and Wallace Hendricks. 1985. ''Police Bargaining, Arbitration, and Fringe Benefits.'' *Journal of Labor Research* 6 (1), 1–20.

Fisher, Glenn W. 1981. ''The Changing Role of Property Taxation.'' In *Financing State and Local Governments in the 1980s*, edited by Norman Walzer and David L. Chicoine. Cambridge, Mass.: Oelgeschlager, Gunn and Hain, Publishers, 37–60.

Florestano, Patricia S. 1981. ''Revenue Raising Limitations on Local Government: A Focus on Alternative Responses.'' *Public Administration Review* 41, 122–131.

Fosler, R. Scott. 1980. ''Local Government Productivity: Political and Administrative Potential.'' In *Fiscal Stress and Public Policy*, edited by Charles H. Levine and Irene Rubin. Beverly Hills, Calif.: Sage Publications, 281–301.

Frankfort-Nachmias, Chava, and David Nachmias. 1992. *Research Methods in the Social Sciences*, 4th ed. New York: St. Martin's Press.

Freeman, Richard B. 1980. ''The Exit-Voice Tradeoff in the Labor Market: Unionism,

Job Tenure, Quits, and Separations.'' *The Quarterly Journal of Economics* 94 (4), 643–673.

———, and Casey Ichniowski. 1988. ''Introduction: The Public Sector Look of American Unionism.'' In *When Public Sector Workers Unionize*, edited by Richard B. Freeman and Casey Ichniowski. Chicago: University of Chicago Press, 1–15.

———, and James L. Medoff. 1979. ''The Two Faces of Unionism.'' *Public Interest* 57, 69–93.

———, and Robert G. Valletta. 1988. ''The Effects of Public Sector Labor Laws on Labor Market Institutions and Outcomes.'' In *When Public Sector Workers Unionize*, edited by Richard B. Freeman and Casey Ichniowski. Chicago: University of Chicago Press, 81–106.

Fuchs, Ester R. 1992. *Mayors and Money: Fiscal Policy in New York and Chicago.* Chicago: University of Chicago Press.

Galenson, Walter. 1986. ''The Historical Role of American Trade Unionism.'' In *Unions in Transition*, edited by Seymour Martin Lipset. San Francisco: Institute for Contemporary Studies, 39–73.

Gallup, George H. 1979. *The Gallup Poll, Public Opinion 1978.* Wilmington, Del.: Scholarly Resources.

Garreau, Joel. 1991. *Edge City.* New York: Anchor Books, Doubleday.

George, Henry. 1879. *Progress and Poverty.* Reprint, 1979. New York: Robert Schalkebach Foundation.

Gerhart, Paul F. 1976. ''Determinants of Bargaining Outcomes in Local Government Labor Negotiations.'' *Industrial and Labor Relations Review* 29 (3), 331–351.

Gold, Steven D. July 1990. *The State Fiscal Agenda for the 1990s.* Washington, D.C.: National Conference of State Legislatures.

———. 1981. ''Property Tax Relief Trends in the Midwest.'' In *Financing State and Local Governments in the 1980s*, edited by Norman Walzer and David L. Chicoine. Cambridge, Mass.: Oelgeschlager, Gunn and Hain, Publishers, 61–87.

———, ed. 1995. *The Fiscal Crisis of the States: Lessons for the Future.* Washington, D.C.: Georgetown University Press.

Goldberg, Joseph P. July 1970. ''Changing Policies in Public Employee Labor Relations.'' *Monthly Labor Review* 93, 5–14.

Goldenberg, Shirley B. 1988. ''Public Sector Labor Relations in Canada.'' In *Public Sector Bargaining*, 2nd ed., edited by Benjamin Aaron, Joyce M. Najita, and James L. Stern, Washington, D.C.: Bureau of National Affairs. 266–313.

Gompers, Samuel. 1971. ''American Federationist, December 1914.'' In *Gompers: Labor and the Employer*. New York: Arno and The New York Times, 127.

———. 1969. ''Annual Report of the A. F. of L. Convention, Rochester, New York, November 1912.'' In *Gompers, Labor and the Common Welfare*. New York: Arno and The New York Times, 48.

Goode, William J. April 1957. ''Community within a Community: The Professions.'' *American Sociological Review* 22 (2), 194–200.

Gotbaum, Victor. 1972. ''Collective Bargaining and the Union Leader.'' In *Public Workers and Public Unions*, edited by Sam Zagoria. Englewood Cliffs, N.J.: Prentice-Hall, 77–88.

Gotlieb, Allan. 1991. *''I'll Be with You in a Minute, Mr. Ambassador'': The Education of a Canadian Diplomat in Washington.* Toronto: University of Toronto Press.

Goulden, Joseph C. 1982. *Jerry Wurf, Labor's Last Angry Man.* New York: Atheneum.

Gramlich, Edward M., and Daniel L. Rubinfeld. 1982. "Voting on Public Spending: Difference between Public Employees, Transfer Recipients, and Private Workers." *Journal of Policy Analysis and Management* 1 (4), 516–533.

Gummesson, Evert. 1991. *Qualitative Methods in Management Research*. Newbury Park, Calif.: Sage Publications.

Hanushek, Eric A. 1994. *Making Schools Work*. Washington, D.C.: The Brookings Institution.

Hayes, Frederick O'R. 1972. "Collective Bargaining and the Budget Director." In *Public Workers and Public Unions*, edited by Sam Zagoria. Englewood Cliffs, N.J.: Prentice-Hall, 89–100.

Heller, Walter. 1979. "Meat-Axe Radicalism in California." In *The Economics of the Tax Revolt: A Reader*, edited by Arthur B. Laffer and Jan P. Seymour. New York: Harcourt Brace Jovanovich, 123–125.

Hills, Stephen M. 1985. "The Attitudes of Union and Nonunion Male Workers toward Union Representation." *Industrial and Labor Relations Journal* 38, 179–194.

Hirschman, Albert O. 1970. *Exit, Voice, and Loyalty*. Cambridge, Mass.: Harvard University Press.

Howard, Christopher, Michael Lipsky, and Dale Rogers Marshall. 1994. "Citizen Participation in Urban Politics: Rise and Routinization." In *Big City Politics, Governance, and Fiscal Constraints*, edited by George E. Peterson. Washington, D.C.: The Urban Institute Press, 153–199.

Howard, Marcia A. Summer 1989. "State and Local Expenditure Limitations: There Is No Story." *Public Budgeting and Finance* 9 (2), 83–90.

Hunt, Janet C., and Rudolph A. White. Winter 1985. "State Employee Bargaining Legislation." *Journal of Labor Research* 6 (1), 63–76.

Huntington, Samuel P. 1981. *American Politics: The Promise of Disharmony*. Cambridge, Mass.: The Belknap Press.

Huxley, Christopher, David Kettler, and James Struthers. 1986. "Is Canada's Experience Especially Instructive?" In *Unions in Transition*, edited by Seymour Martin Lipset. San Francisco: Institute for Contemporary Studies, 113–132.

Ichniowski, Casey. 1988. "Public Sector Union Growth and Bargaining Laws: A Proportional Hazards Approach with Time-Varying Treatments." In *When Public Sector Workers Unionize*, edited by Richard B. Freeman and Casey Ichniowski. Chicago: University of Chicago Press, 19–40.

———. January 1980. "Economic Effects of the Firefighters' Union." *Industrial and Labor Relations Review* 33, 198–211.

———, and Jerry S. Zax. January 1990. "Today's Associations, Tomorrow's Unions." *Industrial and Labor Relations Review* 43, 191–208.

"Initiative Proposals." January issues, 1970 through 1980. *National Civic Review*.

Inman, Robert P. 1979. "Subsidies, Regulations, and the Taxation of Property in Large U.S. Cities." *National Tax Journal* 32, 159–168.

International City/County Management Association. 1979, 1986, 1987, 1988, 1989, 1990. *The Municipal Yearbook*. Washington, D.C.

Jewell, E. Guy. 1973. *Montgomery County Public Schools: The First 100 Years*. 5 vols. Rockville, Md.

Joyce, Philip G., and Daniel R. Mullins. 1991. "The Changing Fiscal Structure of the State and Local Public Sector: The Impact of Tax and Expenditure Limitation." *Public Administration Review* 51 (3), 240–253.

Kaufman, George G., and Kenneth T. Rosen. 1981. *The Property Tax Revolt: The Case of Proposition 13*. Cambridge, Mass.: Ballinger Publishing.

Kearney Richard. 1994. "Monetary Impacts of Collective Bargaining." In *Handbook of Public Sector Labor Relations*, edited by Jack Rabin, Thomas Vocino, W. Bartley Hildreth, and Gerald J. Miller. New York: Marcel Dekker, 73–96.

———. 1992. *Labor Relations in the Public Sector*, 2nd ed. New York: Marcel Dekker.

Kettl, Donald. 1993. *Sharing Power: Public Governance and Private Markets*. Washington, D.C.: The Brookings Institution.

———. 1992. *Deficit Politics*. New York: Macmillan.

Kirlin, John J. 1980. "Accommodating Discontinuity: Adjusting the Political System of California to Proposition 13." In *Fiscal Stress and Public Policy*, edited by Charles H. Levine and Irene Rubin. Beverly Hills, Calif.: Sage Publications, 69–88.

———. 1979. "Proposition 13 and the Financing of Public Services." In *Proposition 13 and Its Consequences for Public Management*, edited by Selma J. Mushkin. Cambridge, Mass.: Abt Books, 65–71.

Kleiner, Morris M., and Daniel L. Petree. 1988. "Unionism and Licensing of Public School Teachers: Impact on Wages and Educational Output." In *When Public Sector Workers Unionize*, edited by Richard B. Freeman and Casey Ichniowski. Chicago: University of Chicago Press, 305–321.

Klinger, Donald E. Fall 1988. "Comparable Worth and Public Personnel Values." *Review of Public Personnel Administration* 9, 45–60.

Kochan, Thomas A. April 1979. "How American Workers View Labor Unions." *Monthly Labor Review* 102, 23–31.

———. February 1975. "City Government Bargaining: A Path Analysis." *Industrial Relations* 14 (1), 90–101.

———. 1974. "A Theory of Multilateral Collective Bargaining in City Governments." *Industrial and Labor Relations Review* 27 (4), 525–542.

———, and Hoyt N. Wheeler. October 1975. "Municipal Collective Bargaining: A Model and Analysis of Bargaining Outcomes." *Industrial and Labor Relations Review* 29, 46–66.

Kurth, Michael M. Fall 1987. "Teachers' Unions and Excellence in Education: An Analysis of the Decline in SAT Scores." *Journal of Labor Research* 8, 351–367.

Kweit, Mary Grisez, and Robert W. Kweit. 1987. "The Politics of Policy Analysis: The Role of Citizen Participation in Analytic Decision Making." In *Citizen Participation in Public Decision Making*, edited by Jack DeSario and Stuart Langton. Westport, Conn.: Greenwood Press, 19–37.

Ladd, Helen F. 1994. "Big City Finances." In *Big City Politics, Governance, and Fiscal Constraints*, edited by George E. Peterson. Washington, D.C.: The Urban Institute Press, 201–269.

———. 1978. "An Economic Evaluation of State Limitations on Local Taxing and Spending Powers." *National Tax Journal* 31, 1–18.

———, and Julie Boatright Wilson. 1983. "Who Supports Tax Limitations? Evidence from Massachusetts' Proposition 2½." *Journal of Policy Analysis and Management* 2 (2), 256–279.

———. 1982. "Why Voters Support Tax Limitations: Evidence from Massachusetts' Proposition 2½." *National Tax Journal* 35 (2), 121–148.

Laffer, Arthur B., and Jan P. Seymour. 1979. *The Economics of the Tax Revolt: A Reader*. New York: Harcourt Brace Jovanovich.

LaJeunesse, Raymond J., Esq. 1984. "Employees' Freedom from Ideological Conformity: A Right without Remedy." *Journal of Labor Research* 5 (3), 266–274.

LeLoup, Lance T. 1988. *Budgetary Politics*, 4th ed. Brunswick, Ohio: King's Court Communications.

Levine, Charles H., ed. 1980. *Managing Fiscal Stress: The Crisis in the Public Sector.* Chatham, N.J.: Chatham House Publishers.

————, and Irene Rubin, eds. 1980. *Fiscal Stress and Public Policy.* Beverly Hills, Calif.: Sage Publications.

Levitan, Sar A., and Frank Gallo. July 1989. "Can Employee Associations Negotiate New Growth?" *Monthly Labor Review* 112, 5–14.

Levy, Frank. Summer 1979. "On Understanding Proposition 13." *The Public Interest* 56, 66–89.

————, Dale Shimasaki, and Bonnie Berk. 1982. "Sources of Growth in Local Government Employment: California 1964–78." *American Economic Review* 72, "Papers and Proceedings," 278–282.

Lewin, David. 1986. "Public Employee Unionism in the 1980s: An Analysis of Transformation." In *Unions in Transition*, edited by Seymour Martin Lipset. San Francisco: Institute for Contemporary Studies, 241–264.

————, Peter Feuille, Thomas A. Kochan, and John Thomas Delaney. 1988. *Public Sector Labor Relations: Analysis and Readings.* Lexington, Mass.: Lexington Books.

Lewis, H. Gregg. 1988. "Union/Nonunion Wage Gaps in the Public Sector." In *When Public Sector Workers Unionize*, edited by Richard B. Freeman and Casey Ichniowski. Chicago: University of Chicago Press, 169–194.

Lipset, Seymour Martin. 1996. *American Exceptionalism: A Double-Edged Sword.* New York: W. W. Norton and Company.

————. 1991. "American Exceptionalism Reaffirmed." In *Is America Different?*, edited by Byron E. Shafer. Oxford: Clarendon Press, 1–45.

————. 1990. *Continental Divide.* New York: Routledge.

————. 1989. "The Failure of the American Socialist Movement." In *Why Is There No Socialism in the United States?*, edited by Jean Heffer and Jeanine Rovet. Paris: Editions de l'école des hautes études en sciences sociales, 23–35.

————. 1986. "North American Labor Movements: A Comparative Perspective." In *Unions in Transition*, edited by Seymour Martin Lipset. San Francisco: Institute for Contemporary Studies, 421–452.

————, and William Schneider. 1987. *The Confidence Gap: Business, Labor, and Government in the Public Mind*, rev. ed. Baltimore: Johns Hopkins University Press.

Lipsky, David P., and John E. Drotning. October 1973. "The Influence of Collective Bargaining on Teachers' Salaries in New York State." *Industrial and Labor Relations Review* 27 (1), 18–35.

Livingston, Frederick R. 1972. "Collective Bargaining and the School Board." In *Public Workers and Public Unions*, edited by Sam Zagoria. Englewood Cliffs, N.J.: Prentice-Hall, 63–76.

Local Government Personnel Association. 1997. *Annual Wage Survey of Benchmark Positions.*

Love, Thomas M., and George T. Sulzner. February 1972. "Political Implications of Public Employee Bargaining." *Industrial Relations* 2, 18–33.

Lowery, David, and Lee Sigelman. 1981. "Understanding the Tax Revolt: Eight Explanations." *American Political Science Review* 75 (4), 963–974.

Lucier, Richard L. 1979. "Gauging the Strength and Meaning of the 1978 Tax Revolt." *Public Administration Review* 39, 371–379.

Macmanus, Susan A. Summer 1991. "Mad about Mandates: The Issue of Who Should Pay for What Resurfaces in the 1990s." *Publius: The Journal of Federalism* 21, 59–75.

———. 1983. "State Government: The Overseer of Municipal Finance." In *The Municipal Money Chase: The Politics of Local Government Finance*, edited by Alberta M. Sbragia. Boulder, Colo.: Westview Press, 145–184.

Macy, John W. 1972. "The Role of Bargaining in the Public Service." In *Public Workers and Public Unions*, edited by Sam Zagoria. Englewood Cliffs, N.J.: Prentice-Hall, 5–19.

Madison, James. n.d. *Federalist 10*. In *The Federalist Papers*. New Rochelle, N.Y.: Arlington House.

Maier, Henry W. 1972. "Collective Bargaining and the Municipal Employer." In *Public Workers and Public Unions*, edited by Sam Zagoria. Englewood Cliffs, N.J.: Prentice-Hall, 53–62.

Maier, Mark H. 1987. *City Unions: Managing Discontent in New York City*. New Brunswick, N.J.: Rutgers University Press.

Martinez-Brawley, Emilia E. 1990. *Perspectives on the Small Community*. Silver Spring, Md.: National Association of Social Workers' Press.

Maryland. 1997. *Annotated Code of Maryland. 1997 Replacement Volume*. Charlottesville, Va.: The Michie Company.

Masters, Marick F., and John Thomas Delaney. Winter 1987. "Contemporary Labor Political Investments and Performance." *Labor Studies Journal* 11 (3), 220–237.

———. Fall 1985. "The Causes of Union Political Involvement: A Longitudinal Analysis." *Journal of Labor Research* 6 (4), 341–362.

May, Peter J., and Arnold J. Meltsner. 1981. "Limited Actions, Distressing Consequences: A Selected View of the California Experience." *Public Administration Review* 41, 172–179.

McLennan, Kenneth, and Michael H. Moskow. 1972. "Multilateral Bargaining in the Public Sector." In *Collective Bargaining in Government: Readings and Cases*, edited by J. Joseph Loewenberg and Michael H. Moskow. Englewood Cliffs, N.J.: Prentice-Hall, 227–234.

Meltsner, Arnold J. 1971. *The Politics of City Revenue*. Berkeley, Calif.: University of California Press.

Meltz, Noah M. 1989. "Interstate vs. Interprovincial Differences in Union Density." *Industrial Relations* 28, 142–158.

Merriman, David. 1987. *The Control of Municipal Budgets*. Westport, Conn.: Quorum Books.

Moe, Terry M. 1981. "Toward a Broader View of Interest Groups." *Journal of Politics* 43, 531–543.

Montgomery County, Maryland. 1997. *Preliminary Official Statement Dated April 11, 1997: Montgomery County, Maryland General Obligation Bonds, $115,000,000 Consolidated Public Improvement Bonds of 1997, Series A*.

———. Fiscal Years 1972 through 1997. *County Executive's Recommended Budget and Public Services Program*. Annual. Rockville, Md.

———. March 1996. *FY 97 Revenue Projections and Assumptions*. Department of Finance. Rockville, Md.

———. December 1996. *Charter of Montgomery County, Maryland*.

————. 1996. *Montgomery County Code 1994*, as amended.

————. April 1986. *Report of the Economic and Budget Strategy Committee*. Rockville, Md.

————. June 1985. *Report of the Compensation Task Force*. 3 vols. Rockville, Md.

————. May 1984. *Report of the Charter Review Commission*. Rockville, Md.

————. May 1980. *Report of the Charter Review Commission*. Rockville, Md.

Moody's Investors Service. July 1977. *Moody's Analytical Overview of 25 Leading U.S. Cities*. New York: Moody's Investors Service.

Moore, William J., and John Raisian. June 1982. "Public Sector Union Wage Effects: A Time Series Analysis." *Monthly Labor Review* 105, 51–53.

Mulrooney, Keith F. 1979. "Tax Restriction: A Public Administrator's View." In *Proposition 13 and Its Consequences for Public Management*, edited by Selma J. Mushkin. Cambridge, Mass.: Abt Books, 75–77.

Nathan, Richard P. 1994. "Deregulating State and Local Government: What Can Leaders Do?" In *Deregulating the Public Service*, edited by John J. DiIulio, Jr. Washington, D.C.: The Brookings Institution, 156–174.

————, and Fred C. Doolittle. 1987. *Reagan and the States*. Princeton, N.J.: Princeton University Press.

National Commission on Excellence in Education. 1983. *A Nation at Risk: The Imperative for Educational Reform*. Washington, D.C.: U.S. Government Printing Office.

National Commission on the Public Service. 1989. *Leadership for America: Rebuilding the Public Service*. Lexington, Mass.: Lexington Books.

National Commission on the State and Local Public Service. 1993. *Hard Truths/Tough Choices: An Agenda for State and Local Reform*. New York: The Nelson A. Rockefeller Institute of Government.

Netzer, Dick. 1983. "Property Taxes: Their Past, Present, and Future Place in Government Finance." In *Urban Finance under Siege*, edited by Thomas R. Swartz and Frank J. Bonello. Armonk, N.Y.: M. E. Sharpe, 51–78.

————. 1966. *The Economics of the Property Tax*. Washington, D.C.: The Brookings Institution.

Niskanen, William A., Jr. 1994. *Bureaucracy and Public Economics*. Aldershot, Hants, England: Edward Elgar Publishing Co.

Oakland, William H. 1979. "Proposition 13: Genesis and Consequences." *National Tax Journal* 32, 387–407.

O'Brien, Kevin M. July 1994. "The Impact of Union Political Activities on Public Sector Pay, Employment, and Budgets." *Industrial Relations* 33 (3), 322–345.

Olson, Mancur, Jr. 1965. *The Logic of Collective Action*. Cambridge, Mass.: Harvard University Press.

Osborne, David, and Ted Gaebler. 1992. *Reinventing Government*. Reading, Mass.: Addison-Wesley Publishing Co.

O'Sullivan, Arthur, Terri A. Sexton, and Steven M. Sheffrin. 1995. *Property Taxes and Tax Revolts: The Legacy of Proposition 13*. New York: Cambridge University Press.

Perry, James L., and Kenneth L. Kraemer. 1993. "The Implications of Changing Technology." In *Revitalizing State and Local Public Service*, edited by Frank J. Thompson. San Francisco: Jossey-Bass Publishers, 225–245.

Petersen, John E. 1981. "Tax and Expenditure Limitations: Projecting Their Impact on Big City Finances." In *The Property Tax Revolt: The Case of Proposition 13*, edited by George G. Kaufman and Kenneth T. Rosen. Cambridge, Mass.: Ballinger Publishing Co., 171–201.

———. 1980. "Changing Fiscal Structure and Credit Quality: Large U.S. Cities." In *Fiscal Stress and Public Policy*, edited by Charles H. Levine and Irene Rubin. Beverly Hills, Calif.: Sage Publications, 179–199.

Peterson, George E. 1982. "The State and Local Sector." In *The Reagan Experiment*, edited by John L. Palmer and Isabel V. Sawhill. Washington, D.C.: The Urban Institute Press, 157–217.

Pfiffner, James P. 1983. "Inflexible Budgets, Fiscal Stress, and the Tax Revolt." In *The Municipal Money Chase: The Politics of Local Government Finance*, edited by Alberta M. Sbragia. Boulder, Colo.: Westview Press, 37–66.

Phares, Donald. 1981. "The Fiscal Status of the State-Local Sector: A Look to the 1980s." In *Financing State and Local Governments in the 1980s*, edited by Norman Walzer and David L. Chicoine. Cambridge, Mass.: Oelgeschlager, Gunn and Hain, Publishers, 145–173.

Piskulich, John Patrick. 1992. *Collective Bargaining in State and Local Government*. New York: Praeger Publishers.

Puryear, David L., and John P. Ross. 1979. "Tax and Expenditure Limitations: The Fiscal Context." *National Tax Journal* 32, 23–35.

Pynes, Joan E., and Joan M. Lafferty. 1993. *Local Government Labor Relations: A Guide for Public Administrators*. Westport, Conn.: Quorum Books.

Quinn, Robert P., and Graham L. Staines. 1979. *The 1977 Quality of Employment Survey*. Ann Arbor: Survey Research Center, University of Michigan.

Quirt, John. 1979. "Aftershocks from the Great California Taxquake." In *The Economics of the Tax Revolt: A Reader*, edited by Arthur B. Laffer and Jan P. Seymour. New York: Harcourt Brace Jovanovich, 126–133.

Rabushka, Alvin, and Pauline Ryan. 1982. *The Tax Revolt*. Stanford, Calif.: The Hoover Institution.

Raskin, A. H. 1972. "Politics Up-Ends the Bargaining Table." In *Public Workers and Public Unions*, edited by Sam Zagoria. Englewood Cliffs, N.J.: Prentice-Hall, 122–146.

Rehfuss, John. 1979. "Citizen Participation in Urban Fiscal Decisions." In International City Management Association, *The Municipal Year Book: 1979*. Washington, D.C., 84–96.

Reid, Gary J. Spring 1988. "How Cities in California Have Responded to Fiscal Pressures since Proposition 13." *Public Budgeting and Finance* 8, 20–37.

Reid, Joseph D., Jr. 1979. "Tax Revolts in Historical Perspective." *National Tax Journal* 32, 67–74.

Riccucci, Norma M. 1990. *Women, Minorities, and Unions in the Public Sector*. Westport, Conn.: Greenwood Press.

Rivlin, Alice M. 1992. *Reviving the American Dream*. Washington, D.C.: The Brookings Institution.

Roberts, Geoffrey. 1988. "Pay in Local Government 1970 to 1986." In *Public Sector Bargaining in the 1980s*, edited by Rene Saran and John Sheldrake. Aldershot: Avebury, 78–87.

Roeder, Phillip W. 1994. *Public Opinion and Policy Leadership in the American States*. Tuscaloosa: University of Alabama Press.

Rubin, Irene S. 1993. *The Politics of Public Budgeting*, 2nd ed. Chatham, N.J.: Chatham House Publishers.

————. 1988. *New Directions in Budget Theory*. Albany: State University of New York Press.

————. 1982. *Running in the Red: The Political Dynamics of Urban Fiscal Stress*. Albany: State University of New York Press.

Saffell, David C. 1984. *State Politics*. Reading, Mass.: Addison-Wesley.

Saltzman, Gregory M. 1988. "Public Sector Bargaining Laws Really Matter: Evidence from Ohio and Illinois." In *When Public Sector Workers Unionize*, edited by Richard B. Freeman and Casey Ichniowski. Chicago: University of Chicago Press, 41–79.

————. April 1985. "Bargaining Laws as a Cause and Consequence of the Growth of Teacher Unionism." *Industrial and Labor Relations Review* 38, 335–351.

Sbragia, Alberta M., ed. 1983a. "Introduction." In *The Municipal Money Chase: The Politics of Local Government Finance*. Boulder, Colo.: Westview Press, 1–8.

————. 1983b. "The 1970s: A Decade of Change in Local Government Finance." In *The Municipal Money Chase: The Politics of Local Government Finance*. Boulder, Colo.: Westview Press, 9–36.

————. 1983c. "Politics, Local Government, and the Municipal Bond Market." In *The Municipal Money Chase: The Politics of Local Government Finance*. Boulder, Colo.: Westview Press, 67–112.

Schick, Allen. January 1988. "Micro-Budgetary Adaptations to Fiscal Stress in Industrialized Democracies." *Public Administration Review* 48, 523–533.

————. 1988. "An Inquiry into the Possibility of a Budgetary Theory." In *New Directions in Budget Theory*, edited by Irene S. Rubin. Albany: State University of New York Press, 59–69.

————. March 1986. "Macro-Budgetary Adaptations to Fiscal Stress in Industrialized Democracies." *Public Administration Review* 46, 124–134.

————. 1980. "Budgetary Adaptations to Resource Scarcity." In *Fiscal Stress and Public Policy*, edited by Charles H. Levine and Irene Rubin. Beverly Hills, Calif.: Sage Publications, 113–134.

Schneider, B. V. H. 1988. "Public Sector Labor Legislation: An Evolutionary Analysis." In *Public Sector Bargaining*, 2nd ed., edited by Benjamin Aaron, Joyce M. Najita, and James L. Stern. Washington, D.C.: Bureau of National Affairs, 189–228.

Schneider, William. 1979. "Punching through the Jarvis Myth." In *The Economics of the Tax Revolt: A Reader*, edited by Arthur B. Laffer and Jan P. Seymour. New York: Harcourt Brace Jovanovich, 114–117.

Schwadron, Terry, and Paul Richter. 1984. *California and the American Tax Revolt: Proposition 13 Five Years Later*. Berkeley: University of California Press.

Sears, David O., Richard R. Lau, Tom R. Tyler, and Harris M. Allen. 1980. "Self-Interest vs. Symbolic Politics in Policy Attitudes and Presidential Voting." *American Political Science Review* 74 (3), 670–684.

Shannon, John. 1981. "The Slowdown in the Growth of State-Local Spending: Will It Last?" In *Financing State and Local Governments in the 1980s*, edited by Norman Walzer and David L. Chicoine. Cambridge, Mass.: Oelgeschlager, Gunn and Hain, Publishers, 223–262.

————, Michael Bell, and Ronald Fisher. 1976. "Recent State Experience with Local Tax and Expenditure Controls." *National Tax Journal* 29, 276–285.

Shapiro, Perry, David Puryear, and John Ross. 1979. "Tax and Expenditure Limitation in Retrospect and in Prospect." *National Tax Journal* 32, 1–10.

Sharp, Elaine B. 1990. *Urban Politics and Administration: From Service Delivery to Economic Development.* New York: Longman.

———. 1984. "Government under Klieg Lights." *Communication Research* 11 (4), 497–517.

Shaw, Lee C. 1972. "The Development of State and Federal Laws." In *Public Workers and Public Unions*, edited by Sam Zagoria. Englewood Cliffs, N.J.: Prentice-Hall, 20–36.

Shefter, Martin. 1985. *Political Crisis/Fiscal Crisis: The Collapse and Revival of New York City.* New York: Basic Books.

Sheldrake, John. 1988. "The Changing Pattern of Collective Bargaining in Local Government." In *Public Sector Bargaining in the 1980s*, edited by Rene Saran and John Sheldrake. Aldershot: Avebury, 57–64.

Spero, Sterling D., and John M. Capozzola. 1973. *The Urban Community and Its Unionized Bureaucracies.* New York: Dunellen Publishing Company.

Stanfield, Rochelle L. December 10, 1983. "The Taxpayers Revolt Is Alive or Dead in the Water—Take Your Pick." *National Journal* 15 (50), 2568–2572.

Stanley, David T. 1980. "Cities in Trouble." In *Managing Fiscal Stress: The Crisis in the Public Sector*, edited by Charles H. Levine. Chatham, N.J.: Chatham House Publishers, 95–122.

Stieber, Jack. 1973. *Public Employee Unionism: Structure, Growth, Policy.* Washington, D.C.: The Brookings Institution.

Straussman, Jeffrey D. 1988. "Rights-Based Budgeting." In *New Directions in Budget Theory*, edited by Irene S. Rubin. Albany: State University of New York Press, 100–123.

———, and Robert Rodgers. Winter 1979. "Public Sector Unionism and Tax Burdens: Are They Related?" *Policy Studies Journal* 8 (3), 438–448.

Susskind, Lawrence E., ed. 1983. *Proposition 2½: Its Impact on Massachusetts.* Cambridge, Mass.: Oelgeschlager, Gunn and Hain, Publishers.

Thompson, Frank J., ed. 1993. *Revitalizing State and Local Public Service.* San Francisco: Jossey-Bass Publishers.

Toulmin, Llewellyn M. 1988. "The Treasure Hunt: Budget Search Behavior by Public Employee Unions." *Public Administration Review* 48, 620–630.

Troy, Leo. 1994. *The New Unionism in the New Society.* Fairfax, Va.: George Mason University Press.

———. Summer 1988. "Public Sector Unionism: The Rising Power Center of Organized Labor." *Government Union Review* 9, 1–35.

———. 1986. "The Rise and Fall of American Trade Unions: The Labor Movement from FDR to RR." In *Unions in Transition*, edited by Seymour Martin Lipset. San Francisco: Institute for Contemporary Studies, 75–109.

———. Summer 1985. "Public Sector Unionism at Home and Abroad." *Government Union Review* 6, 52–75.

———, and Neil Sheflin. 1985. *U.S. Union Sourcebook.* West Orange, N.J.: Industrial Relations Data and Information Services.

———. Spring 1984. "The Flow and Ebb of U.S. Public Sector Unionism." *Government Union Review* 5, 1–149.

Tullock, Gordon. Fall 1974. "Dynamic Hypothesis on Bureaucracy." *Public Choice* 19, 127–131.

Tyler, Gus. March 1972. "Why They Organize." *Public Administration Review* 32, 97–101.

U.S. Department of Commerce, Bureau of the Census. June 1991. *1987 Census of Governments: Public Employment, Labor Management Relations in State and Local Governments*, vol. 3, no. 3. Washington, D.C.: U.S. Government Printing Office.

———. February 1991. *1987 Census of Governments: Public Employment, Compendium of Public Employment*, vol. 3, no. 2. Washington, D.C.: U.S. Government Printing Office.

———. April 1990. *1987 Census of Governments: Compendium of Government Finances*, vol. 4, no. 5. Washington, D.C.: U.S. Government Printing Office.

———. April 1989. *Geographical Mobility: March 1986 to March 1987*. Current Population Reports, Population Characteristics, Series P-20, No. 430. Washington, D.C.: U.S. Government Printing Office.

———. September 1988. *1987 Census of Governments: Government Organization*, vol. 1, no. 1. Washington, D.C.: U.S. Government Printing Office.

———. 1988. *Government Finances in 1986–87*. GF 87–5. Washington, D.C.: U.S. Government Printing Office.

———. May 1985. *1982 Census of Governments: Government Employment, Labor Management Relations in State and Local Governments*, vol. 3, no. 3. Washington, D.C.: U.S. Government Printing Office.

———. December 1984a. *1982 Census of Governments: Public Employment, Compendium of Public Employment*, vol. 3, no. 2. Washington, D.C.: U.S. Government Printing Office.

———. December 1984b. *1982 Census of Governments: Compendium of Government Finances*, vol. 4, no. 5. Washington, D.C.: U.S. Government Printing Office.

———. October 1979. *1977 Census of Governments: Government Employment, Labor-Management Relations in State and Local Governments*, vol. 3, no. 3. Washington, D.C.: U.S. Government Printing Office.

———. July 1979a. *1977 Census of Governments: Public Employment, Compendium of Public Employment*, vol. 3, no. 2. Washington, D.C.: U.S. Government Printing Office.

———. July 1979b. *1977 Census of Governments: Compendium of Government Finances*, vol. 4, no. 5. Washington, D.C.: U.S. Government Printing Office.

———. November 1974a. *1972 Census of Governments: Government Employment, Management-Labor Relations in State and Local Governments*, vol. 3, no. 3. Washington, D.C.: U.S. Government Printing Office.

———. November 1974b. *1972 Census of Governments: Public Employment, Compendium of Public Employment*, vol. 3, no. 2. Washington, D.C.: U.S. Government Printing Office.

———. October 1974. *1972 Census of Governments: Compendium of Government Finances*, vol. 4, no. 5. Washington, D.C.: U.S. Government Printing Office.

U.S. Department of Commerce, Economic and Statistics Administration, Bureau of Economic Analysis. November 1994. *Survey of Current Business*, vol. 74, no. 11. Washington, D.C.: U.S. Government Printing Office.

U.S. Department of Commerce and U.S. Department of Labor. 1976. *Labor-Management*

Relations in State and Local Governments: 1974. State and Local Government Special Studies No. 75. Washington, D.C.

U.S. Department of Labor, Bureau of Labor Statistics. *Current Wage Developments.* Washington, D.C.: U.S. Government Printing Office.

————. *Employment and Earnings.* Washington, D.C.: U.S. Government Printing Office.

U.S. General Accounting Office. September 1988. *Legislative Mandates: State Experiences Offer Insights for Federal Action.* GAO/HRD-88-75. Washington, D.C.: U.S. Government Printing Office.

Valletta, Robert G. April 1989. "The Impact of Unionism on Municipal Expenditures and Revenues." *Industrial and Labor Relations Review* 42, 430–442.

Van Valey, Thomas L., and James C. Petersen. 1987. "Public Service Science Centers: The Michigan Experience." In *Citizen Participation in Public Decision Making,* edited by Jack DeSario and Stuart Langton. Westport, Conn.: Greenwood Press, 39–63.

Walker, Jack L. 1971. "Innovation in State Politics." In *Politics in the American States: A Comparative Analysis,* 2nd ed., edited by Herbert Jacob and Kenneth N. Vines. Boston: Little, Brown and Company, 354–387.

Walzer, Norman, and David L. Chicoine, eds. 1981. "Introduction." In *Financing State and Local Governments in the1980s.* Cambridge, Mass.: Oelgeschlager, Gunn and Hain, Publishers, xvii–xxvi.

Wellington, Harry H., and Ralph K. Winter, Jr. 1971. *The Unions and the Cities.* Washington, D.C.: The Brookings Institution.

Wildavsky, Aaron. 1992. *The New Politics of the Budgetary Process,* 2nd ed. New York: Harper Collins Publishers.

————. 1991. "Resolved, That Individualism and Egalitarianism Be Made Compatible in America: Political-Cultural Roots of Exceptionalism." In *Is America Different?,* edited by Byron E. Shafer. Oxford: Clarendon Press, 116–137.

Wilson, Thomas D., and Ann H. Elder. Spring 1988. "Collective Bargaining: the Unionization and Decentralization of Illinois Counties." *Government Union Review* 9, 23–39.

Winkler, Donald R. 1979. "Fiscal Limitations in the Provision of Local Public Services: The Case of Education." *National Tax Journal* 32, 329–342.

Wolman, Harold. 1980. "Local Government Strategies to Cope with Fiscal Pressure." In *Fiscal Stress and Public Policy,* edited by Charles H. Levine and Irene Rubin. Beverly Hills, Calif.: Sage Publications, 231–248.

Woodbury, Stephen A. January 1985. "The Scope of Bargaining and Bargaining Outcomes in the Public Schools." *Industrial and Labor Relations Review* 38, 195–210.

Yankelovich, Daniel. 1991. *Coming to Public Judgment.* Syracuse, N.Y.: Syracuse University Press.

Yates, Douglas. 1977. *The Ungovernable City: The Politics of Urban Problems and Policy Making.* Cambridge, Mass.: MIT Press.

Yin, Robert K. 1989. *Case Study Research: Design and Methods,* rev. ed. Newbury Park, Calif.: Sage Publications.

Zack, Arnold M. 1972. "Impasses, Strikes, and Resolutions." In *Public Workers and Public Unions,* edited by Sam Zagoria. Englewood Cliffs, N.J.: Prentice-Hall, 101–121.

Zagoria, Sam. 1972. "The Future of Collective Bargaining in Government." In *Public*

Workers and Public Unions, edited by Sam Zagoria. Englewood Cliffs, N.J.: Prentice-Hall, 160–177.

Zax, Jeffrey. Winter 1989. "Employment and Local Public Sector Unions." *Industrial Relations* 28, 21–31.

———, and Casey Ichniowski. April 1990. "Bargaining Laws and Unionization in the Local Public Sector." *Industrial and Labor Relations Review* 43, 447–462.

———. 1988. "The Effects of Public Sector Unionism on Pay, Employment, Department Budgets, and Municipal Expenditures." In *When Public Sector Workers Unionize*, edited by Richard B. Freeman and Casey Ichniowski. Chicago: University of Chicago Press, 323–363.

Index

discretion, 4, 15, 37, 38, 40, 55, 62, 69, 109, 138, 149, 173, 180, 196, 202
downsizing, 79, 195
Dresang, Dennis L., 108
Drotning, John E., 86
Dworak, Robert J., 25, 59, 60, 62–64

Economic Opportunity Act of 1964, 23
education finance, 45, 51, 62
Edwards, Franklin, 85–86
Edwards, Linda N., 85–86
Ehrenberg, Ronald G., 85–86
Elazar, Daniel J., 134
Elder, Ann H., 84
election, 22–23, 27, 38, 41, 54, 57, 64–65, 67, 81, 85, 152–53, 166, 171–72, 174, 180–81, 184, 191–92, 197, 202
employee agenda: economic, 5, 8, 21, 83–87, 176–77, 188, 193, 196–97, 204–6; non-economic, 5, 8, 21, 83–84, 176–77, 188, 193, 197, 204–6
employee benefits, 5, 7, 11, 21, 34, 82–83, 85–87, 108, 140, 156, 158, 177–180, 186, 193–95, 203, 205, 208
Equal Employment Opportunity Commission, 14
Equal Pay Act of 1963, 79
Eribes, Richard A., 41, 50, 57
Erikson, Robert S., 134
exit, 19–26, 31, 201

Fairness In Taxation, 175, 188–89
Faith, Roger L., 26
Farmer, James, 78
female employees, 18, 27, 78–81, 84, 183, 189, 205
Ferguson, Lorna Crowley, 38
Feuille, Peter, 16, 82–83, 85–86
Fiorito, Jack, 21, 27
fire protection employees, 6, 22, 27–28, 31, 54, 62, 66, 74–75, 81–82, 86, 90–98, 123, 133, 153, 155–58, 187, 191, 196
fiscal capacity and fiscal effort, 50
fiscal discontent, 4–9, 15–16, 18, 25, 30, 33–34, 37–41, 44–45, 50, 57, 69, 78, 88–89, 98, 105, 111, 129, 133–34, 138–

40, 143, 145, 147, 149, 162, 164, 172, 174, 187–88, 195–96, 201–6, 208
Fisher, Glenn W., 53
Fosler, R. Scott, 22, 25
Frankfort-Nachmias, Chava, 33
Fraternal Order of Police, 91, 155–56, 182–85
Freeman, Richard B., 5, 26–27, 30, 33, 85–87, 120
free rider, 21, 26
Fuchs, Ester R., 38, 40
functions of government, 6, 86, 89–100, 123, 128–29, 133, 138

Gaebler, Ted, 35, 82
Gallup Poll, 72
Gann, Paul, 57, 60, 173
Ganz, Alex Paul, 65
Garreau, Joel, 14
George, Henry, 52
Gold, Steven, D., 15, 39, 41, 55, 74
Gompers, Samuel, 75
Goode, William J., 91
Gotbaum, Victor, 27–28, 84
Gotlieb, Allan, 22
Goulden, Joseph C., 32, 75, 78, 91, 120
Gramlich, Edward M., 51, 67
Great Depression, 39–40, 53, 84
Great Society, 14, 76
Green, Donald Philip, 62, 64
Gummesson, Evert, 34

Hall, John, 41, 50, 57
Hanushek, Eric A., 18
Harrington, Michael, 14
Harris Poll, 32, 63, 72
Hayes, Frederick O'R., 108, 207
HD states. See high density states
Headlee Amendment, 67
Heldman, Dan C., 11, 85
Heller, Walter, 58
Hendricks, Wallace, 85–86
high density states, 92–107, 110–30, 133–47
highway employees, 6, 90
Hills, Stephen M., 72
Hirschman, Albert O., 4, 19, 20–22, 27, 31

New York City, 28, 32, 38, 40–41, 44–
45, 75, 78–79, 84, 91, 120, 205
New York City Emergency Financial
Control Board, 45
New York City Municipal Assistance
Corporation, 45
New York City Policeman's Benevolent
Association, 91
New York State, 45, 50, 54, 86, 95, 105,
116
Newman, Winn, 80, 198
Niskanen, William A., 54–55
non-instructional education employees, 6,
90, 91
non-residential property, 53, 58–59, 65
non-supervisory employees, 155–56, 176,
182, 186–87
Nordlinger v. Hahn, 63

Oakland, William H., 57, 63
Oates, William, 55
O'Brien, Kevin M., 28, 31, 86–87
occupational community, 6, 21, 90–92,
123, 133, 138, 196, 202, 205
Olson, Mancur, 20–21, 25–26, 30
operating budget, 1, 4–5, 7–8, 11–12, 14,
18; Montgomery County, 158, 160–68,
171–75, 178, 181
organized employees, 4, 6, 7, 34, 71–105,
123, 128–29, 133, 138, 145, 149, 176–
80, 190, 193–97, 202–6
Osborne, David, 35, 82
O'Sullivan, Arthur, 40–41, 51, 60, 65–66
own-source taxes, 7–8, 15, 50, 140, 143,
145, 147, 150, 158, 196, 203–4

Parent Teacher Associations, 23, 168,
170, 187, 190
pay equity, 71, 79–81, 84, 88, 183, 205
pension system, 28, 44, 108, 117; Mont-
gomery County, 155–58, 178–81, 194
Perry, James L., 17
Petersen, John E., 44
Peterson, George E., 39
Petree, Daniel L., 85–86
Pfiffner, James P., 37, 58, 60
Phares, Donald, 54–55
Philadelphia, Pennsylvania, 44, 84

pink collar employees, 79, 176, 183, 189.
See also female workers
Piskulich, John Patrick, 134
pluralism, 20–21, 25, 168
police protection employees, 6–7, 22, 27–
28, 31–32, 54, 62, 66, 74–75, 86, 90–
91, 96, 98, 123, 138, 153, 155–58,
177, 182, 184–87, 190–91, 196–97
political culture, 4, 68, 133–134, 145,
206, 208
political ideology, 133–34, 145, 206, 208
political voice, 5, 8, 21, 26, 108, 120,
151, 188, 190, 197, 206, 208. *See also*
interest group
Port Authority of New York and New
Jersey, 97
Prince George's County, Maryland, 152,
154, 172, 177
private sector employees, 1–5, 8, 11, 25,
27–28, 32–33, 35, 68, 71–77, 83–84,
86, 95, 109, 117, 123, 136–38, 145,
149, 156, 201–5
privatization, 9, 71, 74, 81, 82, 193, 195,
205
propensity: to bargain, 6–7, 117, 123,
128–29, 134, 138, 145, 201–2; to organize, 4, 6–7, 71, 73, 89–90, 105
property tax, 39–68, 158–75
property tax assessment, 40–41, 44, 51–
53; California, 58–60, 63; Massachusetts, 65–67; Montgomery County,
166, 170–74
public hearing, 19, 22–25, 29, 31; Montgomery County, 160–61, 168–72, 178–
179, 183–86, 195, 201–2
public welfare employees, 6, 90–91, 138
Puryear, David L., 38, 55, 64
Pynes, Joan E., 32, 105, 108–9, 117

Quirt, John, 58, 63

Rabushka, Alvin, 56, 63
Raisian, John, 85
Raskin, A.H., 32, 108
Reagan, Ronald, 15, 16, 36, 38, 59
Rehfuss, John, 23, 25
Reid, Gary, 63
Reid, Joseph D., 4, 26, 63

About the Author

ARTHUR W. SPENGLER spent nineteen years on the staff of the county council for Montgomery County, Maryland, serving as its staff director and principal policy advisor for eight years. He has worked as a policy and fiscal analyst for the county and federal governments. Recently, he has been a full-time member of the faculty at George Mason University.

ISBN 1-56720-290-X

90000>

9 781567 202908

HARDCOVER BAR CODE